T0331983

Industrial Forests and Mechanical Marvels

An account of modernization and technological innovation in nineteenth-century Brazil that provides a distinctly Brazilian perspective. Existing scholarship on the period describes the beginnings of Brazilian modernization as a European or North American import dependent on foreign capital, transfers of technology, and philosophical inspiration. Promoters of modernization were considered few in number, derivative in their thinking, or thwarted by an entrenched slaveholding elite; hostile to industrialization. Teresa Cribelli presents a more nuanced picture. Nineteenth-century Brazilians selected among the transnational flow of ideas and technologies with care and attention to the specific conditions of their tropical nation. Studying underutilized sources, Cribelli illuminates a distinctly Brazilian vision of modernization that challenges the view that Brazil, a nation dependent on slave labor for much of the nineteenth century, was merely reactive in the face of the modernization models of the North Atlantic industrializing nations.

Teresa Cribelli is an assistant professor of history at the University of Alabama.

Industrial Forests and Mechanical Marvels

Modernization in Nineteenth-Century Brazil

TERESA CRIBELLI

University of Alabama

CAMBRIDGE
UNIVERSITY PRESS

One Liberty Plaza, 20th Floor, New York, NY 10006, USA

Cambridge University Press is part of the University of Cambridge.

It furthers the University's mission by disseminating knowledge in the pursuit of education, learning and research at the highest international levels of excellence.

www.cambridge.org
Information on this title: www.cambridge.org/9781107100565

© Teresa Cribelli 2016

First published 2016

Printed in the United States of America by Sheridan Books, Inc.

A catalog record for this publication is available from the British Library

ISBN 978-1-107-10056-5 Hardback
ISBN 978-1-107-49665-1 Paperback

Contents

Figures and Map

Figures

Map

Notes on Orthography

Titles of publications are retained in the orthography of the nineteenth century in citations and the bibliography. Personal names, places, publications, and names of institutions have been altered to conform to modern Portuguese spelling in the body of the text.

Abbreviations

MACOP   *Ministério de Agricultura, Comércio e Obras Públicas*
JC   *Jornal do Commercio*
IIFA   *Imperial Instituto Fluminense de Agricultura*

Acknowledgments

I am deeply indebted to the many people and institutions that made this book possible. Foremost I am grateful to my late advisor, John Russell-Wood. Born in Lancashire, England, John traveled far and wide across the Portuguese world up until the very end of his life, bringing his experiences, his compassion, and his keen appreciation of history and the human condition back to his seminar room in Baltimore. I very much wish he were here to see the final result.

I am also grateful to two prolific and accomplished scholars in the history of Latin America: Dr. Franklin Knight, professor emeritus at the Johns Hopkins University, and Dr. Márcia Maria Menendes Motta, professor at the Universidade Federal Fluminense in Rio de Janeiro. The depth and breadth of Franklin's knowledge about Brazil and Latin America has never ceased to astound me, and I am deeply grateful for his insight and encouragement in bringing this project to book form. Indeed, he saw its potential before I did. As for Márcia, *Industrial Forests* would simply not exist without her. She not only pointed me to the paid letters of the *Jornal do Commercio* as a way to locate Brazilian voices on the topic of modernization, but she has remained an unceasing supporter of subsequent revisions and my more recent research. I also extend my gratitude to Márcia's students (all now professors in their own right) who welcomed me into seminars at UFF and answered my questions with enthusiasm and generosity: Graciela Garcia, Marina Machado, Cristiano Luís, Christillino, and Márcio Both.

I am indebted to the staff of the Arquivo Nacional in Rio: Kátia Borges and Sátiro Nunes were especially generous. Likewise I am grateful to the staff in the Rare Works and Periodical room of the Biblioteca

Nacional. Carla Ramos was especially generous in orienting me to the many resources of the library. In São Paulo, Lerice Garzoni, and Dr. Silvia Lara provided invaluable assistance at the Arquivo Leuenroth at the Universidade Estadual de Campinas.

I would like to extend a special thank you to Dr. Monique Sochaczewski-Goldfeld for her on-going support in understanding all things Rio, for our many conversations about Brazilian history, and for her insights into contemporary Brazilian culture. Leo Goldfeld answered my many questions about Brazilian agricultural technology, helping me to understand the specific needs of Brazilian – and tropical – agriculture. I would also like to thank Arthur Ávila of the Universidade Federal do Rio Grande do Sul for our many conversations about frontiers in Brazil and the US. And I am especially grateful to Amilcar Pereira of the Universidade Federal do Rio de Janeiro for our ongoing conversations about the complexities of US and Brazilian history. Elizabeth Mofacto also provided crucial moral support and inspiration as I brought this project to completion. I look forward to future conversations with these scholars and friends as the years progress.

And last but not least, I would like to extend my gratitude to Carmen Alveal and her family: Frederico, Goyo, Joanna, and the late Margarida for the generosity and hospitality they gave to me over many visits to Brazil.

I would also like to thank the professors who oversaw my graduate studies in the History Department and the Department of the History of Science and Technology at the Johns Hopkins University. They unreservedly shared their wisdom, knowledge, support, and encouragement: Richard Kagan, Lou Galambos, Peter Jelavich, Maria Portuondo, and Toby Dietz. I am especially grateful to Ron Walters for his appreciation of history's ironies, as well as his guidance in navigating the job market and the publishing world.

I was part of a truly wonderful cohort at Johns Hopkins, and I learned immensely from conversations both in and outside of my seminars. Thank you to Justin Roberts, Andrew Devereux, Katherine Murphy, Katherine Hijar, Michael Henderson, Mary Ashburn-Miller, Carolyn Salomons, Greg O-Malley, Claire Breedlove, Bill Dixon, Mabel Wong, Stefanie Fishel, Alana Bevan, Eddie Kolla, Martin Carrion, Blake Etheridge, Regina Galasso, Debra Law, Ann de Leon, Kate Moran, Molly Warsh, and Jeremy Arnold.

And last but not least I am thankful that I signed up for Judy Bieber's *History of Brazil* grad seminar at the University of New Mexico all those years ago. It was in her class that I first encountered the fascinating contours of Brazilian history. Since then she has provided on-going encouragement and support. I am very grateful indeed.

I would also like to thank the good folks at the Hispanic Reading Room at the Library of Congress. Carlos Olave in particular helped me find my bearings as a graduate student. Over the years I enjoyed many insightful conversations with Angela Leal at the Oliveira Lima Library, also in Washington, D.C. Wide-ranging conversations with scholars of Brazil and Latin America have also contributed immensely to my development as a scholar. I would like to thank Lise Sedrez, José Pádua, Hal Langfur, Patricia Acerbi, Hendrik Kraay, Celso Castilho, Kari Zimmerman, Ian Read, and Rory Miller for their help along the way and their thoughtful consideration of my research. I am especially grateful for the year I spent in central New York with Heather Roller. Our conversations about Brazil, academia, snow, and motherhood were sustaining. Likewise, I would like to thank Colin Snider for our many inspiring conversations over the years.

I would also like to thank the anonymous readers of this manuscript. Their suggestions and comments made this a much stronger book.

I am very appreciative of the support – institutional, professional, and scholarly – that I have received at the University of Alabama. The conversations I have shared with my colleagues have helped immensely as I navigated the ins and outs of being an assistant professor. Thank you Steve Bunker, Jennifer Purvis, Erik Peterson, Lisa Lindquist-Dorr, Janek Wasserman, Bart Elmore, Andrew Huebner, Jenny Shaw, Heather Kopelson, Kari Frederickson, Harold Selesky, John Giggie, David Beito, Sharony Green, Mike Innis-Jimenez, Steve Kosiba, Karina Vasquez, Sarah Moody, and John Beeler. I proffer a special thanks to Margaret Abruzzo for coming up with the title for *Industrial Forests*. I would also like to thank Alana Baldwin and Christina Frantom of the Faculty Resource Center for their assistance in creating the graphics, maps, and illustrations for this book. They were patient and supportive as I requested revisions and new versions. Mary Meares and Viktoria Harms, my colleagues in other departments, provided a different kind of support in yoga class each week. Additionally, I have worked with outstanding students here at UA. I am grateful to Brian Royster and David Nazworth for their research assistance, and I am thankful for Tori Robinson's excellent work on one of the graphics used in this book. Thank you all for making the University of Alabama such a pleasant place to work.

I would also like to acknowledge the institutions that supported my travel to distant archives to research the theme of Brazilian modernization. First and foremost is the History Department of the Johns Hopkins University for a dissertation fellowship and funding for summer research travel. The J. Brien Key Fellowship and the Program in Latin American Studies at Johns Hopkins also underwrote research costs in Brazil. I am deeply grateful for the Fulbright IIE fellowship for facilitating the bulk of the research for this book. The Spencer Baird Fellowship at the Dibner Library of Science and Technology located at the Smithsonian Institution Library also provided invaluable research material for this project.

I am equally grateful to friends and family for both the material and less tangible ways in which they contributed to the completion of this book. Foremost is my mother, Susan Cribelli, eminent proofreader, footnote checker, and expert on commas. My sister, Rebecca Cribelli, was an untiring cheerleader, especially in moments of doubt. Daniel Levine listened to my ideas for many hours and pointed me to readings that enriched my understanding of modernization. Aaron and Rhoda Levine provided moral support and many good dinners for two very poor graduate students. My father Frank Cribelli's love for history and his keen flair for storytelling are two qualities that have influenced me deeply, and for which I am grateful.

Finally, I want to thank all the fierce women who raised me and taught me to question and explore the world around me: Sandra Miller, Nancy Turner, Patricia Bulthaup, Mary MacDonald, and my grandmothers and great-grandmother, Mary Cribelli, Elizabeth Jones, and Grace Crowe.

Preface

Brazil was very distant in time and place for a young girl growing up in Greeley, Colorado, in the 1970s and 1980s. Everyone in my elementary school knew about the soccer sensation Pelé. I recall reading about him in my Scholastic newsletter and seeing his quick soccer moves on television. My classmates and I were also fascinated with the exotic and vibrant, but in other ways dimly imagined Amazon forest. Beyond these brief glimpses, Brazil rarely appeared in our everyday world. The first time I began to think about the possibilities of Brazil beyond what I had been exposed to in these small bits and pieces, was, oddly enough, a science fiction story about the aftermath of nuclear war in the United States that I read as a teenager in the mid-1980s. In the story, Brazil had risen to become the dominant political and technological power in the western hemisphere after the United States was destroyed by nuclear bombs. The narrative began two-and-a-half centuries after the fall of the United States when geologist Cristovão Hoffman crashed his helicopter in what had once been Los Angeles while on a reconnaissance mission to locate natural resources for the Brazilian government.[1] From there the story followed the romance between Hoffman and a young woman who rescued him. Though at fifteen I appreciated the tragically romantic bent of the story, the most striking aspect – and the piece that stuck with me all of these years – was the idea that a nation outside of the United States or Europe might inherit the mantel of technological hegemon. This

---

[1] Joan D. Vinge, "Phoenix in the Ashes," in *Phoenix in the Ashes* (New York: Bluejay Books, 1985), pp. 1–34.

MAP 1. Map of mid-nineteenth-century Brazil (map design: Alana Baldwin and Alex Hauser).

book is not science fiction, but my work nods to this teenage experience through its exploration of Brazil's pathway to modernization, a nation on the periphery of the North Atlantic industrial powers that has not yet been fully recognized for its technological achievements.

Nineteenth-Century Modernization in Brazil

Luís Carlos Martins Pena's 1842 romantic comedy *Os Dois ou o Inglês Maquinista* dramatizes the tensions surrounding the clandestine African slave trade in Rio de Janeiro (officially abolished in 1831), the increasing presence of British merchants and engineers on the city's streets, and the arrival of the steam machine, a new technology that signaled the beginning of modernization in nineteenth-century Brazil.[1] Gainer, an English carpetbagger machinist plying his trade in the Brazilian capital, constructs a machine that instantaneously (and, pointedly – with no labor) transforms an entire cow into an array of perfected products ready for market: sugar, combs, hats, polished shoes, and cuts of steak.[2] Gainer's invention receives a skeptical welcome from the play's handsome and wily protagonist Felício, a native of Rio. The Brazilian archly observes that the Englishman's intricate and seemingly magical machine is too good to be true.[3] Counterposed to the scheming English machinist is a Brazilian

---

[1] The Slave Trade was legally abolished by treaty with Britain in 1831, though illegal slave imports continued, increasing in the 1830s and 1840s to meet the demands of the expanding coffee sector in Brazil.

[2] Luís Carlos Martins Pena, *Os Dous ou o Inglez Machinista*, in *Comédias* (Rio de Janeiro: H. Garnier, n.d.), pp. 127–28.

[3] This Brazilian description of an early encounter with the new inventions of the nineteenth century echoes a more somber portrayal of factory machinery by US writer Herman Melville. In his 1855 short story, "The Tartarus of Maids," the "inscrutable intricacy" of the newly invented paper machines of a Massachusetts mill illustrates the wonder inspired by nineteenth-century technology combined with dismay at the soul-crushing repetitiveness of mechanized work reflected in the wan faces of factory workers. Herman Melville, *Great Short Works of Herman Melville* (New York: HarperCollins Press, 2004), pp. 221–22. Also cited in Judith A. McGaw, *Most Wonderful Machine: mechanization and social change in Berkshire paper making, 1801–1885* (Princeton, NJ: Princeton University Press, 1987), pp. 3–4.

villain Negreiro (equally the target of Felício's scorn), a wealthy slave importer baldly named for his illicit profession.[4] Through these characters Pena inserts reactions to the beginning of modernization in Brazil into a traditional theatrical narrative of heroes, ingénues, and villains. In doing so, he gestures to the promise and apprehensions unleashed by a then emerging transatlantic modernity and distills a complicated social process into characters embedded within the Brazilian context.

This early representation of technology in Brazilian literature juxtaposes two of the most important issues of the period: Brazil's continuing use of – and indeed, growing dependence on – slavery in an increasingly abolitionist world, and the arrival of the steam machine, the harbinger of even more technological advances to come. For Felício, the character with whom we are meant to empathize (and the one who wins the heart of Mariquinha, the young woman that both Negreiro and Gainer court), neither the greedy excesses of Negreiro nor the scheming opportunism of Gainer pose desirable options; neither Brazil's past nor England's present offer appropriate models for the future. Exploring this dilemma provides a point of entry for understanding Brazilian perspectives on modernization. Though powerful conservative factions remained ardent supporters of slavery up until abolition in 1888, the institution's impending demise cast a long shadow over the reign of Emperor Pedro II (1840–89). Negreiro and his ilk were not the future that many Brazilians envisioned for their nation, despite the ongoing reliance on slavery that drove the clandestine trade until it was definitively ended in 1850. Likewise, new technologies in agriculture and industry were both enthusiastically admired and greeted with skepticism as many outside innovations proved disappointing – at worst oversold, or at best simply impractical for the different geography, climate, infrastructure, and social organization in Brazil. Furthermore, the liberal, English industrial capitalistic system was ultimately potentially dangerous to the social organization of this highly stratified and slavery-dependent tropical nation. Brazil had created a social order that could not become "English" without – it was feared – possibly destroying itself. The specter of slave revolts and mass uprisings coupled with prevailing racist notions about the inability of Africans and their descendants to operate or produce technology made elites cautious about adopting any new system that might uproot their power and privilege. Pena's example therefore provides a useful schematic: the existence of a *Brazilian* way to adopt the social and technological advances of the age in service of

---

[4] *Negro* referred to an African or African-descended person, while *negreiro* was both a slave trader and the name for a slave ship.

the nation's progress. Elites, while embracing ideologies and technologies from Europe and beyond did not merely follow in the footsteps of the North Atlantic industrializing nations, they forged their own path based on their material realities, hopes, and fears.

With the aim of understanding the motivations behind Brazilian visions of modernization in the nineteenth century, this work examines how certain sectors of society (specifically, literate white males with connections to Rio) thought about and responded to the technological, economic, and social innovations unfolding in the late colonial period and across the nineteenth century, especially the transformative years of 1850–89 following the political consolidation of the post-independence Brazilian Empire (1822–89). Although modernization is a twentieth-century word that expresses a specific vision of economic and social development relevant to the Cold War era, I use the term here to describe the nexus of transformations that spread across Europe, the Americas, and beyond as a result of the technological, bureaucratic, and economic innovations that emerged in the eighteenth and nineteenth centuries. Modernization had many facets, be they the accumulation of capital and the rise of industrialization, the emergence of a concept of a uniform civil or mass society and the institutional and social innovations that served its collective needs such as public education, national banks, nationalized legal codes and languages, the compilation of statistics, and the surveying of state territories.[5] Though modernization was never a term used by the Brazilian actors of this study, this definition broadly captures the changes they envisioned and enacted for their nation.

[5] Craig Calhoun, ed., *Dictionary of the Social Sciences* (Oxford: Oxford University Press, 2002), s.v. "modernity."

Marshall Berman offers an eloquent description of modernization and modernity:

The maelstrom of modern life has been fed from many sources: great discoveries in the physical sciences, changing our images of the universe and our place in it; the industrialization of production, which transforms scientific knowledge into technology, creates new human environments and destroys old ones, speeds up the whole tempo of life, generates new forms of corporate power and class struggle; immense demographic upheavals, severing millions of people from their ancestral habitats, hurtling them halfway across the world into new lives; rapid and often cataclysmic urban growth; systems of mass communication, dynamic in their development, enveloping and binding together the most diverse people and societies; increasingly powerful national states, bureaucratically structured and operated, constantly striving to expand their powers; mass social movements of people, and peoples, challenging their political and economic rulers, striving to gain some control over their lives; finally, bearing and driving all these people and institutions along, an ever-expanding, drastically fluctuating capitalist world market.

All That is Solid Melts into Air: The Experience of Modernity (New York: Simon & Schuster, 1982), p. 16.

The meaning of modernization employed here should not be confused with modernization theory, a development model created in the middle of the twentieth century as a solution to the underdevelopment of the so-called Third World, especially Latin America where poverty was seen as a national security threat by US policymakers.[6] Conceived as a counter to Soviet-style communism, modernization theory promoted the creation "... of a dynamic market-based economy ... as a generator of wealth at the societal level and as a distributor of wealth across the society."[7] The promoters of modernization theory argued that economic growth led to political stabilization and eventually the establishment of democratic institutions.

Modernization: Brazil and Beyond

Processes of nineteenth-century modernization have long intrigued scholars of Brazil, as is evident from a rich body of scholarly work on the development of the industrial, banking, insurance, communication, and transportation sectors.[8] Of these, two early works, Richard Graham's

---

[6] Rafael R. Ioris, *Transforming Brazil: A History of National Development in the Postwar Era* (New York: Routledge, 2014), p. 3.

[7] Calhoun, *Dictionary of the Social Sciences*, s.v. "modernization theory." For a recent treatment of the history of modernization theory in the United States, see Nils Gilman, *Mandarins of the Future: Modernization Theory in Cold War America* (Baltimore: The Johns Hopkins University Press, 2003).

[8] In addition to Graham and Eisenberg, the following selected works treat aspects of modernization in the imperial period: Humberto Bastos, *O pensamento industrial no Brasil* (São Paulo: Martins Ed., 1952); Geraldo de Beauclair, *Raízes da Indústria no Brasil: a pre-indústria fluminense, 1808–1860* (Rio de Janeiro: Studio F&S Editora, 1992), and *A Construção Inacabada: a economia brasileira, 1822–1860* (Rio de Janeiro: Vício de Leitura, 2001); E. Bradford Burns, *The Poverty of Progress: Latin America in the Nineteenth Century* (Berkeley: University of California Press, 1983); Edgard Carone, *O Centro Industrial do Rio de Janeiro e sua importante participação na economia nacional: 1827–1977* (Rio de Janeiro: Ed. Cátedra/Centro Industrial, 1978); Warren Dean, *The industrialization of São Paulo, 1880–1945* (Austin: Published for the Institute of Latin American Studies by the University of Texas Press, 1969); Marshall Eakin, *British Enterprise in Brazil: the St. John d'el Rey Mining Company and the Morro Velho Gold Mine, 1830–1960* (Durham, NC: Duke University Press, 1989); Peter L. Eisenberg, *The Sugar Industry in Pernambuco: Modernization without change, 1840–1910* (Berkeley: University of California Press, 1974); Noah Elkin, "Promoting a New Brazil: National Expositions and Images of Modernity, 1861–1922" (Ph.D. dissertation, Rutgers University, 1998); Francisco Foot, *Trem Fantasma: A Modernidade Na Selva* (São Paulo: Companhia das Letras; São Paulo: Editora Schwarcz, 1988); Celso Furtado, *Economic Development of Latin America* (Cambridge: Cambridge University Press, 1970); Richard Graham, *Britain and the Onset of Modernization in Brazil: 1850–1914* (Cambridge: Cambridge University Press, 1968); Stephen Haber, ed., *How Latin America Fell Behind:*

Great Britain and the Onset of Modernization in Brazil: 1850–1914 (1968), and Peter Eisenberg's *The Sugar Industry in Pernambuco: Modernization without Change, 1840–1910* (1974), were important scholarly milestones in the English-language historiography on Brazil that investigated the beginning of modernization during the reign of Pedro II (1840–89). The former illuminated the British role in Brazilian modernization, while the latter described the technological advances that improved sugar production in northeastern Brazil even as the social standing and living conditions of those on the lowest rungs of society remained the same.

More recent Brazilian scholarship on modernization explores new lines of inquiry. Leandro Malavota, for example, sheds light on Brazilian

Essays on the Economic Histories of Brazil and Mexico, 1800–1914 (Stanford: Stanford University Press, 1997); Anne G. Hanley, *Native Capital: Financial Institutions and Economic Development in São Paulo, Brazil, 1850–1920* (Stanford: Stanford University Press, 2005); Álvaro Antonio Klafke, "O Império na provincia: construção do estado nacional nas páginas de O *Propagador da Indústria Rio-grandense- 1833–1834,*" (Master's thesis, Universidade Federal do Rio Grande do Sul, Brazil, 2006); Douglas Cole Libby, "Proto-Industrialization in a Slave Society: The Case of Minas Gerais," *Journal of Latin American Studies*, 23:1 (Feb., 1991), pp. 1–35; Heitor Ferreira Lima, *História do Pensamento Econômico no Brasil* (São Paulo: Editora Nacional, 1976); Eulalia Maria Lahmeyer Lobo, *História do Rio de Janeiro (Do Capital Comercial ao Capital Industrial e Financeiro)*, 2 vols., (Rio de Janeiro: Instituto Brasileiro de Mercado de Capitais, 1978); Lourenço, Fernando Antonio, *Agricultura Illustrada: liberalismo e escravismo nas origins da questão agraria brasileira* (Campinas, SP: Editora Unicamp, 2001); Nícia Vilela Luz, *Luta pela industrialização no Brasil* (São Paulo: Editora Alfa Omega, 1975); Sérgio de Oliveira, *Entrepreneurship in Nineteenth-Century Brazil: The Formation of a Business Environment* (New York: St. Martin's, 1999); Maria Fernanda Vieira Martins, "O Imperial Instituto Fluminense de Agricultura: elites, política e reforma agrícola (1860–1897)," (Master's thesis, Universidade Federal Fluminense, 1995); Caio Prado Júnior, *História Econômica do Brasil* (São Paulo: Editora Brasiliense, 1976); Eugene Ridings, *Business Interest Groups in Nineteenth-Century Brazil* (Cambridge: Cambridge University Press, 1994); Luiz Werneck da Silva, "Isto é o que me parece: a Sociedade Auxiliadora de Indústria Nacional (1827–1904) na formação social brasileira: a conjuntura de 1871 até 1877" (Master's thesis, Universidade Federal Fluminense, 1979); Stanley J. and Barbara H. Stein, *The Colonial Heritage of Latin America: Essays on Economic Dependence in Perspective* (New York: Oxford University Press, 1970); Stanley Stein, *The Brazilian Cotton Manufacture: Textile Enterprise in an Underdeveloped Area, 1850–1950* (Cambridge, MA: Harvard University Press, 1957), and *Vassouras, a Brazilian Coffee County, 1850–1900* (Cambridge, MA: Harvard University Press, 1957); William Summerhill, *Order Against Progress: Government, Foreign Investment, and Railroads in Brazil, 1854–1913* (Stanford: Stanford University Press, 2003); Barbara Weinstein, *The Amazon Rubber Boom 1850–1920* (Stanford: Stanford University Press, 1983), and *The Color of Modernity: São Paulo and the Making of Race and Nation in Brazil* (Durham, NC: Duke University Press, 2015) and Paulo Alfonso Zarth, *Do Arcaico ao Moderno: o Rio Grande do Sul agrário do século XIX* (Ijuí, RS: Editora UNJUI, 2002).

efforts to promote technological innovation through patents. In 1809, one year after the arrival of the Portuguese court in Rio, Dom João VI (then the crown prince) issued the world's fourth modern patent law (following Great Britain, France, and the United States) for Portugal and its colonies. "Patents of introduction" were a unique feature of the law in Brazil (updated after independence in 1830) that provided short-term monopolies of fifteen years to importers of foreign inventions with the aim of encouraging technological dissemination even in the absence of Brazilian innovators. As Malavota shows, the evolution of Brazilian patents in the 1800s demonstrated creativity, foresight, and a keen awareness of North Atlantic legal innovations that resulted in debates and legislation intended to spur economic development in Brazil.[9]

Carlos Gabriel Guimarães' research on the interplay of English and Brazilian interests in the nation's nascent banking sector sheds new light on the domestic and international relationships embedded within this important facet of modernization. A central prong of Guimarães' analysis is the deconstruction of the mythic image of nineteenth-century entrepreneur, banker, and industrialist, the Baron of Mauá (Irineu Evangelista de Souza, 1813–89). Jorge Caldeira and other scholars have cast Mauá as a misunderstood visionary thwarted by conservative, slave-owning agragian elites from bringing industrialization and economic development to Brazil.[10] Guimarães paints a more complex picture of Mauá and his period in which Brazilian and British interests often coincided; both political conservatives and liberals had business and political relationships with the entrepreneur and indeed supported his many technological projects (railroads, for example); and Mauá (unlike the antislavery advocate he is presented to be in the 1999 film based on Jorge Caldeira's research), invested in the slave trade through his numerous commercial enterprises when it was profitable to do so.[11] In Guimaraes' work, the trajectory of nineteenth-century Brazilian economic development emerges as a more complex story than the backward,

---

[9] Leandro Malavota, *A Construção do Sistema de Patentes no Brasil* (Rio de Janeiro: Editora Lumen Juris, 2011), p. 25.

[10] Carlos Gabriel Guimarães, *A presença inglesa nas finanças e no comércio no Brasil Imperial: os casos da Sociedade Bancária Mauá, MacGregor & Cia. (1854–1866) e da firma inglesa Samuel Phillips & Cia. (1808–1840)* (São Paulo: Alameda Casa Editorial, 2012), pp. 32–4.

[11] *Mauá – O Imperador e o Rei*. Directed by Sérgio Rezende. Rio de Janeiro: Riofilms, 1999.

slave-owning plantation elites, British banking interlopers, and thwarted industrialists sometimes blamed for the nation's underdevelopment. In Guimarães' words, Brazil was a "seignorial slave society . . . immersed in a process of expansion of capitalism" and needs to be understood as such in order to avoid anachronistic renderings of economic development as exemplified by the Mauá myth.[12]

A new investigation of Brazilian economic development extends to the twentieth century in Rafael Ioris' analysis of the reception of and support for the postwar economic policies of President Juscelino Kubitschek by previously understudied sectors of Brazilian society. Through the consultation of new sources from the press and underutilized institutional archives, Ioris demonstrates how an expanding domestic consumer market, the mobilization of São Paulo autoworkers, and a growing and vibrant national cultural scene shaped and transformed more traditional conservative politics and the developmentalist policies of postwar Brazil. Together, this recent Brazilian scholarship adds new depth to our understanding of state-supported economic development while also bringing the voices of actors from different (and previously ignored) sectors of Brazilian society into focus, as in the case of Ioris. Most importantly, these works demonstrate that Brazilian economic development in the nineteenth and twentieth centuries was more complex than the reactive enterprise it has sometimes been described to be.

My project expands on these lines of inquiry by focusing on Brazilian perspectives on modernization during the transformative period of the nineteenth century. One analytical thread aims to understand debates published in government reports, journals, illustrated weeklies, national and international exhibition catalogs, and the public opinion sections of newspapers from an explicitly Brazilian perspective, rather than through the lens of foreign influence or as a primarily economic process. The sentiments expressed in public letters enliven the transformations then underway in Brazil and offer a human voice to both counter and complement statistical analysis and economic data. These sources also provide insight into attitudes about modernization where economic sources have not survived or do not exist. By contrasting official documents with the usually anonymous public letters printed in one of Rio's most important newspapers of record, the *Jornal do Commercio*, Brazilian attitudes about the technological and social transformations of the period come

[12] Guimarães, pp. 46–7.

into view. Each of the following chapter topics first evolved out of public letters and paid articles published in the *Jornal do Commercio*.

First, a brief review of selected scholarship on the English Industrial Revolution, one of the most important topics of eighteenth- and nineteenth-century modernization, is in order. Late eighteenth- and nineteenth-century advances in agricultural technology and industry in Europe – and England in particular – were integral to conversations about modernization in Brazil. The profound changes that resulted from the English Industrial Revolution (1760–1840) emerged as a subject of scholarly inquiry even as it was still unfolding in the nineteenth century. Looking back on more than a century and a half of scholarship on the topic, historians in the 1980s and 1990s set out to analyze the conflicting interpretations of the roots, causes, and outcomes of industrialization. In her classic 1992 synthetic analysis, Pat Hudson argued that the Industrial Revolution was more than a series of events centered in mechanized factories, or even the direct result of mechanization and capital accumulation per se. Instead, it was a complex socio-economic, political, and cultural process that unfolded over many decades and depended on the participation of diverse sectors of society. Industrialization, she contended, must therefore be understood as more than an economic process alone, despite a long-standing focus on this aspect in scholarship. The availability of economic data (primarily from larger enterprises) was (and is) more readily available and quantifiable than the sometimes nebulous and harder to study cultural and social relationships that undergirded new industrial work systems, one reason many of the early studies of the Industrial Revolution focused on economic growth.

Hudson concluded that the Industrial Revolution was indeed revolutionary in terms of its economic and social impact, but this was neither a full-speed-ahead gallop into exclusively mechanized production nor did it result in the overnight creation of uniform economic growth. Traditional modes of production continued alongside factory machines, and in some cases even outperformed mechanical innovations well into the nineteenth century.[13] The late eighteenth-century success of English calico print production, for instance, depended less on mechanization and more "on a cheap workforce prepared to carry out labour-intensive processes on a

---

[13] Pat Hudson, *The Industrial Revolution* (London: Edward Arnold, 1992), p. 46. *See* also, Maxine Berg and Pat Hudson, "Rehabilitating the Industrial Revolution." *The Economic History Review*, New Series, Vol. 45, No. 1 (Feb., 1992), pp. 24–50; and David Cannadine, "The Present and the Past in the English Industrial Revolution 1800–1900." *Past and Present*, 103 (1984), pp. 131–72.

new scale and under new organization and discipline in a competitive setting."[14] In the agricultural sector, machinery that reduced the number of workers needed during sowing in some cases resulted in a shortage of hands during the crucial, labor-intensive harvest period, making it difficult for farmers to bring in their crops.[15] These points are important to remember when considering the relative backwardness of less developed nations like Brazil. While the intention here is not to diminish the importance of factory mechanization – and the economic and social reorganization it entailed – but rather to note that machinery was not always the most efficient or advantageous mode of production in spurring economic growth. In fact, manual labor, traditional modes of production, and slavery employed in nations and colonies on the periphery of the first wave of European and US industrialization contributed enormously to the economic success of the Industrial Revolution. Slave-produced cotton from the US South, as is well known, fueled textile production in Northern factories as well as Britain until supply chains were disrupted by the Civil War.[16]

This work also situates nineteenth-century Brazilian modernization within a recent historiography that further challenges and adds nuance to the traditional, triumphalist narrative of the English Industrial Revolution. Jeff Horn's examination of France's delayed industrialization compared to England revealed that the fear of popular revolts after the French Revolution resulted in industrialists taking a more cautious approach to negotiations with factory laborers in the late 1700s. This reticence translated into greater rights and freedoms for French workers than were attained by their counterparts in England. By the 1830s, after the specter of political violence unleashed during the French Revolution had receded, French factory owners backed by the state were more willing to press their demands upon the laboring classes in a manner that echoed the coercive and sometimes violent treatment of protesting English laborers around the turn of the nineteenth century.[17] Concern with social upheaval was

---

[14] Hudson, p. 48. [15] Hudson, p. 69.

[16] Ed Baptist's recent work on the role of slavery in the production of one of the most important raw materials of the Industrial Revolution, cotton, demonstrates the link between burgeoning textile production in the industrializing North and slave labor in the South, *The Half has never Been Told: Slavery and the Making of American Capitalism* (New York: Basic Books, 2014), pp. 317–324.

[17] Jeff Horn, *The Path not Taken: French Industrialization in the Age of Revolution, 1750–1830* (Cambridge, MA; The MIT Press, 2006), Chs. 4–6; for works on the coercive tactics employed against workers in England, *see* Hudson, p. 32; and E. P. Thompson, *The Making of the English Working Class* (New York: Vintage Books, 1963).

also present in nineteenth-century Brazil, albeit for different reasons, as will be explored further in Chapters 2 and 6. Likewise, the collected essays in Horn, Rosenband, and Smith's *Reconceptualizing the Industrial Revolution* challenge the established narrative of England as an exceptional site for the first wave of industrialization, while still acknowledging its important role. A central contribution of the volume is the extension of the context of the Industrial Revolution beyond England with essays that consider Brazil, India, Japan, Russia, German, the United States, and Scandinavia.[18]

A re-visioning of Latin American industrialization has also emerged in recent scholarship. Fernando Rocchi's study of Argentina between 1870 and 1930, for example, contradicts the traditional narrative of a nation dependent on agricultural exports with a conservative landholding elite hostile to industry that resulted in sluggish manufacturing development before 1914 (a sentiment that echoes the Mauá myth in Brazil). Rocchi argues that a "middling industrialization" that served a fledgling domestic consumer market was more robust during the period than previously acknowledged. Furthermore, Rocchi demonstrates that a section of powerful landholding elites supported industries that employed key agricultural commodities produced in Argentina.[19] Yovanna Pineda also examines industrial production during the years of 1890–1930, arguing that despite Argentina's less robust industrial development compared to North Atlantic nations, the state nonetheless steadfastly supported industrialization, recognizing that it "helped Argentina stay globally connected," through the importation of the latest technology and by providing access to foreign investment. These recent works demonstrate that Latin American nations were fully aware of the potential benefits of industrialization despite the ongoing importance of the agrarian sector to their economies.[20]

Whereas the previously mentioned scholars bring to light understudied aspects of Argentine industrialization, Edward Beatty's work on technology transfer to Mexico between 1870 and 1930 explores the reasons why the adoption of sewing machines, bottle-making factories, and the cyanide

---

[18] Jeff Horn, Leonard N. Rosenband, and Merritt Roe Smith, eds., *Reconceptualizing the Industrial Revolution* (Cambridge, MA: MIT Press, 2010).

[19] Fernando Rocchi, *Chimneys in the Desert: Industrialization in Argentina During the Export Boom Years, 1870–1930* (Stanford: Stanford University Press, 2006), chs. 1 and 2.

[20] Yovanna Pineda, *Industrial Development in a Frontier Economy: The Industrialization of Argentina, 1890–1930* (Stanford: Stanford University Press, 2009), p. 17.

process for gold mining did not result in the establishment of domestically produced innovation or the dissemination of Mexican technological expertise. Many of the barriers to industrialization in Mexico outlined by Beatty (namely the high cost of freight and difficulty of transportation before the establishment of the railway in combination with the scarcity of raw materials for textile and paper production) were significant challenges in Brazil as well.[21] My work contrasts with Beatty in that I show where Brazilians successfully assimilated and reproduced technological systems including improvements and adjustments to railroad equipment that rendered trains and locomotives more efficient. Brazilians also engineered significant innovations for coffee production both within their nation and abroad. Brazil's competitive advantage in producing coffee, a crop that can only be grown in the subtropics and tropics, spurred the development of technology to meet the nation's unique needs, especially as the end of slavery neared. Mexico was also hindered by its proximity to the United States where US technicians and railway managers dominated certain technological sectors to the detriment of Mexican engineers, unlike the case of Brazil and Chile where distance and higher shipping costs contributed to the development of domestic technological expertise, a topic I explore further in Chapter 5.[22] My work converges with Beatty in explorations of the social disruptions – both imagined and real – that accompanied technological modernization in Brazil.

Sources

The inspiration for this project grew out of the rich variety of public letters and articles published in the *Correspondências* and *Publicações a Pedido* sections of the *Jornal do Commercio* from the late 1840s until the end of the Brazilian Empire in 1889. The *Correspondências* section was akin to a modern-day letter-to-the-editor column and included commentaries on politics, the economy, modernization, and other issues of the moment. *Publicações a Pedido*, loosely translated as "publications by request," (*apedidos*) covered some of the same topics as the *Correspondências* section, but letters and articles were published for a fee. Political letters appeared in both sections, while advertisements, eulogies,

---

[21] Edward Beatty, *Technology and the Search for Progress in Modern Mexico* (Berkeley, CA: University of California Press), 2015, pp. 159–62.

[22] By the 1880s, Chile produced its own locomotives and rolling stock. Arnold J. Bauer, "Industry and the Missing Bourgeoisie: Consumption and Development in Chile, 1850–1950," *Hispanic American Historical Review* 70:2, (May 1990), p. 229.

and amateur poetry were printed exclusively in the latter. It is unknown what selection criteria existed for each, or the amount charged for an *apedido*, though the fee was presumably calculated per word or line. While the cost was probably not prohibitive (the section was popular), it was most likely beyond the reach of the less affluent. Indeed, one contributor declared that he was unwilling to continue a heated debate in the *Jornal do Commercio* because he did not have money to waste on publication fees. The cost of publishing an article, along with Brazil's low literacy rate, would have restricted *apedido* submissions to those with the financial means, personal motivation, and sufficient leisure to follow political discussions in the newspaper. By the 1860s, the *Correspondências* section appeared irregularly and eventually disappeared, while the *Publicações a Pedido* grew steadily from an average of 74.3 submissions per month consulted in 1850 to 751 per month by 1889. Accordingly, the majority of the letters and articles cited in this study are *apedidos*. James Fletcher, a North American missionary, offers the following observation on the popularity of this printed forum in Rio's newspapers:

The press being free, I doubt whether any journals in the United States, England, or the Continent, contain so many communications from subscribers as those of Rio de Janeiro. As all of these *communicações* [sic] must be accompanied with the cash [sic], journalism in Brazil is a lucrative "institution."[23]

The profitability of *apedidos*, as Fletcher suggests, was probably one factor in the decline of the *Correspondências* section by the 1860s.

As a genre, the *Publicações a Pedido* represented a broad, sometimes eclectic, spectrum of public sentiment. Letters and articles ranged widely, from criticism or support of legislation and politics to amateur poetry, angry complaints about every variety of government shortcoming (from slow mail carriers to the poor condition of roads) as well as usually anonymous and often vitriolic personal and political attacks, as scandalized foreigners noted.[24] Grateful citizens banded together to publicly thank firefighters, engineers, boat captains, midwives, and doctors for jobs well done. Other *apedidos* advertised products: everything from medicinal tonics to men's hats appeared with the changing seasons. The yellow fever epidemic of 1850 resulted in grief-stricken eulogies, heartbreaking in their plaintiveness, as well as medical testimonials for miracle cures.

---

[23] James C. Fletcher, D. P. Kidder, *Brazil and the Brazilians*, 9th ed. (Boston: Little, Brown, and Company, 1879), p. 252.

[24] Hendrik Kraay, *Days of National Festivity in Rio de Janeiro, Brazil, 1823–1889* (Stanford: Stanford University Press, 2013), p. 115.

Sometimes *apedido* debates unfolded across multiple newspapers. Critics of Brazil's first major macadamized road, the União e Indústria, printed their complaints in the *Correio Mercantil* while supporters responded in the *Jornal do Commercio*. Some *apedidos* were composed of only a few short lines, while others filled up ten columns or more, and a few were virtual serial publications that spanned the course of many months. Most writers concealed their identities with pseudonyms, though declarations from notable persons appeared periodically, including the aforementioned Baron of Mauá, André Rebouças (1838–98), Miguel Calmon du Pin e Almeida, (the Marquis of Abrantes, 1796–1865, a senator, planter, and president of the Sociedade Auxiliadora), and Joaquim Nabuco (an abolitionist, politician, and diplomat). Local and national notables also frequently published under pseudonyms. What did not appear, or were at best concealed through anonymity, were letters from or about women (except in a few rare cases), slaves, or the illiterate poor.

Due to the volume of material (by the 1880s, some months contained nearly 1,000 paid articles and letters), I focused on *apedidos* published in January, May, and September for the years 1850, 1855, 1860, 1865, 1870, 1875, 1880, 1885, and 1889 (the fall of Brazil's constitutional monarchy). I chose these months in an effort to sample different periods of the year: January, because it launched the beginning of the year and included the annual political and economic retrospective of the *Jornal do Commercio*. May and September provided an equidistant sample and overlapped with the parliamentary session that convened from early May to early September.[25] I also consulted supplemental dates in search of responses to specific projects such as national exhibitions and railroad inaugurations. Undoubtedly, the method employed here has bypassed potentially enlightening *apedidos* and additional topics on modernization, but the high volume of paid letters and articles necessitated a systematic approach. Following is a list of topics on modernization encountered in the *Correspondências and Publicações a Pedidos* sections, in descending order based on frequency of submissions:

Railroads
Roads
Machinery (agricultural)

---

[25] May to September corresponded to the dry, cool season, facilitating travel from interior and distant provinces. Jeffrey Needell, *The Party of Order: The Conservatives, the State, and Slavery in the Brazilian Monarchy, 1831–1871* (Stanford: Stanford University Press, 2006), p. 37.

Navigation
National Industry
Coffee Machinery
Agricultural Improvement
Engineering
Gas Illumination
Intellectual Property (patents)
Canals
Industry
Telegraphs

Additional topics related to modernization but not listed here include: slavery, European immigration, and state-sponsored immigration
colonies. The latter was presented as a way to provide a docile source of
labor in answer to an anticipated shortage of workers as the abolition
of slavery loomed. Furthermore, many Brazilian elites called for European immigration as a way to simultaneously replace slaves and "whiten
the nation." By mid-century, immigration was promoted as a remedy for
reducing the nation's sizable Afro-descended population vis-à-vis European immigrants and their descendants, a notion born out of the perception that Afro-Brazilians were culturally and biologically unsuited for
modernization.[26]

Notwithstanding the short run of many periodicals and a readership
limited to a literate minority (16 percent of the population, mostly male,
could read at the time of the first official census in 1872), Brazil became
home to a vibrant newspaper culture after the arrival of the Portuguese
Court in Rio de Janeiro in 1808 when the printing press was legalized
in the colony for the first time.[27] The Brazilian press was noted for its

---

[26] Discussions of "whitening" are explored in George Reid Andrews, *Blacks and Whites in
São Paulo, 1888–1988* (Madison, WI: University of Wisconsin Press, 1991), pp. 133–34;
and Thomas Skidmore, *Black into White; Race and Nationality in Brazilian Thought*
(Oxford: Oxford University Press, 1974). For a recent exploration of the linkage between
whiteness, modernization, and progress in Brazil, see Barbara Weinsten, *The Color of
Modernity: São Paulo and the Making of Race and Nation in Brazil*.

[27] Lilia Mortiz Schwarcz, *As barbas do imperador: D. Pedro II, um monarca nos trópicos*
(São Paulo: Campanhia das Letras, 2003), p. 78. For works on the print media in
nineteenth-century Brazil, see Joaquim Marçal Ferreira de Andrade, *História da fotoreportagem no Brasil: a fotografia na imprensa do Rio de Janeiro de 1839 a 1900* (Rio
de Janeiro: Elsevier Editora Ltda., 2004); Marcelo Balaban, *Poeta do Lápis: sátira e
política na trajetória de Angelo Agostini no Brasil Imperial (1864–1888)* (Campinas,
SP: Editora Unicamp, 2009); Kraay, *Days of National Festivity...*; Maria Beatriz Nizza
da Silva, *A Gazeta do Rio de Janeiro (1808–1822): cultura e sociedade* (Rio de Janeiro:

lack of censorship by the 1830s and throughout most of the imperial period, a fact made all the more remarkable given that the importation of newspapers and other publications were censored and strictly controlled by the Portuguese authorities throughout the colonial period. Though many centuries behind the official arrival of the printing press in other New World colonies, Brazil nonetheless became home to two of the longest-lasting, continuously published newspapers in Latin America: the aforementioned *Jornal do Commercio* (Rio de Janeiro, 1827) and the *Diário de Pernambuco*, founded two years previously in Recife. Among the many newspapers printed in Rio, Brazil's political and cultural center in the nineteenth century, the *Jornal do Commercio* stands out for its wide-ranging and numerous public submissions, its national audience, and its status as paper of record for the period. In the 1880s, one foreign observer noted the popularity of the *Jornal do Commercio* as reading material for men on board the train from Rio to São Paulo, linking two of the most important innovations of the century: railways and mass-produced publications.[28] Few other sources provide such a broad window into public reactions to modernization, however limited newspaper readership may have been to the masculine, literate, and at least moderately affluent sectors of society. The high volume of *apedidos* published each month underscores the popularity of the section, providing a useful lens for examining public reactions to modernization across the nineteenth century.

By 1876, the *Jornal do Commercio* distributed 15,000 copies daily, three times the amount published by one of its nearest competitors in the capital, the *Diário do Rio de Janeiro*, which had a daily run of 5,000 copies.[29] The *Jornal do Commercio* was also distributed nationally; individuals from far-flung provinces regularly contributed to the *Publicações a Pedido* section. While the popularity of the newspaper diminished by the end of the 1880s and other dailies eventually surpassed it in terms of circulation, it nonetheless remained an important venue for political,

---

Editora UERJ, 2007); Mauro César Silveira, "As marcas do preconceito no jornalismo brasileiro e a história do *Paraguay* Illustrado," *Revista Brasileira de Ciências da Comunicação* 30:2, pp. 41–66; and Nelson Werneck Sodré, *História da imprensa no Brasil* 4ª ed. (Rio de Janeiro: Mauad, 1998, 2004).

[28] Kraay, p. 271.

[29] By the 1870s, the *Jornal do Commercio* employed eight editors and eighty correspondents in Brazil, the United States, and Europe. An additional 242 employees worked behind the scenes. *The Empire of Brazil at the Universal Exhibition of 1876* (Rio de Janeiro: Tip. e Lith. do Imperial Instituto Artístico, 1876), pp. 226–7.

economic, and social commentary. Furthermore, the increasing number of *apedidos* published by the end of the 1880s indicates that they remained a vital forum and most likely were an important source of revenue for the paper.

Another key source for this work is *O Auxiliador da Indústria Nacional*, a scientific and technological journal published by Brazil's most important industrial and agricultural society, the Sociedade Auxiliadora da Indústria Nacional (Society for the Promotion of the National Industry). The long run of *O Auxiliador* (1833–92) demonstrated a long-standing and ongoing interest in technological development in Brazil, with an emphasis on agricultural improvement. Within the society, an emerging class of professionalized engineers and scientists joined forces with progressive planters and merchants to promote economic growth through technological means. Together, the *apedidos* and articles of *O Auxiliador* present a lively and creative discourse on the benefits and risks of Brazilian modernization.

Finally, nineteenth-century Brazil was home to a variety of illustrated weeklies. Innovations in lithograph technology, printing presses, and inexpensive paper that drove down the cost of reproducing images facilitated the growth of the mass-produced illustrated press across the North and South Atlantic. Illustrated publications ranged from the French satirical *La Silhoutte* (founded in 1829) and *La Caricature* (1830), to the first illustrated newspaper *The Illustrated London News* (1842), to monthly variety magazines in the United States such as *Harper's New Monthly Magazine* (1850) and *Scribner's Monthly* (1870). The Brazilian illustrated press followed suit with satirical publications such as *O Mosquito* (1872), the *Semana Illustrada* (1860), and the *Revista Illustrada* (1876). There is a well-established scholarship on the Brazilian illustrated press, particularly in the realm of political satire and news reporting.[30] But whereas scholars have used illustrated publications to explore Brazilian politics and topics such as abolition, I have consulted these publications in order to shed light on Brazilian attitudes toward technology and modernization expressed in visual sources. Indeed, the illustrated press, like Martins Pena's play at the beginning of this chapter, provides insight into the ways in which technology was at times perceived in a less positive light by Brazilian observers, providing a counternarrative to celebrations of technology in *apedidos*, *O Auxiliador*, and exhibition catalogs.

[30] See Andrade, *História da fotoreportagem*; and Marcelo Balaban, *Poeta do Lápis*.

Background and Historical Context

Before continuing, a brief summary of the trajectory of Brazilian history is in order, especially as it relates to late colonial economic production, independence, and the ongoing practice of slavery in nineteenth-century Brazil. Agricultural production and resource extraction characterized Brazil's economic development during more than three hundred years of Portuguese colonial rule (1500–1822), with sugar, diamonds, gold, and tobacco comprising the main exports to markets in Europe and Africa. Beginning in 1530 with the transfer of sugar cultivation from Portuguese Africa to Brazil, enslaved indigenous Brazilians, and later African slaves provided the bulk of the labor force for the colony by the 1600s. Africans were especially important on the labor-intensive sugar plantations of the northeastern coastal regions established in the sixteenth and seventeenth centuries, and in the gold and diamond extraction that drew settlers to the interior from the coast after the 1680s. Placer mining in the densely forested interior captaincy of Minas Gerais (the primary mining region) demanded intensive manual labor and technological knowledge; both needs were met by ongoing imports of captive Africans. The high demand for African slave labor in the pursuit of these economic activities over the course of the colonial period resulted in a majority nonwhite population (both slave and free) in Brazil by independence. Slavery also became crucial to the social structure of Brazilian society, undergirding social status and economic production simultaneously. In a colony where manual labor was disparaged, an individual's relationship to slavery as a large or small slaveholder, free, freed-person, or slave was a key factor in social position.

By the middle of the eighteenth-century, Brazilian sugar production (the heyday of sugar exports dated from 1550 to the 1670), and gold and diamond mining (1680s to the 1760s) were in decline.[31] Other factors contributed to the colony's diminishing productivity as well. The Spanish and Portuguese waged a costly battle for supremacy in the Río de la Plata region over the course of the eighteenth century, where

---

[31] Dauril Alden, *Royal Government in Colonial Brazil: With Special Reference to the Administration of the Marquis of Lavradio, Viceroy, 1769–1779* (Berkeley: University of California Press, 1968), pp. 11–12; Stuart Schwartz, "A Commonwealth within Itself: The Early Brazilian Sugar Industry, 1550–1670," Stuart Schwartz, ed., *Tropical Babylons: Sugar and the Making of the Atlantic World, 1450–1680* (Chapel Hill: University of North Carolina Press, 2004), pp. 158–200. For gold mining, see Charles Boxer's classic study, *The Golden Age of Brazil, 1695–1750: Growing Pains of a Colonial Society* (Berkeley: University of California Press, 1962).

cattle ranching was becoming a lucrative industry. The ascendancy of the British Empire, especially after the Seven Year's War (1756–63) put additional pressure on the Spanish and Portuguese Empires in the Americas as control of shipping and military concerns rose to the forefront.[32] Additionally, new ideas of the Enlightenment, especially discussions about free trade, technological innovation, and the replacement of slave with free labor circulated in the North Atlantic and soon reached South American shores.

It was in this scenario of declining profits, international political rivalry, and new economic ideologies that the "enlightened despot," the Marquis of Pombal (Sebastião José de Carvalho e Melo 1699–1782), enacted a series of Enlightenment-influenced policies engineered to diversify, expand, and improve Brazil's colonial economy. Serving as Secretary of State (1750–77) in the court of Dom José I, Pombal was careful to engineer policies designed to increase profits in Brazil without introducing potentially dangerous social ideologies that might encourage opposition to colonial rule. Foremost among the economic reforms enacted by the Marquis was the improvement of existing crops (sugar and tobacco), the acclimatization of introduced cultivars, and the location of Brazilian species that could be developed into new commodities. Under these reforms, the colony experienced a period of agricultural diversification and increased productivity (the cultivation of indigo and cotton were among the most successful of these), but gains were designed to benefit the metropole over the colony.[33]

The challenge to British authority by a ragtag rebellious colonial army in North America in 1776 furrowed the brows of Portugal's inner governing circle, a worry that eventually bore out in the ultimately toothless, but nonetheless alarming small-scale conspiracy in Minas Gerais in 1789 to overthrow Portuguese control. The *Inconfidência Mineira* (Minas Conspiracy), as it was called, was followed nine years later by the *Inconfidência Baiana* (Bahian Conspiracy, or the Revolt of the Tailors) in 1798 in Salvador, Bahia. In the first instance, the crown was dismayed by the location of the conspiracy in the heart of the mining region. Especially worrisome was the discovery of multi-language editions of the most important Enlightenment thinkers of the age found among the libraries

---

[32] Kenneth Maxwell, *Paradox of the Enlightenment* (Cambridge: Cambridge University Press, 1995), pp. 117–18; Dauril Alden, *Royal Government in Colonial Brazil: With Special Reference to the Administration of the Marquis of Lavradio, Viceroy, 1769–1779* (Berkeley: University of California Press, 1968), pp. 110–12.

[33] Alden, pp. 372–83.

of the conspirators.[34] The second revolt, led by free mulatto tailors in one of Brazil's most important trading ports, raised the specter of the Haitian Revolution, especially because ringleaders invoked the liberal social values of the Enlightenment.[35] All of these events point to the fact that by the last decade of the eighteenth century change was in the air across the Atlantic. Though no revolt or conspiracy in Brazil during this period led to a wide-scale challenge to Portuguese authority, independence was nonetheless not far off after the turn of the nineteenth century.

Brazil's transition from colony to independent nation diverged in important ways from the rest of the Americas. Whereas the Spanish and British colonies (excepting Canada) fought wars of independence against their rulers, in Brazil the colonial relationship was turned on its head when the Portuguese court (numbering around 15,000 aristocrats, bureaucrats, and other notables) fled Napoleon's invasion of the Iberian Peninsula and arrived in Rio under British escort in 1808.[36] The relocation of the court, presided over by Prince Regent Dom João VI (ruling in his mentally ill mother's stead), quickly improved Brazilian fortunes. The same year, João VI opened Brazilian ports to free trade with "friendly nations," referring specifically to England, now a protector of the Portuguese and their colonies during the French occupation of Portugal. The prince also legalized the printing press, as previously mentioned, and issued new legislation intended to encourage economic development in the colony, including the enactment of a modern patent law and the reversal of a 1785 edict outlawing manufacturing in the colony. The transfer of a European court to a colonial city, even an important one such as Rio, necessitated numerous cultural improvements as well, including the construction of a theater and educational institutions, appropriate housing for the aristocrats and bureaucrats of the court, and new shops to accommodate European tastes in the realm of fashion and victuals. The sudden proximity of the Portuguese government also resulted in greater access for Brazilian colonials to the resources and favors of the crown and state.

---

[34] For a full treatment of the Minas Conspiracy, see Kenneth Maxwell, *Conflicts and Conspiracies: Brazil and Portugal 1750–1808* (Cambridge: Cambridge University Press, 1973), especially chs. 5 and 6.

[35] Maxwell, pp. 218–25. See also Donald Ramos, "Social Revolution Frustrated: The Conspiracy of the Tailors in Bahia, 1798," *Luso-Brazilian Review*, 13:1 (Summer 1976), pp. 74–90.

[36] See Kirsten Schultz for a description of the debates about and impact of the transfer of the monarchy to Rio, *Tropical Versailles: Empire, Monarchy, and the Portuguese Royal Court in Rio de Janeiro, 1808–1821* (New York: Routledge, 2001).

The crown prince and the colony's fortunes continued to rise together when Brazil was elevated to the status of kingdom in 1815, equal to the kingdoms of Portugal and the Algarves, followed by João VI's acclamation in 1816. João VI ruled from Rio for a total of fourteen years, returning to Portugal as king in 1822, seven years after Napoleon's defeat. He left behind his son, the intemperate Pedro I, in Rio, to rule as regent in his stead. With the support of Brazilians who were resistant to seeing their newly elevated kingdom returned to its former status of colony upon the return of the king to Lisbon, Pedro I declared independence in 1822, becoming emperor of the new Empire of Brazil.

With his coronation the same year, Pedro I oversaw the foundation of the longest-lasting monarchy in the New World, although his role in it was short-lived. He reigned until 1831 when he abdicated the throne and returned to Portugal, leaving behind his five-year-old son, Pedro II, in Rio under the protection of a regent. Though defending his daughter's claim to the Portuguese crown in Lisbon was a significant factor in his decision to abdicate, the emperor also faced increasing hostility from an alliance of Brazilian-born liberal radicals and more moderate reformists. At first officially hailed as the new nation's liberator, the emperor's volatile personality and escalating disagreements about the limitations of his power vis-à-vis those of the congressional body put him at odds with his Brazilian-born constituency. Brazilian radicals, known as the *exaltados* (enraged ones), and reformists resented the domination of Pedro I's cabinet by Portuguese-born statesmen and accused the emperor of absolutism, a central factor in his decreasing popularity in Brazil.[37]

The regency period, before the young Pedro II ascended to the throne in 1840 at the age of fourteen, was far from a politically stable period as significant threats to the new empire's unity erupted across the country. Revolts from the far north in Pará (1835) and Maranhão (1838) to Rio Grande do Sul in the far south (1835) challenged state sovereignty and threatened to dissolve the empire before it had fully consolidated. For this reason, Pedro II was hastily crowned emperor in 1840 at the age of fourteen, four years before his majority. Though regional revolts continued into the 1840s, Pedro II provided a paternalistic figure (despite his youth) around which national unity solidified. By 1850, regional revolts and disagreements were resolved and modernization became a key

---

[37] Jeffrey Needell, *The Party of Order: The Conservatives, the State, and Slavery in the Brazilian Monarchy, 1831–1871* (Stanford: Stanford University Press, 2006), pp. 40–1.

preoccupation of the state.[38] Displaying political acumen at a young age and invoking the powers granted to him through the Modifying Power (the ability to dissolve congressional bodies), Pedro II presided over a stable government for the next forty-nine years as the New World's longest-reigning constitutional monarch.

Returning to the beginning of Pedro II's regency, the 1830s proved decisive in the development of Brazilian politics. During the politically turbulent years of the 1830s after Pedro I's abdication, the clash between liberals, moderates, and conservatives over opposing visions of governance resulted in the rise of the self-styled Party of Order, or conservative party, by the end of the decade.[39] While liberals advocated for constitutional reform and weaker powers for the emperor, and those on the radical side promoted the establishment of a republic in Brazil, the conservative party supported a constitutional monarchy that represented the political and economic interests of the elite merchant and landowning class, a key objective of which was the maintenance of slavery. Indeed, during the push for his abdication, one of the central grievances against Pedro I was the aforementioned abolition of the slave trade in a treaty with Great Britain signed by the emperor in 1826 and put into effect in 1831. Powerful Brazilian interests resented the emperor's failure to consult with the congressional body in his negotiations with the British, the result of which was Brazilian resistance to the enforcement of the slave trade and the continuing clandestine importation of African captives into Brazil, as Martins Pena's play illustrated at the beginning of this chapter. Strong ties to slaveholding interests within the conservative party resulted in the centrality of the issue throughout the imperial period, especially as slave-produced coffee exports boomed after the 1840s. Slavery was always in the background, when not at the fore, of debates about modernization in Brazil.

Three hundred years of slavery in Brazil resulted in a large African-descended population by the nineteenth century, a matter that modernizers fretted over as the inevitability of abolition loomed by the end of the 1860s. Discussions about the need to transition from slave to free labor appeared periodically after independence, though the topic of abolition only gained widespread traction after the 1870s, as we will explore

---

[38] Needell, p. 33.

[39] Roderick Barman, *Citizen Emperor: Pedro II and the Making of Brazil, 1825–91* (Stanford: Stanford University Press, 1999), p. 61; and *Brazil, the Forging of a Nation* (Stanford: Stanford University Press, 1988), ch. 6. See also Needell, ch. 2.

shortly. Discussions about the meaning of the role of free labor in promoting industry, the perceived necessity of securing reliable sources of agricultural labor to replace slaves, the need to improve cultivation practices with technology, and the growing anxiety over the racial complexion of the Brazilian population at a time when European powers espoused ideologies of scientific racism surfaced in the writings of modernizers throughout this period. Because slavery was central to the Brazilian economy, politics, society, and, therefore by extension, modernization itself, we now turn to a brief summary of the pathway to abolition during this period.

Shortly after independence, Brazilian statesman José Bonifácio da Andrada e Silva (1763–1838) called for the end of slavery and its replacement with agricultural technology and free labor in his 1825 treatise on the topic. Central to his argument (and this was later reflected in the writings of the Sociedade Auxiliadora) was the need to end the dual system of slash-and-burn cultivation and slave labor on the basis that captive Africans were an "un-civilizing" force in the Brazilian countryside and a key factor in the destruction of the nation's valuable tropical forests.[40] This stance was echoed by antislavery proponent and member of the Sociedade Auxiliadora, Frederico Burlamaque (1803–66), in his 1837 treatise calling for the replacement of slave labor with agricultural technology and European immigrants.[41] Burlamaque feared that the ongoing importation of African slaves into Brazil would have an increasingly debilitating effect on Brazilian society, which he saw manifested in the "rustic" habits of the rural population, slave and slaveholder alike. While both advocates called out slavery as a barbaric and cruel institution, their motivations for its termination centered on concerns of "civilizing" or Europeanizing Brazil rather than for purely moral reasons.

Together these publications demonstrate that antislavery sentiments were on the minds of notable Brazilians, though the first step toward ending slavery came with the abolition of the slave trade in 1850, this time brought to a definitive end through government enforcement. The termination of slave imports was a significant start toward ending the practice,

---

[40] José Bonifácio de Andrada e Silva, "Representação à Assemblea Geral Constituinte e Legislativa do Imperio do Brasil Sobre a Escravatura," (Paris: Tip. de Firmin Didot, 1825) in *Obras Científicas e Sociais de José Bonifácio de Andrada e Silva, coligadas e reproduzidas por Edgard de Cerqueira Falcão*, Vol. II (São Paulo: Revista dos Tribunais, 1963), pp. 133–36.

[41] Frederico Burlamaque, *Memoria analytica a'cerca do commercio dos escravos e a'cerca dos malles da escravidão domestica* (Rio de Janeiro: Tip. Commercial Fluminense, 1837).

but resistance to outright abolition remained strong as the expanding coffee sector in the southeastern states spurred a thriving internal trade of slaves from the declining sugar-producing regions of the north to plantations in Rio de Janeiro, Minas Gerais, and São Paulo after 1850.[42] The next major government-supported step toward abolition came twenty-one years later with the passage of the Law of Free Birth in 1871. As the name suggests, the law was designed to manumit children born to slave mothers after the 1871 enactment of the law through either government indemnification at the age of eight or upon majority at age twenty-one.[43] Though passage of the law improved Brazil's image in the North Atlantic where slavery was increasingly disparaged, especially after the end of slavery in the United States in 1865, it changed little in practical terms or in the lived experience of most enslaved Brazilians. Additionally, though opponents of slavery spoke out against the institution throughout this period, official support for slavery continued until a revival of abolitionist sentiment gained traction after 1879, culminating in full abolition in 1888 with the signing of the *Lei Áurea* (Golden Law) by Princess Isabel acting in the capacity of regent while her father Pedro II traveled in Europe.[44] The law ended more than three hundred years of legal slavery in the tropical nation.

Sociedade Auxiliadora da Indústria Nacional

It was against this political and economic backdrop that the Sociedade Auxiliadora da Indústria Nacional, the publisher of *O Auxiliador*, came into existence. Founded in the early years of independence, scholars have disagreed to what extent the society played a role in transmitting

---

[42] See Robert Conrad's classic study on the end of slavery in Brazil, *The Destruction of Brazilian Slavery, 1850–1888* (Berkeley: University of California Press, 1972), ch. 4.

[43] Conrad, ch. 7.

[44] Conrad, 270–4; Hendrik Kraay describes manumission ceremonies sponsored by Isabel and enacted at official state celebrations and on the birthdays of the princess and her mother, the empress Teresa Cristina, in the 1880s, *Days of National Festivity*, pp. 333–8. Recent scholarship provides a rich exploration of abolition activism in the 1870s and 1880s, see, for example, Celso Castilho and Camillia Cowling, "Funding Freedom, Popularizing Politics: Abolitionism and Local Emancipation Funds in 1880s Brazil," *Luso-Brazilian Review* 47:1 (2010), pp. 89–120, and Celso Castilho, "Performing Abolitionism: The Social Construction of Political Rights in 1880s Recife, Brazil," *Hispanic American Historical Review*, 93:3 (2013), pp. 377–409. For insight into the abolitionist sentiments of the elite, see Joaquim Nabuco's classic 1883 treatise *Abolitionism: The Brazilian Antislavery Struggle* (Urbana, IL: University of Illinois Press, 1977).

Enlightenment thought in the Brazilian Empire. Maria Odila da Silva Dias argues that the Sociedade Auxiliadora was essential for linking the generation of Brazilian-born and Coimbra University-trained scientists (where elite Brazilians went to receive a university education) of the late colonial and early independence period to their counterparts in the later part of the century.[45] José Murilo de Carvalho challenges Odila, arguing that two distinct periods of a Luso-Brazilian Enlightenment developed in the nineteenth century. The first generation faded away at the end of Pedro I's reign in 1825, and the second emerged in the 1870s with the creation of new scientific and educational institutions.[46] Among these numbered the revived Museu Nacional (National Museum) in 1876, which became an important site for botanical research under the direction of naturalist Ladislau Netto.[47] While acknowledging a new vigor in the development of Brazilian science and technology in the 1870s, I side with Odila in arguing that the Sociedade Auxiliadora was an important site of engagement with Enlightenment thought throughout the nineteenth century. This position is supported by the botanical information contained in exhibition catalogs of the 1860s in addition to the scientific articles published in the society's journal.[48] The fact that some of the most ardent supporters

---

[45] Maria Odila da Silva Dias, "Aspectos da ilustração no Brasil," *Revista do Instituto Histórico e Geográfico Brasileiro*, 278 (1968), p. 163.

[46] José Murilo de Carvalho, *A Escola de Minas de Ouro Preto: o peso da glória* (Rio de Janeiro: FINEP, and São Paulo: Editora Nacional, 1978), pp. 18–21. Other important sites for the study of science and technology in the nineteenth century were the Academies of Medicine in Salvador and Rio de Janeiro, and the Navy Arsenal in Rio de Janeiro. The Escola Militar in Rio de Janeiro was transformed into a modern Polytechnic school in 1874, and the Escola de Minas was founded in Ouro Preto in 1876.

[47] Netto published a treatise on Brazilian plant species in 1866, *Apontamentos sobre a colleção das Plantas Economicas do Brasil para a exposição internacional de 1867* (Paris: Ballière, 1866).

[48] Another node in this argument that is not pursued here are the different pathways through which Enlightenment thought was disseminated in Brazil. Patrícia Barreto attributes the omission of the Sociedade Auxiliadora in the historiography of Brazilian science to a failure to recognize the importance of salons and associations in disseminating scientific information in eighteenth- and nineteenth-century Brazil as opposed to the formal universities and institutions established in Europe, Patrícia Regina Corrêa Barreto, "Sociedade Auxiliadora da Indústria Nacional: o templo carioca de palas atena," (Ph.D. dissertation, Universidade Federal do Rio de Janeiro, 2009), pp. 133–5. Silvia Fernanda Mendonça Figueirôa observes that this Eurocentric framework has also resulted in the oversight of Brazilian scientists' contributions to European and North American expeditions, an assessment shared by Marcus Vinicius de Freita, Silvia Fernanda Mendonça Figueirôa, *As Ciências Geológicas no Brasil: Uma História Social e Institucional, 1875–1934* (São Paulo: Hucitec, 1995), pp. 16–18; and Marcus Vinicius de Freita, *Hartt: Expedições pelo Brasil Imperial* (São Paulo: Metalivros, 2001), p. 157.

of science and technology in the service of economic development from the 1840s to the 1870s were also society members further supports this claim. Among these numbered agronomist Frederico Burlamaque, engineer, abolitionist, and advocate for land reform, André Rebouças, the aforementioned industrialist the Baron of Mauá, politicians and members of the emperor's Council of State, José Maria da Silva Paranhos, (the Viscount of Rio Branco, 1819–80), and the Marquis of Abrantes, as well as the emperor Dom Pedro II (1825–91).[49]

Officially founded by decree in 1827 under the patronage of Pedro I, the Sociedade Auxiliadora was the project of a wealthy Rio merchant and ennobled courtier in Pedro I's inner circle, Ignácio Álvares Pinto de Almeida. Indicative of the high regard of French Science and culture in nineteenth-century Brazil, the society was modeled after the Société d'Encouragement pour l'Industrie Nationale founded in France in 1801. Likewise, similar institutions were established in Spain and Spanish Latin America in the late eighteenth and early nineteenth centuries.[50] The Sociedade Auxiliadora functioned as an independent advisory organ for the state from which it also received the majority of its funding.[51] Aside from financial support, the society maintained ties to the government through the appointment of prominent politicians to leadership roles, including the Viscount of Rio Branco who served as president from 1865–80.[52]

The Sociedade Auxiliadora also oversaw the creation of partner institutions, including the more famous Instituto Histórico e Geográfico Brasileiro founded in 1838, and the Imperial Instituto Fluminense de

[49] Luiz Werneck da Silva was the first to observe the absence of the Sociedade Auxiliadora in the historiography on Brazil, "Isto é o que me parece," vol. II, pp. 8–18. Richard Graham's classic *Britain and the Onset of Modernization in Brazil, 1850–1914* makes no mention of the Sociedade Auxilidora despite the author's treatment of the industrial projects of members André Rebouças and the Baron of Mauá. Likewise, Nancy Stepan's *The Beginnings of Brazilian Science: Oswaldo Cruz, Medical Research and Policy, 1890–1920* (New York: Science History Publications, 1976), does not reference the Sociedade Auxilidora's role in nineteenth-century Brazilian science despite the wide-ranging scientific topics published in the society's journal.

[50] Stuart McCook, *States of Nature: Science, Agriculture, and Environment in the Spanish Caribbean, 1760–1940* (Austin: University of Texas Press, 2002), pp. 16–20; and Maria Portuondo, "Plantation Factories: Science and Technology in Late Eighteenth-Century Cuba," *Technology and Culture*, 44:2 (2003), pp. 232–3.

[51] Werneck da Silva, "Isto é o que me parece", pp. 61–71; Barreto, "Sociedade Auxiliadora da Indústria Nacional," p. 49 and pp. 158–69.

[52] Heloisa Maria Bertol Domingues, "A Sociedade Auxiliadora da Indústria Nacional e as Ciências Naturais no Brasil Império" in Maria Amélia M. Dantes, ed., *Espaços da Ciência no Brasil: 1800–1930* (Rio de Janeiro: Editora Fiocruz, 2001), p. 85, and pp. 92–4.

Agricultura established in 1860 in partnership with the newly created Ministério de Agricultura, Comércio, e Obras Públicas (Ministry of Agriculture, Commerce, and Public Works). Designed as an experimental agricultural school overseen by society member and close friend of Pedro II, Luís Pedreira do Couto Ferraz (The Baron of Bom Retiro, 1818–86), the institute was located on the grounds of the Jardim Botânico in Rio de Janeiro. One of its principal objectives was the "expansion and improvement" of the original garden established by João VI in 1808.[53] IIFA produced a quarterly journal, the *Revista Agrícola do Imperial Instituto Fluminense de Agricultura*, which covered the latest developments in agricultural improvement, including the institute's experiments with indigenous and acclimatized plants.[54] The publication supplemented and often overlapped the content of O *Auxiliador*. Sociedade Auxiliadora members regularly contributed to both journals.

The central aim of the Sociedade Auxiliadora was the dissemination of the latest in scientific and technological advances, especially, as mentioned previously, for agricultural improvement and as a way to transition from slave to free labor. In addition to O *Auxiliador*, the society produced supplemental publications on modern agricultural techniques and machinery, oversaw the assessment of patent applications, and organized and participated in national and international exhibitions. Until Brazilian patent law was updated in 1882, the Society played a central role in the patent approval process. After inspection of an invention (Brazilian patents required that a scale model of each invention accompany the application) by the appropriate committee, the Sociedade Auxiliadora was authorized to grant preliminary patents for machinery, manufacturing processes, and chemicals. Approved applications were forwarded to the Ministry of Agriculture for the issuance of an official government patent, usually granted for a period of twenty years.[55] Additionally, regular meetings were held at the society's Rio offices where a library and depository for machines were also maintained, albeit not always in optimal condition as society members sometimes complained. Though the society did not possess a lab or other equipment for experiments, machinery demonstrations for didactic purposes and patent assessments were held on site.

The Sociedade Auxiliadora was also instrumental in organizing five national exhibitions in Rio in the 1860s and 1870s from which Brazil's

---

[53] Geraldo de Beauclair Mendes de Oliveira, *A Construção Inacabada*, pp. 112–13.
[54] *Ibid.*, pp. 112–13.
[55] The Junta do Comércio oversaw patent applications before 1860.

displays for international exhibitions in the US and Europe were selected, a project overseen by the Ministry of Agriculture.[56] The Ministry oversaw the directives and funding for the collection of exhibition materials, and provincial presidents were tasked with organizing the local and regional exhibitions that provided industrial products and raw display items for Rio. Through these venues, interior regions were represented on the international stage in North Atlantic exhibition halls. Exhibition catalogs represented an ambitious effort at compiling a truly national "inventory of Brazil's industry" – both manufactured goods and natural resources – and were especially important in collecting and disseminating information on Brazilian botanical species. In addition, Sociedade Auxiliadora members attended and gave lectures, maintained correspondence with scientists and agriculturalists abroad, debated economic theories, disseminated seeds, livestock, and machinery beyond Rio, and translated and wrote articles on the latest agricultural, scientific, and technological advances of the period.

Plan of the Work

This project examines Brazilian modernization through three central facets: the issues that Brazilians discussed in public forums concerning modernization; the resurrection of currents of Brazilian economic thought that drew from a variety of Enlightenment thinkers ranging from Carl Linnaeus to Adam Smith; and by bringing to light Brazilian inventive activity in the patent record for a society considered technologically backward, even hostile to innovation. Though many of the ideas in play in Brazil in this period bear signs of foreign manufacture, elites did not merely imitate or import their ideologies about modernization from abroad, as is sometimes asserted; they created their own modernity reflective of their particular circumstances, culture, and context.[57] Emília Viotti da Costa

---

[56] Noah Elkin, "Promoting a New Brazil," pp. 44–5. Sociedade Auxiliadora members also served as administrators and jury members at both national and international exhibitions.

[57] For a discussion of the circulation and acceptance of European ideas in the Brazilian context, see Roberto Schwarz, *Misplaced Ideas: Essays on Brazilian Culture*, John Gledson, ed., (London: Verso, 1974, 1992); Maria Sylvia de Carvalho Franco, "As idéias estão no lugar," *Cadernos de debate*, 1976), pp. 59–64; Elías José Palti, "The Problem of 'Misplaced Ideas' Revisited: Beyond the 'History of Ideas' in Latin America," *Journal of the History of Ideas*, 67:1 (January 2006), pp. 149–79; and José Murilo de Carvalho, "História intelectual no Brasil: a retórica como chave de leitura," *Topoi* 1 (2000), pp. 123–52.

eloquently challenges the notion that Brazilian elites blindly absorbed foreign philosophies of progress:

There is no doubt . . . that Brazilian reformers quoted European authors to support their opinions. However, one cannot assume that they had those opinions *because* they had read European authors. In fact, the opposite might be true. It might be more correct to say that their desire to change society in certain ways predisposed them to prefer some European authors over others. Otherwise, how can we explain their preference for Comte over Marx or for Spencer over Fourier?[58]

Invoking Costa's tone, this work seeks to provide a more complex picture of modernization from a Brazilian perspective. Auguste Comte's vision of a society ordered around the discovery of each individual's proper social and economic role through positive science appealed to Brazilians who wished to avoid the social upheaval occasioned by the end of slavery in Haiti and the United States, or the conflicts that unfolded in industrializing nations.[59] Additionally, threads of Carl Linneaus' political economy of national self-sufficiency surfaced in nineteenth-century Brazilian visions of modernization. The Swedish naturalist designed his system of biological classification in part to promote the exploitation of his nation's natural resources in support of social and economic development.[60] Economic self-sufficiency was appealing to would-be modernizers in a tropical country rich with native flora and a long history of successfully acclimatized cultivars (sugar, for example) that could not be cultivated or produced in temperate climates. Finally, Brazil's patent record reveals cutting-edge innovations in the coffee sector, the nation's most important agro-industrial export in the nineteenth century. Importantly, coffee technology evolved both alongside slave labor and as a remedy to the institution's eventual demise, countering the notion that innovation was antithetical to economic systems based on slavery.

This project concentrates on the years between 1850 and the end of the empire in 1889. The definitive end of the Slave Trade in 1850, after a series of unenforced laws and treaties, provides a useful launching point

---

[58] Emília Viotti da Costa, "Brazil: The Age of Reform, 1870–1889," in *The Cambridge History of Latin America*, Vol. V, c. 1870–1930 (Cambridge: Cambridge University Press, 1986), pp. 726–7; see also da Costa's chapter on Liberalism, *The Brazilian Empire: Myths and Histories* (Chicago: The University of Chicago Press, 1985), ch. 3.

[59] See Riolando Azzi, *A concepção da ordem social segundo o positivismo ortodoxo brasileiro* (São Paulo: Edições Loyola, 1980), pp. 87–101.

[60] Emma Spary, "Political, Natural, and Bodily Economies," in N. Jardine, J. A. Secord, and E. C. Spary (eds.), *Cultures of Natural History* (Cambridge: Cambridge University Press, 1996), pp. 178–9.

as it foreshadowed the demise of slavery and brought debates about the use of wage labor and mechanization to the forefront, as we have seen. Questions centered on how best to transition to a wage economy: Rehabilitate slaves and educate the poor in state-run agricultural and industrial schools? Replace slaves with technology-savvy European immigrants, as mentioned earlier? Eliminate the need for slave laborers with more efficient agricultural machinery? Revive depleted coffee plantations with modern fertilizers and plows and make them available to Brazilian-born colonists? Furthermore, how was Brazil to make the transition to a free labor economy while avoiding social and economic disruption? As one modernizer proposed, Brazil needed to establish industrial societies across the nation with the aim of birthing a "beneficial revolution," a controlled progress that brought material improvement without social upheaval. Brazilians also considered to what extent other models of modernization were appropriate for their context, for example, how best to integrate factories into Brazilian society and prepare the poor for industrial work? In this light, the United States emerged as a role model for many members of the Sociedade Auxiliadora. Like Brazil, it was a nation of continental scale with an expanding (and often violent) agricultural frontier. Additionally slavery remained important to the US economy into the 1860s, another factor, though rarely directly commented upon, for comparison in the eyes of society members.

Also by the 1860s increased population growth raised the question of food production and spurred investigations into more efficient agricultural methods. A central purpose of the IIFA was the dissemination of agricultural technology and the development of new industries derived from species native to Brazil (sugar, coffee, and cotton – three important agricultural exports – were introduced species) in order to diversify the economy. From the 1850s to the 1880s, articles in O *Auxilador* and the *Jornal do Commercio* demonstrated an increasing sophistication in the discussion of innovative agricultural technologies and their local application.

Before beginning, it is important to disentangle Brazilian modernization from the welter of social values and contexts with which these notions are often conflated in the Anglo-American cultural and academic milieu. To suggest, as I have done in the foregoing, that Brazilians actively engaged in shaping their own modernity does not mean they shared the same moral progressivism. The Brazilian elite's invocations of progress and civilization adhered to a general notion of material, moral, and economic improvement shared with their counterparts in the North Atlantic industrializing nations, but they did not necessarily aim for identical social outcomes. While many desired the material improvements and comforts offered by modernization, they hoped to avoid the social disruptions that accompanied it. Even Brazilian liberals such as Joaquim Nabuco (1849–1910) and Rui Barbosa (1849–1923), who advocated for the reform of economic and social policies, especially the abolition of slavery, did not believe that a liberal and democratic government based on expanded suffrage was a viable system for Brazil.[61] Beyond the initial step of emancipation, those who desired modernization were cautious on the matter of potentially disruptive social innovations.

One prevailing perception in Brazilian historiography is that the nation's dependence on slavery prohibited technological innovation. While to an extent this was true, the patent record at the National Archives and the preponderance of advertising for new machines and technologies in the *Jornal do Commercio* and other publications counter this notion. Machines increasingly played a part in the daily life of Brazilians of the Second Empire, from the railways that steamed through the tropical forest to the mule-drawn streetcars that made an appearance on the streets of Rio de Janeiro and other cities. By the 1860s, sewing machines appeared in urban households, and agricultural equipment, from steam-powered corn huskers to coffee drying systems, churned on rural *fazendas* (plantations) and were often operated by slaves. Coal-fired steam machines powered mechanized hat production in Rio de Janeiro in the 1870s and 1880s, seed oil processing in Alagôas in the 1850s, and agricultural operations throughout rural areas. Steam machines even occasioned one of the first environmental complaints of the era. In 1885, a group of disgruntled neighbors complained to the Rio city council that "*fábricas a vapor*" (steam-powered manufactories) be prohibited in the city center as the residents of *Sete de Setembro* street were forced to keep their windows shut to prevent the coal smoke of the steam machines from "turning their clothes black," an especially irksome problem for those who worked as seamstresses and tailors nearby.[62] For good or ill, modernization was an increasingly important component of daily life during the period of the Brazilian Empire.

With this in mind, existing academic discourses according to which Brazil's "failure to launch" by the standards of the economic and industrial development of England or the United States in the nineteenth

---

[61] Graham, pp. 265–76.
[62] "Industria Nacional," *Publicações a Pedido, JC*, September 18, 1880.

century, merit re-examination.[63] I propose that neither did Brazil fail to modernize nor did Brazilians refrain from vigorously engaging with technological and economic changes. Economic historian Geraldo de Beauclair argues for instance, that while Brazil did not experience an industrial *revolution*, it did undergo a steady increase in the establishment of factories and the *evolution* of new technologies throughout the nineteenth century.[64] As other scholars have indicated, the adoption of new technological systems such as the railroad during this period set the stage for later economic development, demonstrating that Brazil was not the technologically backward and reactionary nation it is sometimes presented to be.[65] It is precisely this native story that this work seeks to uncover.

As stated at the beginning of this chapter, the seminal works of Peter Eisenberg and Richard Graham were important for understanding the beginning of modernization in nineteenth-century Brazil. Graham documented the influence of Great Britain in the realms of capital investment, technology transfer, consumer goods, and the spread of social philosophies such as the Social Darwinism of Herbert Spencer. His reliance on foreigners' observations, while perceptive and illuminating, represented a decidedly non-Brazilian perspective that projected foreign preconceptions about race, climate, and notions of progress that were sometimes extraneous and thus erroneous to the Brazilian reality. For instance, many observers were ignorant of the limitations and basic requirements of tropical agriculture in what historian Paulo Zarth, invoking the work of Russian economist Alexander Chayanov, describes as "local economic logic":

[Chayanov's] critique of the idea of a capitalist rationality in opposition to a noncapitalist irrationality is useful in studying the agricultural history of [Rio Grande do Sul] in the nineteenth century. We will demonstrate ... that local economic activities have specific characteristics that are difficult to capture in a rational capitalist model without running the risk of distorting reality.[66]

Chapter 4 shows that the absence of plows and fertilizers in Brazilian agriculture (a chief complaint among many foreign observers) and

---

[63] See, for example, Stephen Haber, *How Latin America Fell Behind.*

[64] Beauclair, *A Construção Inacabada*, ch.1.

[65] See Jorge Caldeira, *Mauá: empresário do Império* (São Paulo: Companhia das Letras, 1995). The 1999 film *Mauá – o Imperador e o Rei* portrays nineteenth-century Brazil as a backward slavocracy governed by a conservative planter class. The present work aims to present a more nuanced vision of nineteenth-century Brazil.

[66] Zarth, pp. 25–6.

agriculturalists' reliance on slash-and-burn cultivation continued in the tropical nation because it simply worked better and was considerably less expensive and less risky than untried machinery and manufactured fertilizers. Though the publications of important Brazilian organizations such as the Sociedade Auxiliadora also reflected frustration with the continuation of slash-and-burn cultivation that undergirded coffee expansion, domestic perspectives provide a more nuanced view on the perceived backwardness of the nation's agriculture. The Sociedade Auxiliadora, for instance, advocated for the introduction of agricultural machinery, the diversification of crops beyond the sugar/coffee axis, and supported the creation of educational institutions such as IIFA for educating poor Brazilian children in scientific agriculture. Brazilian organizations were modeled after their counterparts in Europe, North America, and to a lesser extent, other Latin American nations to be sure, but they nonetheless reveal decidedly domestic perspectives. Brazilians sought to rationalize agricultural and industrial production in line with what they perceived to be their nation's most important competitive advantage: the long growing season of their tropical climate and the nation's immense natural wealth, especially its tropical forests.

Peter Eisenberg's study showed how technological modernization does not necessarily result in a parallel social transformation. The wage laborers attached to the industrial nexus of the modern *engenhos centrais* (centralized sugar mills that gradually replaced planter-owned milling operations located on individual *fazendas*) found themselves in virtually the same material circumstances as the slaves and free poor of previous generations of agricultural workers. Neither were the mechanized central mills, heavily subsidized by the government beginning in the 1880s, enough to save Brazil's ailing sugar industry. Planters were reluctant to supply cane to mills for economic reasons, but equally important, as Eisenberg observes, they did not desire to relinquish the social prestige associated with the *senhor de engenho* (plantation and mill owner).[67]

The analysis of scholars like Eisenberg assumes the covariance of social liberalization with the introduction of new technologies and capitalist economic organization, a central tenant of modernization theory. In nineteenth-century Brazil this was not necessarily the goal. Brazilian elites, planters and urban groups alike, might have desired progress but they wished to avoid the messy social upheaval instigated by processes of modernization in other nations, be it the reorganization of

---

[67] Eisenberg, 221.

agricultural labor and production or industrial manufacturing. The traditional interests (ranchers, planters, and merchants) of Rio Grande do Sul, for instance, used the term *"transformar para preservar"* (transform in order to preserve) to indicate that for them modernization was not about changing the social system.[68] Even the progressive members of the Sociedade Auxiliadora wanted to first perfect agricultural production through improved machinery before encouraging the widespread establishment of manufacturing industries. While they advocated for the rehabilitation of freed slaves through agricultural education, they also hoped to avoid the clashes between workers and industrialists then occurring in Europe or, worse, the slave uprising of the previous century in Haiti.

Finally, relying on economic statistics for understanding Brazilian modernization, as Hudson observed about the Industrial Revolution, only captures part of the picture. Export commodities often only appear in official documents such as tariff calculations and ship registries. Such analyses overlook experiments with other crops undertaken by Brazilian agriculturalists. The willingness of Brazilian *fazendeiros* (planters), for example, to experiment with indigo, cinchona bark, and numerous other native species refutes the notion that they stubbornly clung to the cultivation of a narrow range of tried and true export crops. In the first of Brazil's national exhibitions in 1861, for example, the northeastern provinces displayed hundreds of samples of indigenous plant materials in the hope of finding economic uses for them. These included lumber, fruits, fibers, oils, and resins, from the forest and *sertão* (backlands) in addition to experimental crops such as indigo or tea. Together, they reveal the recognition of Brazil's rich forests and biological diversity as potential sources of new raw materials for domestic manufacturing and international markets. To be sure, carnaúba wax (a product of the carnaúba palm tree from the northeast and Amazonian regions used in the manufacture of candles) never became as economically significant as tropical products like coffee or sugar. But this is a matter of economic contingency, marketing savvy, the characteristics of the species, and even passing fashion; it does not negate the energies that would-be innovators put into its exploration and commercial application of these natural resources. Brazil's failures at diversifying agricultural production can tell us as much as its successes.

In examining a Brazilian perspective of modernization in the nineteenth century, I invoke a word culled from the sources cited herein: *aperfeiçoar*. The term, defined as "to perfect" or "to improve," captured

[68] Zarth, p. 286.

the sense in Zarth's example of "*transformar para preservar.*" Brazilians, among them promoters of free market liberalism and the most conservative defenders of the status quo alike, desired gradual improvement and hoped to avoid too much change too fast. They wanted to manage and direct the forces of progress. This was not the open-ended bombast of the United States' Manifest Destiny with a seeming unlimited western frontier in which human ambition and technological achievement went hand in glove. This cautious sense of *aperfeiçoar* is conveyed in a report by the Industrial Association of Rio de Janeiro, an organization founded in the 1880s with the goal of promoting industrial manufacturing in Brazil. One member of the association called for the "*aperfeiçoamento progressivo*" (progressive improvement) of Brazilian economic production to include both mechanically refined agricultural products and manufactured goods accomplished carefully through managed steps.[69] *Aperfeiçoamento* expressed the over-arching Enlightenment ideal of material and moral progress but matched to a Brazilian vision based on order and tranquillity. Yet this conservative approach did not mean elites were fearful of any transformation whatsoever; they merely aimed to channel change into what they saw as the most desirable – and controllable – outcomes. A further exploration of this term, and the equally important *indústria* (industry) are included in Chapter 2 and set the stage for an understanding of Brazil's conservative modernization.

Brazil's prodigious forests, so long admired by foreign travelers, emerge as a vital component in visions of national economic development in Chapter 3. Efforts to develop native flora into raw materials and products for both domestic and foreign industry demonstrated that Brazilians actively sought to diversify economic production beyond the nation's traditional export commodities. From a scheme to fuel steam locomotives with native tree nuts (a precursor to modern-day biofuels?) to the unsuccessful promotion of mate as a replacement for tea and coffee in foreign markets, this chapter demonstrates a deeply creative and newly scientific engagement with native resources. Whereas England and the United States had coal-fired "satanic mills" of heavy industry, Brazilians looked to their "industrial forests" to provide all of the blessings of modern prosperity with none of its associated maladies, and indeed, the more enlightened use of Brazil's plant resources was cast as a way to eliminate slave labor and to stop the environmental destruction associated with coffee production.

---

[69] *Archivos da Exposição da Industria Nacional: actas, pareceres e decisões do jury geral da Exposição da Industria Nacional realizada no Rio de Janeiro in 1881*, p. CLVII.

To achieve a greater scientific understanding of native forest resources, the Sociedade Auxiliadora and the Ministry of Agriculture reported on potentially economically useful species in government publications and national exhibition catalogs. Sociedade Auxiliadora members also railed against the slash-and-burn techniques that characterized Brazilian agriculture, a destructive practice that they felt forestalled a more sustained and rational exploitation of Brazil's natural resources.

Chapter 5 examines one of the most troublesome aspects of Brazilian modernization: the difficulty of establishing modern transportation networks (macadamized roads, railway networks, and steamship lines) across the nation's vast expanses. The lack of improved roads inspired impassioned and bitter complaints from the general public in the 1850s and 1860s, before the widespread establishment of railroads in the 1870s began to ease the transportation bottleneck in Brazil's interior regions. The difficulties of overland transportation, due to the vagaries of tropical weather and the challenging topography that included dense forests and mountains combined with a chronic lack of public monies for road-building projects, vexed provincial presidents, and the public alike. Complaints about muddy roads and unexplored rivers also filled annual provincial reports from all parts of the empire. Once transportation projects were underway, foreign engineers of Brazil's first railroads met enormous challenges in conquering the coastal escarpment of Rio de Janeiro and São Paulo provinces that resulted in delays and unexpected expenses. Furthermore, railroads constructed in less challenging territory often crossed sparsely settled lands with an insufficient population base or agricultural production to make the enterprise feasible without government subsidies. Brazil's rivers were both a boon and a bane for internal transportation; many waterways were not uniformly navigable due to falls and shallows, or were only useful for part of the year. Others, such as the Amazon in the north and the Paraná that linked the western province of Mato Grosso to the nations of the Río de la Plata further south, provided ample opportunities for the introduction of steamship lines, as the Baron of Mauá successfully achieved in the case of the Amazon.

Despite the initial difficulties that the topography posed for engineers, and the competition for scarce capital, railroads were ultimately successful in ending the transportation bottleneck and facilitating economic growth, especially in São Paulo province. Yet the success of Brazilian railroads in spurring agricultural production, both for export and domestic consumption, did not result in large-scale industrialization linked to the railroad sector as occurred in the United States, England, and Germany. Brazil's factor endowments of iron and coal proved difficult to exploit or were of insufficient quality for the task at hand, and less-expensive foreign production of rails and locomotives further discouraged domestic production. Yet despite these challenges, railroad workshops in Rio de Janeiro and São Paulo emerged as important local sites for innovation, including the construction of railroad cars, forged iron implements, and machines for local use. Establishing modern transportation networks proved an enormous challenge, but these initial efforts resulted in large payoffs by the end of the century.[70]

Chapter 6 turns to the letters of the *Jornal do Commercio* for a closer analysis of the debates and tensions that surrounded the introduction of railways and wage labor in the capital city of Rio de Janeiro. Ironically, the "civilized" locomotive brought with it the "uncivilized" railroad worker. Conflicts over the proper behavior of conductors and engineers filled the pages of the *Jornal do Commercio*, revealing tensions over the social ramifications of the new technology as it affected the arrangement of public space, gender relations, and introduced a new class of worker into a slave society: the wage laborer. The final section of this chapter examines efforts to fold factory owner/factory worker relationships into the paternalistic social order of Brazilian slave society. Factory-sponsored schools were exemplified as the best pathway to "civilize" hirelings and prepare them for the discipline necessary for industrial production. Guidance was provided under the benevolent patronage of the factory manager or owner. Together, these examples demonstrate the tensions and adjustments necessitated by the introduction of new technological and economic systems as they related to and affected the prevailing social hierarchy, and they underscore the fact that Brazilian modernizers hoped to perfect, not radically transform, their society.

---

[70] William Summerhill observes that railways spurred domestic agricultural production and provided a solid base for Brazil's economic growth in the late nineteenth and early twentieth century, *Order Against Progress: Government, Foreign Investment, and Railroads in Brazil, 1854–1913* (Stanford: Stanford University Press, 2003), pp. 4–5.

2

The Vocabulary of Brazilian Modernization

In January of 1849 an announcement appeared in the *Jornal do Commercio* celebrating the achievements of the young scholars at the Instituto Collegial de Novo Friburgo, a private secondary school located in the mountains north of Rio de Janeiro.[1] One enterprising youth, João Francisco Carneiro Vianna, received a gold medal for his "good conduct, industry, and completion of studies in preparation for his future career."[2] The next day a sardonic response from a humble shoemaker calling into question the nature of the industry taught at the school appeared in the *Correspondências* section of the *Jornal do Commercio*:

I ... read the article by Mr. Freese. I read it and re-read it and I experienced palpitations of pleasure as it seemed that I had finally encountered that which I have so long desired for my sons ... mechanical instruction alongside a basic education. The article stated that nearly all of the students had received distinctions in *industry* [emphasis in the original]. Everywhere in the article I encountered this word that so pleased me, and I even saw that the student awarded the gold medal owed this honor to his *indefatigable industry*. Yet I am still in need of clarification: what are the branches of industry taught in Mr. Freese's establishment? For what *industry* did the student João Francisco Carneiro Viannadeserve so elevated an honor? Was it tailoring, carpentry, or blacksmithing? I see much discussion of industry in the article, but I would like this [term] better explained ... I am a bit thick and it is difficult for me to understand such matters, especially when described with such grand words ...[3]

---

[1] The Institute was founded in 1841 by Swiss immigrant Johannes Heinrich Freese, Jorge Miguel Mayer, "Raízes e crise do mundo caipira: o caso de Nova Friburgo," (Ph.D. dissertation, Universidade Federal Fluminense, 2003), p. 235.
[2] "Instituto Collegial de Nova Friburgo," *Publicações a Pedido, JC*, January 4, 1849.
[3] "Instituto Collegial de Nova Friburgo," *Correspondencias, JC*, January 5, 1849.

This curious letter stands out among the usual collection of complaints and announcements printed in the *Jornal do Commercio*. First, it challenged the definition of a term (industry) then in flux across the Atlantic and especially in Europe where the rise of industrial manufacturing in the eighteenth century spurred discussions about economic production and modes of labor. Brazil fully participated in this conversation; by the early nineteenth century, *indústria* signified both economic production and material development broadly writ. Second, the letter slyly criticized the growing number of Brazilian *bacharéis* (young men with bachelor's degrees in the liberal arts) employed in the state bureaucracy. The shoemaker emphatically wished to avoid this fate for his three sons, declaring that the *bacharéis* were a "plague" that had "already caused enough trouble for Brazil." His hope was that his sons would " . . . study any one of the mechanical arts, shoemaking, tailoring, carpentry, goldsmithing, or watchmaking . . . " along with traditional instruction in reading, writing, and arithmetic in order to "avoid the predicament in which I find myself as I struggle to write these lines . . . "[4]

Conspicuously, rather than directly criticizing the unambiguously non-industrial liberal arts curriculum of the Institute, the shoemaker lampooned the young João Vianna's "indefatigable industry."[5] Though this is only one letter among many hundreds printed that year in the *Jornal do Commercio*, the seemingly innocent questioning of the term *indústria* in this example reveals a deeper – and very pointed – criticism of the low regard for *artes mecânicas* (mechanical arts or artisanal trades) in nineteenth-century Brazilian society. To drive his point home, the author also spoofed the rather lofty name of the institute:

[4] *Ibid.*

[5] The original announcement of the *Instituto Collegial* lists a standard nineteenth-century liberal arts program that clearly excluded training in the mechanical arts:

Roman Catholic Christian Doctrine, the Old and New Testaments and religious history;
Calligraphy and Arithmetic;
Commerce and Accounting (both single and double entry);
Mathematics;
Greek, Latin, Portuguese, Physics, and Chemistry;
Improvisatory exercises, with the goal of facilitating and exercising the intellectual faculties;
Music, dance, design, fencing . . . and other military exercises;
Gymnastic and athletic exercises,"

"Instituto Collegial de Nova-Friburgo," January 4, 1849.

The very title of the article is confusing. *Instituto-collegial!* It sounds a very grand thing, but I cannot quite fathom its meaning! I borrowed my neighbor the *boticário's* (pharmacist) dictionary and I found [each word] in the dictionary, but when I put them together they make no sense... [6]

Speaking tongue-in-cheek, the shoemaker cleverly inferred that *bacharéis* were parasitical dependents on the state coffers whose work did little to contribute to the material development of the nation. Indeed, a professional, white-collar middling class emerged to meet the needs of the expanding state bureaucracy in Rio following independence from Portugal in 1822. Through the 1840s white-collar professions grew hand in hand with the artisanal trades, but by the year of the shoemaker's letter in 1849 the state bureaucracy increasingly served the burgeoning coffee economy, narrowing pathways to wealth and consolidating economic and political power in the hands of an oligarchy to the detriment of artisans like the shoemaker.[7] Furthermore, Brazil's reliance on slave labor – and the ongoing association of slavery with manual labor – contributed to the negative perception of the *artes mecânicas* (manual arts).[8] At the midpoint of the nineteenth-century the liberal professions of doctor, lawyer, or bureaucrat commanded more social prestige than the manual trades, creating a demand for liberal arts schools, to the detriment of the *artes mecânicas.*[9]

[6] "Instituto Collegial de Nova Friburgo," January 5, 1849.

[7] Zephyr Frank uses the term "middling class" (rather than "middle class") to describe the social group to whom the shoemaker would have belonged in mid-nineteenth-century Brazil. Franks's middling group included tinsmiths, blacksmiths, tailors, street vendors, low-level bureaucrats, and small-scale slaveholders and property owners, many of whom were non-white and even included freedmen and women. Higher-ranking government jobs were usually held by the lighter-complexioned European-descended *bacheréis* disdained by the shoemaker in the previous examples, *Dutra's World: Wealth and Family in Nineteenth-Century Rio de Janeiro* (Albuquerque: University of New Mexico Press, 2004), p. 8.

[8] The 1831 edition of the *Diccionario da Lingua Portuguesa* defined "artes mecânicos":

Arts and mechanical works, as distinguished from Liberal Arts, are manufactured, and include works produced by hand and foot, for example, shoemaking, tailoring, hatmaking, carpentry, etc., which are not learned through scientific principle; those who perform manual labor in contrast to reason or science. (*Artes, Obras Mecanicas,* oppostas às *Liberaes* são todas as de manufacturas, e de trabalhos de mãos, e pés, *v.g.* as de sapataria, alfayates, capelheiros, carpinteiros, etc., todas as que se não aprendem por princípios scientificos; as que practicão os mesteres, contrap. ás de *razão,* ou scientificas.)

Diccionario da Lingua Portugueza, composto por Antonio de Moraes Silva, 4th ed. (Lisbon: Impressão Regia, 1831), s.v. "mecanico".

[9] André Luiz Alípio de Andrade, "Variações sobre um tema: a Sociedade Auxiliadora da Indústria Nacional e o debate sobre o fim do tráfico de escravos (1845–1850),"

The Brazilian shoemaker's defense of mechanical arts echoed an important theme in eighteenth-century French Enlightenment discourse: the valorization of artisanal crafts alongside the liberal arts. *Encylopédie* author Denis Diderot championed the mechanical arts as an "equally subtle and complex production... of the human mind" in an attempt to change negative perceptions of manual labor in the highly stratified aristocratic society of his day.[10] In the spirit of Diderot, the shoemaker drew attention to what he saw as a harmful prejudice within Brazilian society. The manual trades were the only true source of wealth creation, he argued, though he also intimated that both the liberal arts and *indústria* were necessary for material progress, an informed citizenry, a vital economy, and self-liberation for those on the margins of patronage networks. Furthermore, his musings revealed that in Brazil – a so-called backward agricultural nation deeply reliant on slave labor – the new economic and moral values conveyed by "indústria" had an identifiable "impact on consciousness," in the words of Leo Marx. In this sense, the shoemaker's definition of *indústria* demonstrated the need for new vocabulary to express emerging modes of economic production and social organization.[11] While one should not assign too much weight to the meaning of *indústria* expressed in a single letter, a broader discussion of this shifting term is corroborated in multiple sources. The journals of the Sociedade Auxilidora Nacional and the Imperial Instituto Fluminense de Agricultura, provincial presidential reports, national and international exhibition catalogs, and patent applications invoked, debated, and defined the term in the same spirit as the anonymous shoemaker.

The letter also raises many unanswerable questions. Was the writer truly a shoemaker? Was he a Brazilian eager for more economic and educational opportunities for the artisanal class? Was he a politician poking fun at the overwrought title of the institute and the future *bacharéis* it would produce for comfortable employment in the state bureaucracy? Was he influenced by contemporary currents of political economy or a believer in the personal and economic liberation promised by Enlightenment liberalism? His satirical observations suggest that he might be more than he stated in the letter. Though he claimed to have only a basic

(Master's thesis, Universidade Estadual de Campinas, Instituto de Economia, 2002), p. 48.

[10] William Hamilton Sewell, *Work and Revolution in France: the language of labor from the Old Regime to 1848* (New York: Cambridge University Press, 1980), pp. 64–6.

[11] Leo Marx, *The Machine in the Garden: Technology and the Pastoral Ideal in America* (New York: Oxford University Press, 1964, 2000), endnote, p. 166.

education, his eloquence and clever rhetorical tactics suggest otherwise. On the other hand, nineteenth-century Brazil was an era of autodidacts. Joaquim Machado de Assis, Brazil's most celebrated author of the period, was self-taught. Moreover, self-effacement was a rhetorical strategy used in editorial statements; contributors often softened (perhaps sarcastically at times) their strong positions behind a humble tone and professions of ignorance. Whatever the true identity of the shoemaker, the letter demonstrates that multiple views of industry – and of the liberal ideologies behind the term – circulated in nineteenth-century Brazil. Furthermore, the fact that the writer expressed his views in a very visible public forum (albeit anonymously) attests to the strong feelings of many Brazilians when it came to economic development and modernization.

The shoemaker's letter also suggests that his understanding of *indústria* was colored by both external and local influences; the latter dimension might be easy to miss without a consideration of the greater social context of mid-nineteenth-century Brazil. This chapter seeks to provide this context by examining the emerging economic, technological, and social meanings of two key terms: *indústria* (industry), and *aperfeiçoar* (to perfect or to improve), as they were expressed in period sources. By the 1890s, Brazilians assigned explicitly economic and technological definitions to the terms from the perspective of a nation both dependent on slave labor and desiring to modernize without the social turmoil of the European Revolutions or the violence of the Haitian Revolution and the US Civil War. The question surfaced repeatedly, particularly in the writings of the Sociedade Auxiliadora: What type of *indústria* was best suited to a tropical and "essentially agricultural" nation? Which *aperfeiçoamentos* and *indústrias* would engender economic and moral improvements in Brazilian society while also avoiding social upheaval?

Linked but subordinate to *indústria* and *aperfeiçoar* were other key terms including *melhorar* (to improve) and the related *melhoramentos materiais* (material improvements), *civilizar* (to civilize), *moralizar* (to moralize), and *progresso* (progress). Together, these words represented a vocabulary in gestation as older social and economic meanings gave way to concepts that described the new technological and economic realities of the nineteenth century. The premodern sense of *indústria* – as expressed in the Latin phrase quoted on the cover of *O Auxiliador da Indústria Nacional*, "vires industria firmat" (industry confirms their strength – a quote from Virgil) – meant "diligent action or skill."[12] *Indústria* referred

---

[12] Cover, *O Auxiliador*, January 1860.

to the moral quality of a person's character, a virtuous and productive ethos expressed through the skillful management of one's household, laborers, property, and family. By the end of the nineteenth century in Brazil, the term explicitly referred to "creative economic production," and in particular, goods produced through mechanized processes
in factories.[13] The anonymous shoemaker invoked the new economic
meaning of the term in 1849, though portions of the older virtuous sense
of industry endured, as will be demonstrated later in this chapter.

This exploration of *indústria* and *aperfeiçoar* is based on their frequency in articles, exhibition publications, provincial reports, public letters, patent applications, and, in the case of the former, in the name of the
Sociedade Auxiliadora itself. *Progresso* (progress), prominently displayed
alongside *Ordem* (order) on the Brazilian flag after the formation of the
Republic in 1889, conveyed a lofty yet vague sense of Enlightenment-
inflected belief in material and moral advancement without specifics of
how this was to be achieved.[14] *Progresso* was regularly invoked in O *Auxiliador* where its range of meanings included both material and economic
development. The term also described improved machinery. *Progresso*
additionally could mean an "entrepreneurial or innovative drive," as indicated in a report on experiments with tea cultivation in Brazil in the 1860s
where the author complained that the "cruel monopoly of preferred tea
varieties in the marketplace . . . has killed [Brazilian agriculturalist's] spirit
of progress." The most noble – and often opaque – sense of *progresso* was
invoked in publications for and about international exhibitions where it
conveyed an over-arching narrative of ever forward-moving material and
moral improvement.[15] An amusing invocation of *progresso* and *melhoramentos materiais* captures this sense in the 1855 novel of Joaquim Manoel
de Macedo, *A Carteira do Meu Tio (My Uncle's Purse)*. The novel's protagonist, a youth traveling through the interior with the self-serving aim
of observing the Brazilian population on his way to becoming a politician,

---

[13] Herausgegeben von Otto Brunner, Werner Conze, Reinhart Koselleck, eds., *Geschichtliche Grundbegriffe: Historisches Lexikon zur politisch-sozialen Sprache in Deutschland* (Stuttgart: Klett-Cotta, 1982), p. 239. My thanks to Janek Wasserman for trans-
lating this example.

[14] Brazilian Positivists successfully lobbied for the inclusion of the term on the national flag
after the establishment of the Republic in 1889, José Murilo de Carvalho, Clifford E.
Landers, trans., *The Formation of Souls* (Notre Dame: University of Notre Dame Press,
2012), pp. 115–17.

[15] "Relatorio Sobre o Fabrico das Amostras de Chá remettidas a Exposição Nacional
com a Marca a Margem," *O Auxiliador*, January, 1862, p. 8; Conde de Villeneuve,
"Exposições: Exposição Internacional de Antuerpia em 1885," *O Auxiliador*, Março
1886, p. 83.

encounters a remote innkeeper feverishly spouting the buzzwords of the day in a manic mantra of progress, "... big business, canals, railroads, immigrant colonies, mining, steamships ... material progress! ... material improvements! ... everything material! everything material!"[16] As this overwrought example shows us, material progress was very much on the minds of Brazilians at mid-century. In contrast to *progresso* and related words in the previous examples, *ordem* rarely appeared in the sources consulted for this project, although it was a concept vital to Brazilian political life.[17]

The terms *civilizar* and *moralizar* were discussed as a way to remedy the backwardness of the Brazilian poor and the rapacious slash-and-burn cultivation practices of coffee planters.[18] But these terms appeared less frequently and either espoused vague or what seems to twentieth-century eyes fantastical courses of action (one modernizer hoped to civilize the poor by planting "physically and morally purifying" Eucalyptus trees near their dwellings), or expressed a general desire to Europeanize the poor and marginalized in Brazil.[19] In contrast, the frequency and specificity embodied in the terms *indústria* and *aperfeiçoar* reveal a concrete trail of changing meanings and their "impact on consciousness" during the period of the empire. These terms thusly provide a fine-grained lens through which the meanings of progress, order, and material improvements in the context of nineteenth-century Brazil come into focus. As the shoemaker's letter demonstrated, such terms reflected the visions and tensions of a society in transformation.

Indústria

Nineteenth-century Brazil was not industrial in the sense that mechanized centers of production – be they rural factories or urban workshops – played a large role in economic production. By this definition swathes of

---

[16] Joaquim Manoel de Macedo, *A Carteira do Meu Tio* (Rio de Janeiro: Tip. Paulo Brito, 1855), pp. 54–5.

[17] See Jeffrey Needell, *The Party of Order: The Conservatives, the State, and Slavery in the Brazilian Monarchy, 1831–1871* (Stanford: Stanford University Press, 2006), pp. 1–6 and 95–6.

[18] For a discussion of *civilizar* and *civilização* see Heloisa Maria Bertol Domingues, "A Noção de civilização na visão dos construtores do Império. (A Revista do Instituto Histórico e Geográfico Brasileiro: 1838–1850/60)," (Master's thesis, Instituto de Ciências Humanas e Filosofia, Centro de Estudos Gerais, Universidade Federal Fluminense, 1989).

[19] J. A. D'Azevedo, "Eucalyptos Globulus: Sua Descoberta e Introducção," *Revista Agricola do Imperial Instituto Fluminense*, March 1874, No. 1, p. 28.

Europe and the United States were also not yet industrial during the same period. The Brazilian economy depended on a constellation of agricultural and wild-harvested exports: rubber, nuts, sugar, leather, wood, and especially coffee. Indeed, for much of the period of this study, *indústria* was most often linked to agricultural production, as the cover of O *Auxiliador* examined later in this chapter demonstrates. Yet mechanized factories and workshops appeared early in the century after the arrival of the Portuguese court in 1808, which ended the 1785 ban on manufacturing in the colony. Between 1809 and 1849, 101 factories were established in Niteroi and Rio de Janeiro – among them silk, paper, and wallpaper factories, foundries, glassworks, chemical works, and even a chocolatier and oilcloth factory.[20] In 1821, a newly constructed paper mill outside the city attracted the attention of the young Pedro I who, along with his wife and infant, inspected its clattering, water-powered paper pulpers early one morning, attesting to the noteworthiness of new manufacturing establishments for the period.[21] Manufactories may not have been widespread, but machine-based production became increasingly visible in Brazil, accompanied by the evolving definition of *indústria*. By the 1850s, provincial reports from the north to south noted the presence of factories, mills, and steam engines. A new leather manufactory complete with a "water-powered machine" established by an "honest and hardworking Frenchman" in Bahia in 1843 attested to the enthusiasm with which such establishments were described beyond Rio.[22] Though Brazil was not an industrial nation by the midpoint of the nineteenth century, rich and poor alike were increasingly exposed to mechanized production in urban and rural settings.

Brazil was also directly linked to the industrial boom in England through close-knit trade relations. Though Brazilians inhabited the

---

[20] Eulalia Maria Lahmeyer Lobo, *História do Rio de Janeiro: do capital comercial ao capital industrial e financeiro* (Rio de Janeiro: Instituto Brasileiro de Mercado de Capitais, 1978), pp. 114–15; and Urias A. da Silveira, *Fontes de Riqueza dos Estados Unidos do Brasil* (S.L.P.: S.C.P., 1890), as cited in Erdna Perugine, "A Palavra Indústria na Revista O Auxiliador da Indústria Nacional 1833–1843," (Master's thesis, Universidade de São Paulo, 1978), pp. 25–6.

[21] Thomas Bennett, *A voyage from the United States to South America, performed during the years 1821, 1822, & 1823. Embracing a description of the city of Rio Janeiro, in Brazil, of every port of importance in Chili; of several in Lower Peru; and of an eighteen months cruise in a Nantucket whaleship. The whole interspersed with a variety of original anecdotes*, 2 ed., (Newburyport, MA: Herald Press, 1823), pp. 14–15.

[22] *Falla que recitou o presidente da provincia da Bahia, o conselheiro Joaquim José Pinheiro de Vasconcellos, n'abertura da Assembléa Legislativa da mesma provincia em 2 de fevereiro de 1843* (Bahia: Tip. de J.A. Portella e Companhia, 1942 [sic]), p. 12.

periphery in relation to Europe's core, they encountered the new products and technologies of the era first-hand through commercial networks. Brazil's long coastline and port cities, principally Rio, provided it with ready access to overseas markets. US visitor Daniel Kidder observed in the 1830s that Rio's enviable central location on "the great highway of nations" linked the tropical nation directly to Europe, Bombay, Canton, Chile, Australia, and the Pacific Islands, and later became an important rendezvous point for ships sailing between the western and eastern coasts of North America.[23] Rio became a key port for provisioning and repairing hundreds of California Gold Rush ships on their way from the Eastern US to the gold fields in the 1840s and 1850s. From colonial times Brazilian ports also served as major entrepôts for ships traveling to and from Europe and Africa. After the arrival of the Portuguese court in 1808 and the establishment of a monarchy after independence the colony received numerous European visitors and entrepreneurs who informed Brazilians of the latest North Atlantic technologies, as evidenced by the arrival of the daguerreotype camera a few months after it was made commercially available in France.[24] The *Jornal do Commercio* celebrated "the first photographic demonstration" of the camera "made before Brazilian eyes," in Rio in January of 1840, a machine so marvelous, the paper declared, that it had to be witnessed in person to be fully appreciated.[25] Though located under the distant Southern Cross, Brazilian ports were well integrated into the global movement of information, technology, and capital.

Other factors contributed to Brazil's advantageous position for participating in the global movement of technology and capital in the nineteenth century. The relatively peaceful transition of Brazil from colony to independence allowed for continuity in political leadership and maintained existing socioeconomic hierarchies. Though regional rebellions in the early imperial period were an enormous drain on public coffers and manpower, these were neutralized by the 1850s under the centralized administration of the empire located in the "court city" of Rio de Janeiro.

[23] Daniel P. Kidder, *Sketches of Residence and Travels in Brazil Embracing Historical and Geographical Notices of the Empire and its Several Provinces* (London: Wiley and Putnam, 1845), pp. 171–2.

[24] French photographer Louis Compte's daguerreotype of the imperial palace in Rio circa 1840 is considered the first photographic image recorded in Brazil, Marçal Ferrera de Andrade, *História da fotorreportagem no Brasil: a fotografia na imprensa do Rio de Janeiro de 1839 a 1900* (Rio de Janeiro: Elsevier Editora Ltd., 2004), p. 12.

[25] As cited in George Ermakoff, *Rio de Janeiro, 1840–1900: uma crônica fotográfica* (Rio de Janeiro: Casa Editorial, 2006), p. 25.

Brazilian elites then increasingly turned their attention to improving the economic prospects and material conditions of their country, including the establishment of communication networks with North Atlantic nations through steamship lines and telegraph cables. Brazil's close links to Great Britain provided access to capital, new technologies such as the steam engine and railroad, and trained technological specialists (machinists and engineers). France was also influential in the transfer of technology; many of the patents registered in Brazil during this period were for French inventions. Although Great Britain hindered Brazilian economic development through its preferential trade agreements and manufactured imports that undercut Brazilian producers, it also provided valuable access to technological innovation in the form of machinery, railroad construction, scientific knowledge, and investment capital.[26]

Transatlantic Transformations

We owe many of the material and theoretical innovations that underpin our modern economies and technologies to the nineteenth century. The railway, the telegraph, the light bulb, photography, the typewriter and sewing machine, the periodic table of the elements, standardized time zones, and less lofty inventions such as the adhesive postage stamp owe their provenance to innovators working in this century. The production of new technologies and goods – or the application of science to manufacturing in the case of the periodic table of the elements – arose under new work regimes that amplified human labor through machinery purchased with newly available capital. From this novel work system – centered in factories – the modern concept of industry as "systematic work or labour ... especially in the arts or manufactures" emerged.[27] By the end of the nineteenth century in Brazil and beyond, industry almost exclusively referred to the economic production of goods in mechanized factories. The term's premodern denotation of diligence, skill, dexterity, or cunning faded to a secondary meaning across the Atlantic at the dawn of the twentieth century.

The term "industry" entered the English language by the 1400s via the French. Its earliest definition, "the application of skill, cleverness, or

---

[26] Richard Graham, *Britain and the onset of modernization in Brazil: 1850–1914* (Cambridge: Cambridge University Press, 1968), ch. 5.

[27] *The Oxford English Dictionary* (Oxford: Clarendon Press, 1989), 2nd ed., s.v. "industry."

craft; a device, contrivance; a crafty expedient," and "[an] intelligent or clever working, [or] skill," resembled the premodern sense conveyed in Virgil's phrase quoted earlier. Within a century industry more explicitly conveyed, "a particular form or branch of productive labour; a trade or manufacture."[28] The transformation of a raw material into an item of greater monetary value through the application of labor is the explicit definition given by Sir James Steuart, Adam Smith, and David Ricardo, and now referred to as the Labor Theory of Value.[29] By the end of the nineteenth century, industry almost exclusively referred to mechanized production, diminishing the visibility of the laborer in the process.

Scottish political economist Sir James Steuart in his 1767 publication *An Inquiry into the Principals of Political Oeconomy*, declared "[l]abour, which through its alienation creates a universal equivalent, I call industry."[30] Under Steuart's definition, industry transformed raw material into a finished product of greater value that commanded a standard monetary value in the marketplace. In other words, the term no longer referred exclusively to a quality (skill or dexterity) but to an economic process. Steuart also further distinguished coerced labor from free labor. Slave labor – the unskilled power of human muscle compelled to produce goods by force – did not and could not result in industry because slaves had no motivation to improve the end result of their labor, nor were they free to enjoy the fruits of their work. Free labor allowed the possibility for innovation, and by extension, the ability to increase the economic value of the finished product, which in turn further motivated the laborer to improve the product. According to Steuart, the result was a virtuous and self-sufficient cycle of product development through intelligent labor that also resulted – and this was essential to Steuart's definition – in the political liberation of the individual.[31] In this example of slave and free labor, Steuart's industry still contained a seed of its ancient moral value,

---

[28] *The Oxford English Dictionary* ... s.v., "industry."

[29] *Dictionary of the Social Sciences*, ed. Craig Calhoun (Oxford: Oxford University Press, 2002, 2012), s.v., "labor theory of value."

[30] As cited in Karl Marx, *A Contribution to the Critique of Political Economy* (Moscow: Progress Publishers, 1970), p. 58.

[31] Steuart continues, "INDUSTRY is the application to ingenious labour in a free man, in order to procure, by the means of trade, an equivalent, fit for the supplying of every want ... *Industry* ... likewise implies something more than labour. *Industry*, as I understand the term, must be voluntary; *labour* may be forced: the one and the other may produce the same effect, but the political consequences are vastly different," Sir James Steuart, *An Inquiry into the Principles of Political Oeconomy, Vol. I*, ed. Andrew S. Skinner (Chicago: University of Chicago Press, 1966). p. 146.

but it was now applied to modern modes of production. Importantly for Steuart, only industry resulted in social and political freedom.

Industry (*industrie*) also described the changing economic system in France as evidenced in Denis Diderot's and Jean Le Rond d'Alembert's *Encyclopédie*, published between 1751 and 1772. Two entries divided the definition of *industrie* between its "metaphysical" qualities and its political and economic aspects as they related to the economies of modern states. The former definition distinguished industry from artistic talent, that is, the ability to discern taste ("an aesthetic sensibility for perceiving beauty and its opposite, flaws"), and intellectual prowess or "genius" ("the vivacity of emotion, the grandeur and power of imagination, and the activity of the conception of ideas"). Defined as a more practical quality, *industrie* reflected "a calm and extensive imagination, an ease of perception, and the quick grasping of ideas." It was furthermore " ... guided by science, ... [the consideration] of a material's [natural] properties, and/or the simple laws of motion," demonstrating that *industrie* conveyed a scientific, or rational, understanding of the natural world.[32] The last sense is echoed in the Brazilian use of the term, especially as it related to agricultural improvement. The second entry for *industrie* explicitly referred to the growth of the manufacturing sector in England, a development, the *Encyclopédie* authors argued,that served as an aspirational model for "all the trades and professions" in France.[33] *Industrie* also directly benefited the state's treasury through increased tax revenue, the *Encyclopédie* asserted; in sum, *industrie* was beneficial to individual and nation.

The multiple meanings assigned to the term industry in Enlightenment thought also resonated in Brazil. Returning to the Brazilian shoemaker, what appears to be a simple commentary about the type of industry taught at Mr. Freese's secondary school indeed offers up a more complicated polemic on social rights, the role of skilled labor in the economy, and the lack of educational opportunities than is apparent at first glance:

I am a poor shoemaker supporting my wife and children by my labor, and I wish to give my sons the education that I was not able to obtain for myself ... I want my sons to learn any of the mechanical arts: cobbling, tailoring, carpentry, watch making, etc. because I understand very well that *he who possesses [such a skill] is truly independent* (emphasis mine).[34]

---

[32] *Encyclopédie, ou dictionnaire raisonné des sciences, des arts et des métiers, etc.*, Denis Diderot and Jean le Rond d'Alembert, eds., University of Chicago: ARTFL Encyclopédie Project (Spring 2013 Edition), Robert Morrissey, ed., http://encyclopedie.uchicago.edu/, s.v. "INDUSTRIE (*Métaphys*)."

[33] *Encyclopédie*, s.v. "INDUSTRIE (Droit polit. & Commerce)."

[34] "Instituto Collegial de Nova Friburgo," January 5, 1849.

The shoemaker asserted that an individual trained in the mechanical arts was empowered to earn his bread by his own labor and skill, freed from dependence on a patron or employer. This last point was especially important; Brazilian patronage networks were the pathway to the attainment of government jobs, political office, or professorial chairs in the schools of medicine or law. In Brazilian slave society, patronage networks also took expression through godmother and godfather relationships, as well as the relationship between large landowners and *agregados* – poor rural inhabitants whose informal agreements with landholders ranged from sharecropping, to supplying votes for local elections, to providing firepower in land conflicts with rival planters.[35] Furthermore, self-employment in the trades was less socially prestigious than a *bacharel* employed in the civil service. Manual and artisanal labor was still strongly stigmatized by its association with slavery. Indeed, in nineteenth-century Brazil slaves worked as skilled artisans in a number of trades: tailoring, cooking, barbering, carpentry, blacksmithing, and shoemaking, to name a few.[36] *Indústria* offered the promise of economic independence but not social independence, respect, or upward mobility.

In 1861, Sociedade Auxiliadora member Raphael Archanjo Galvão Filho also identified the low value of artisanal trades and lack of industrial education as the reason for an absence of "entrepreneurial spirit" in Brazil:

It is evident that the majority of Brazilians do not pursue careers in workshops, the mechanical arts, or agriculture. They dedicate themselves to the study of letters, and aspire to secure public employment. In this way they diminish the number of hands available to... develop industries... [which results] in many individuals without vocations...[37]

The lack of regard for industrial labor in an aristocratic slave society aggravated Sociedade Auxiliadora members. They lobbied for agricultural and industrial education as the means to transform Brazilians into good workers, including the poor, freed slaves and free mixed-race

---

35 Marina Machado, *Diccionário da Terra*, ed. Márcia Motta (Rio de Janeiro: Civilização Brasileira, 2005), s.v. "Agregado." For a discussion of the role of patronage networks in the imperial period see Richard Graham, *Patronage and Politics in Nineteenth-Century Brazil* (Stanford: Stanford University Press, 1990).

36 See Frank, *Dutra's World*, pp. 27–8 and 47–50.

37 Raphael Archanjo Galvão Filho, "Industria Metallurgica. Artes e Productos Chimicos. Relatorio do Terceiro Group," in Antônio Luiz Fernandes da Cunha, *Relatorio Geral da Exposição Nacional de 1861 e Relatorios dos Jurys Especiaes Colligidos e Publicados por Deliberação da Commissão Directora* (Rio de Janeiro: Tip. Diario do Rio de Janeiro, 1862), p. 346.

populations. They also targeted *fazendeiros*, or more specifically their sons, envisioning agricultural schools as the best way to change backward agricultural practices such as slash-and-burn cultivation. They argued that an industrial and agricultural education would directly contribute to the economic and social health of the nation while also maintaining stability.[38] Inspired by Adam Smith (a topic that will be examined further shortly), society member and editor of *O Auxiliador*, Frederico Burlamaque, saw manufacturing industry as an important auxiliary to agriculture and an industrial education as a remedy for the shameful "ignorance of everyday practical knowledge of the nature of the material world by those destined to liberal careers."[39] In 1851 the provincial president of São Paulo observed that a traditional primary education did little to help students "acquire [training in a useful] industry," condemning them instead to work as "domestic servants or tavern cashiers." He thought it expedient to send ten of the "most indolent" students (suggesting that industry also civilized the slothful) of the Seminario de Santa Anna in São Paulo to the Navy Arsenal in Rio where they would be educated in "whichever industry would be most useful for themselves and the nation."[40] In 1855 two workshops were opened at the seminary, one for tailoring and one for shoemaking, with the triple objective of providing the community with badly needed artisans, bringing in revenue for the seminary, and training students in a skill "useful to them, and to the province."[41] Together these examples demonstrate that disseminating industrial knowledge was very much on the minds of Brazilians at the midpoint of the nineteenth century. By the 1860s, the economic sense of industry predominated (whether agricultural or manufactured), though the term also contained a kernel of its older, moral sensibility of skill or diligence. Though conservative economic interests within late colonial and nineteenth-century Brazilian society famously asserted that

[38] Marcus Vinícius Fonseca, *A Educação dos Negros: uma nova face do processo de abolição da escravidão no Brasil* (Bragança Paulista, São Paulo: Coleção Estudos CDAPH, 2002), p. 35.

[39] Frederico Leopoldo Cesar Burlamaque, "Sala das sessões do Imperial Instituto Fluminense de Agricultura, 24 de Outubro de 1860," *O Auxiliador*, January 1861, p. 5.

[40] *Discurso com que o illustrissimo e exm. o senhor conselheiro dr. Vicente Pires da Motta, presidente da provincia de São Paulo, abbrio [sic] a Assembléa Legislativa Provincial no dia 15 de fevereiro de 1851* (São Paulo: Tip. do Governo, 1851), p. 16.

[41] *Discurso com que o illustrissimo e excellentissimo senhor dr. José Antonio Saraiva, presidente da provincia de S. Paulo, abrio a Assembléa Legislativa Provincial no dia 15 de fevereiro de 1855* (São Paulo: Tip. 2 de Dezembro de Antonio Louzada Antunes, 1855), p. 38.

the nation was first and foremost "agricultural" – industry and industrial educational was nonetheless championed as an essential (albeit subordinate to agriculture) component of the Brazilian economy particularly by the Sociedade Auxiliadora.[42]

Nowhere was the term *indústria* more prominent than in the publications of the Sociedade Auxiliadora. It referred to the economy in its broadest sense (defined as a large-scale system of production and exchange) that also contained more specific branches of production, usually divided into *indústria fabril* (manufacturing industry), *indústria agrícola* (agricultural industry), and *indústria comercial* (commercial industry, i.e., merchants).[43] The Visconde de Cairu (José da Silva Lisboa, 1756–1835), Brazil's first interpreter of Adam Smith's political economy, used the term "indústria geral" to describe the total economic output of a nation. Additional phrases, *indústria extractiva* (extractive industry, i.e., mining), *indústria de transporte* (transportation industry), and *indústria botânica* (economic botany), attested to the wide variety of economic activities discussed in nineteenth-century Brazil.[44] Illustrative of the multiple meanings of industry across the Atlantic, this expansive sense of *indústria* was not limited to Brazil, as Ruth Oldenziel observes about the nineteenth-century United States:

An early nineteenth-century speaker could discuss manufacturing, industry, and industriousness, referring to any kind of production mechanical or otherwise that could even include agriculture; could mention science and useful knowledge in one breath without sensing any contradiction; could marvel about the wonderful inventions and discoveries that ran the whole gamut from languages to mechanical devices; and could speak of technology referring to academic knowledge as well as to the skills of millers, bakers, farmers, teachers, and innkeepers.[45]

Erdna Perugine's exploration of the word *indústria* as it appeared in *O Auxiliador* from 1833–43 demonstrates a similar semantic range.

---

[42] José de Murilo de Carvalho, *A construção da ordem: a elite política imperial;* and *Teatro de Sombras: a política imperial,* 2nd ed. (Rio de Janeiro: Civilização Brasileira, 2006), pp. 254–5; and Ilmar Rohloff de Mattos, *O Tempo Saquarema* (São Paulo: Editora Hucitec, 1987), pp. 34–7.

[43] Manuel de Oliveria Fausto, "Industria," *O Auxiliador da Indústria Nacional,* No. 1, July 1854, pp. 12–16.

[44] Geraldo de Beauclair, *Raízes da Indústria no Brasil* (Rio de Janeiro: Studio F&S Editora, 1992), pp. 15–16; and José Luiz Werneck da Silva, "Isto é o que me parece: a Sociedade Auxiliadora da Indústria Nacional (1827–1904) na Formação Social Brasileira. A Conjuntura de 1981–1877," vol. I, (Master's thesis, Universidade Federal Fluminense, Niterói, 1979), p. 83.

[45] Ruth Oldenziel, *Making Technology Masculine: Men, Women, and Modern Machines in America, 1870–1945* (Amsterdam: Amsterdam University Press, 1999), p. 19.

Industry appears in three central clusters of meaning: nature, human, and nation (Fig. 2.1). "Nature" referred to the spontaneous production of organic or inert material of the nonhuman world, be it flora, fauna, or mineral. In reference to the human individual, industry contained both its premodern moral association and a modern sense of work ethic. Industry as it related to the nation conveyed progress manifested through material work; wealth creation generated through economically productive activities; and the identification and creation of new agricultural and manufactured commodities. As the inclusion of industry in the title of the Sociedade Auxilidora suggests, the term also represented the overarching economic, social, and material development of the nation.

The influence of the French Physiocrats on Brazilian economic thought – and subsequently on definitions of *indústria* – was apparent in the primacy placed on agricultural production by prominent nineteenth-century actors including Brazilian statesmen and the members of the Sociedade Auxiliadora.[46] Central to Physiocratic doctrine was the argument that only agriculture provided a reliable – and renewable – source of wealth with other branches of production and commerce serving as auxiliaries.[47] Adam Smith also argued that industry was secondary to agriculture, an influence that is readily apparent in *O Auxiliador*.[48] The continental emphasis on agricultural production fit well with the long-standing view of Brazil as a paradise resplendent with natural riches that dated to the earliest years of colonization.[49] In the eyes of the Sociedade Auxiliadora, Brazil's tropical abundance gave it a competitive advantage in producing agro-industrial commodities for domestic and international

---

[46] José Agosto Pádua, *Um Sopro de Destruição: Pensamento Político e Crítica Ambiental no Brasil Escravista (1786–1888)* (Rio de Janeiro: Jorge Zahar Editor, 2002), p. 18; Agricultural improvement and the role of agriculture in national economies were important topics in eighteenth-century Enlightenment thought; J. H. Galloway, "Agricultural Reform and the Enlightenment in Late Colonial Brazil," *Agricultural History*, 53:4 (1979), p. 765.

[47] Elizabeth Fox-Genovese, *The Origins of Physiocracy: Economic Revolution and Social Order in Eighteenth-Century France* (Ithaca: Cornell University Press, 1976), p. 223; and Liana Vardi, *The Physiocrats and the World of the Enlightenment* (Cambridge: Cambridge University Press, 2012), p. 3.

[48] Dr. Manuel de Oliveria Fausto, "Industria," *O Auxiliador*, July 1854, pp. 12–16; Andrade, "Variações Sobre um Tema...," pp. 9 and 58; Adam Smith, *An Inquiry into the Nature and Causes of the Wealth of Nations* (Chicago: University of Chicago Press, 1976), pp. 401–2.

[49] Patrícia Regina Corrêa Barreto, "Sociedade Auxiliadora da Indústria Nacional: o templo carioca de Palas Atena," (Ph.D. dissertation, Universidade Federal do Rio de Janeiro, 2009), ch. 2.

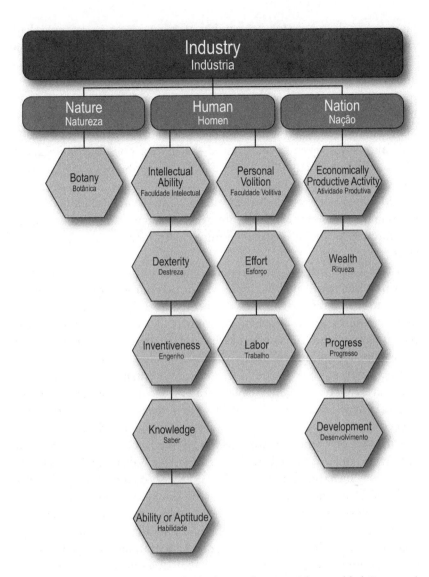

FIGURE 2.1. Table of semantic fields for "indústria." I have added "economic botany" to the category of "Nature." Adapted from Erdna Perugine, "A Palavra Indústria na Revista O Auxiliador da Industria Nacional 1833–1843," (Master's thesis, Universidade de São Paulo, 1978), p. 111. Table design: Tori Robinson.

markets. If the powerful "principles of science and agronomy" had resulted in an agricultural revolution in Great Britain, a small nation "less favored by nature [than Brazil]" with its "disagreeable climate and...sterile soils," what might the fertile Brazilian provinces accomplish with "the same methods appropriately modified" to their particular agricultural needs? Were Brazilian agriculturalists not capable of "far superior results?"[50] The *uberdade* or "super-fertility" of Brazil's soils and forests even overshadowed the human populace as an agent of economic productivity in *O Auxiliador*. Contributors to the journal bitterly decried the backward triumvirate of rapacious *fazendeiros*, brutalized slaves, and unenlightened agricultural laborers planting export crops in the ashes of the burned forest that threatened to stop the rational development of Brazil's natural resources even before it had a chance to start.[51]

The nation's tropical vitality as the genesis of industrial productivity appeared frequently in visual representations. Four illustrations from the 1860s to the 1880s provide a visual metaphor of the industrial potential of the nation's forests; each illustration places the symbols of industry – steam engines, railroads, plows, and a factory – within a tropical stage embedded within the forest. While lush foliage also symbolized the Brazilian nation, the rhetoric of the Sociedade Auxilidora and Brazilian national exhibition catalogs demonstrated that the naturally abundant tropical environment was also intrinsically industrial. All that Brazilians needed was to harness this innate industrial potential to the market. This Brazilian vision of the generative powers of the forest as the birthplace of industry contrasted strongly with Romantic poet William Blake's "satanic mills" that menaced the industrializing English countryside, or Charles Dickens' bleak industrial "wilderness of smoke and brick" in the fictional factory town of Coketown. For these authors, industry sterilized the natural world and reduced its human inhabitants to ashen, empty-eyed survivors.[52] In contrast, the Brazilian illustrations conveyed a vision of harmonious industrial development that proceeded without violence or exploitation, nourished by and sheltered in the forest.

A depiction of the Fábrica de Papel de Orianda (The Orianda Paper Factory) founded outside Petropólis in 1851 by Sociedade Auxiliadora member The Baron of Capanema (Guilherme Schüch, 1824–1908),

---

[50] *O Auxiliador*, January 1860, p. 48.   [51] Pádua, *Um Sopro de Destruição*, pp. 174–9.
[52] Leo Marx, *The Machine in the Garden*, pp. 18–19; Charles Dickens, *Hard Times* (Oxford: Oxford University Press, 2006), p. 88.

FIGURE 2.2. "Fábrica do Barão de Capanema, Petrópolis." *Source*: Agostinho José de Mota, photograph of original painting, n/d. Courtesy of Acervo da Fundação Biblioteca Nacional, Brazil, Iconografía, Pasta de Fotografías diversas, tam. B, Nº XV.

illustrates this theme (Fig. 2.2). The forest surrounds the mill, both revealing it and concealing it. Indeed, at first glance the Orianda mill is barely visible, only after closer scrutiny do the contours of roof and smokestack emerge from the dense foliage. Yet the mill is the focal point of the illustration, and the plume of smoke rising from the chimney – a visual trope for progress – represents a beneficial industry. A young boy and girl seated at the side of the road to the factory add an idyllic element to the picture, evoking a quiet scene of rural order and tranquility. In contrast to the narrative of declension at the center of British Romanticism, Capanema's factory is organically protected, even nurtured by the forest.

A similar treatment of tropical vitality providing the stage for technological development appears in the frontispiece of Antônio Diodoro de Pascual's *Ensaio Critico sobre a viagem ao Brasil em 1852 de Carlos B. Mansfield*, a rebuttal of an English traveler's narrative criticizing Brazil's lack of material and social progress.[53] In this portrayal, the Brazilian nation is represented in the figure of an indigenous man gazing over his shoulder to the horizon (Fig. 2.3).

The illustration can be read in two overlapping ways: the native serves as an intermediary between nature and machine within a purely Brazilian context, illustrating the level of progress that the nation had achieved by the early 1860s. At this time, the romanticized image of the Brazilian Indian was emerging as a standard symbol of the nation.[54] In an alternate reading, the illustration is a visual rebuttal of the European portrayal of Brazil as uncivilized and backward; the indigenous figure discloses the nation's increasing level of material development to the international community and challenges the European vision of the tropics as inimical to industry. What comes to the fore in both readings is the native's revelatory gesture as he pulls back a curtain of vines from the first plane of vision, inviting the observer to look upon a distant scene: a railroad and a steamship moving to the horizon in a visual metaphor for Brazilian technological progress. The vista highlights prominent Rio landmarks, including what appears to be the São Cristovão Palace (Pedro II's residence), on a hill above the city. In the foreground are the *Arcos da Lapa*, an eighteenth-century aqueduct admired by foreign visitors and considered one of Rio's most important architectural structures. Not only does the illustration counter the European perception of the tropics as dangerous, messy, and difficult to control, but Brazil's tropical abundance

---

53 Frontispiece, Antônio Diodoro de Pascual, *Ensaio Critico sobre a Viagem ao Brasil em 1852 de Carlos B. Mansfield* (Rio de Janeiro: Tip. Universal de Laemmert, 1861), Division of Rare and Manuscript Collections, Cornell University Library; Charles Mansfield, *Paraguay, Brazil, and the Plate* (Cambridge: Macmillan, 1856).

54 See Tracy Devine Guzmán, *Native and National in Brazil: Indigeneity after Independence* (Chapel Hill: University of North Carolina Press, 2013), pp. 63–84; and Hendrik Kraay, *Days of National Festivity in Rio de Janeiro, Brazil, 1823–1889* (Stanford: Stanford University Press, 2013), pp. 223–7, and 237–8.

A de Pinho. Lith.

J Risso

FIGURE 2.3. Frontispiece. *Source*: Antônio Diodoro de Pascual, *Ensaio Crítico sobre a Viagem ao Brazil em 1852 de Carlos B. Mansfield* (Rio de Janeiro: Tip. Universal de Laemmert, 1861). Courtesy of Cornell University Library, Division of Rare and Manuscript Collections.

provides a fertile stage for the enlightened transformation of organic *nature* into mechanical *progress*.[55] The connection to the natural world remains central to the illustration; the luxurious foliage is pulled away to frame the passage of steamship and locomotive on the distant horizon; both remain firmly contained within a tropical frame.

An 1876 advertisement for the Fábrica C. F. Cathiard (C. F. Cathiard Factory), a shoe manufactory, published in O *Mosquito* echoes the association of tropical vitality – the spontaneous productivity of Brazilian forests – with the factory (Fig. 2.4). Tropical palm fronds and philodendron leaves pull back like theater curtains to reveal three stages. The top stage discloses a scene of genteel Carioca society wearing refined, costly, and distinctively European clothing. An impressive steam engine dominates the bottom left scene, while to the right workers toil at workbenches and polishing belts. The production line is not an artisanal workshop; the workers are arranged in an organized system following Adam Smith's classic example of the division of labor in a pin factory.[56] In each scene the focus of the action – manufacturing or leisure culture – takes place in the second plane of vision, partially obscured by the tropical foliage occupying the first plane. The reader of O *Mosquito* gazes into a private world of privileged consumption and industrial activity, ultimately observing himself as a sophisticated consumer of a product manufactured with the latest technology embedded within the forceful tropical fertility of the nation.

A final example of the association of Brazil's fertility with technological progress is exemplified by the 1882 cover illustration for O *Auxiliador* (Fig. 2.5). Farm machinery and a plow take center stage in the illustration. A railroad – the hero of industrialization – steams above the plow, visually demonstrating the link between rural production and urban and overseas markets. The inclusion of a plow in this scene may read as quaint to modern eyes, but innovations in plow blades greatly improved eighteenth- and nineteenth-century cultivation practices and crop yields in Europe and North America, the fact of which society members were keenly aware. John Deere's 1837 polished-steel sodbuster plow was crucial for transforming previously impenetrable Midwestern grasslands into one of the most productive agricultural regions in the United States, spurring

---

[55] Lygia Segala and Paulo M. Garchet, "Prescriptive Observation and Illustration of Brazil: Victor Frond's Photographic Project (1857–1861)," *Portuguese Studies*, 23:1 (2007), p. 63, n. 27; and Nancy Stepan, *Picturing Tropical Nature* (Ithaca, NY: Cornell University Press, 2001), pp. 48–9.

[56] Smith, pp. 8–9.

FIGURE 2.4. Advertisement for the "Imperial Steam-Powered Shoe Factory of C. F. Cathiard," showing the association of Brazilian industry with the tropical landscape. *Source*: *O Mosquito*, May 10, 1876, p. 8. Courtesy of the Acervo da Fundação Biblioteca Nacional, Brazil.

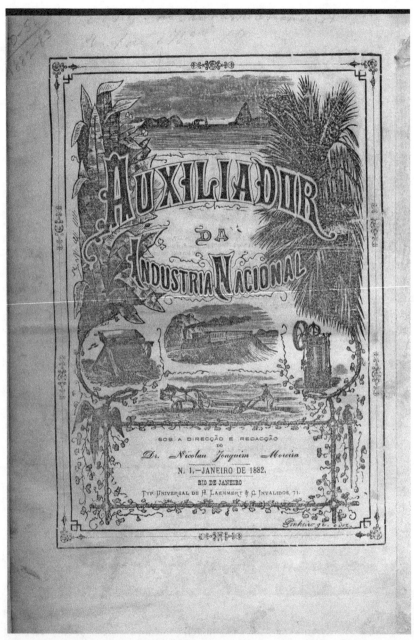

FIGURE 2.5. Cover of O *Auxiliador da Indústria Nacional*, January 1882.
Courtesy of the Library of Congress.

further agricultural innovations. On the right side of the illustration is a multi-use, steam-powered pump or mill, and to the left stands a Brazilian machine designed for processing manioc root, an important national crop. Tropical foliage again frames a theater of progress contained within and emerging from tropical vegetation that is abundant and nurturing, linking the forest to nation and economy.

Provincial Reports

The category of *indústria* in the annual provincial reports submitted to the central government in Rio sheds further light on the developing economic connotation of the term by the 1860s. Report categories included agriculture, industry, public works, prisons, the catechism of indigenous groups, roads and road-building, education, public health, navigation, public illumination, and churches. Industry appeared frequently though irregularly as a separate category, and it was often conflated with agriculture, the main economic activity across the provinces.

The quality and depth of provincial reports varied greatly depending on the discretion, interest, personality, and resources available to the president (the equivalent of a governor and usually a national politician appointed from Rio) or vice-president (usually a local politician). Some years included detailed statistical data on trade, while others contained only meandering discussions of political economy or, as was common from the 1850s to the 1870s, bitter complaints about the lack of well-engineered provincial roads. Despite the lack of consistency from year to year and the fact that provincial presidents (if not necessarily locally rooted presidents) probably most often represented the economic ideologies of Rio, the appearance of *indústria* in reports from across the provinces demonstrated the broad dissemination of the evolving economic sense of the term.

In 1862 provincial president Dr. Francisco Carlos de Araújo Brusque, a native of São Paulo province, approached his presidential duties in Pará with gusto, compiling a detailed report of the state of industry in twenty-six Paraense towns and villages. The category of *indústria* appeared in the reports for Pará for 1862, 1863, and 1864 during his tenure, but did not appear again until the 1882 report, indicating that terminology and data collection very much depended on the outlook of each individual president.[57]

---

[57] *Relatorio apresentado à Assembléa Legislativa da provincia do Pará na primeira sessão da XIII legislatura pelo exm.o senr. presidente da provincia, dr. Francisco Carlos de*

The majority of provincial industrial establishments in the 1862 report were located in the capital city of Belém and processed agricultural and forest products such as sugar, manioc, tropical plant oils, and timber for domestic and export markets:

> There exist in this municipality 1,273 industrial establishments employing 7,596 hands, as follows:
>
> 7 *engenhos* (mills) for the fabrication of sugar, 2 powered by steam, and 5 by water.
>
> 30 *engenhos* (mills and distilleries) for the fabrication of *aguardente* (sugar cane liquor), 5 powered by steam, 15 by water, and 10 by animal.
>
> 9 *engenhos* (mills and distilleries) for fabricating *aguardente* and sugar, 4 powered by steam and 5 by water.
>
> 10 *engenhos* (sawmills) for processing lumber, 5 powered by steam and 5 by water.
>
> 3 *engenhos* (mills) for drying and processing rice.
>
> 7 *engenhos* (mills) for processing coffee beans, 1 powered by animal and 6 manually.
>
> 1,165 establishments for producing manioc flour.
>
> 15 brickyards for the fabrication of tiles and bricks.
>
> 9 *fábricas* (workshops) for processing lime.
>
> 6 *fábricas* (pottery works) for making pottery.
>
> 6 *fábricas* (workshops) for extracting and processing oils.
>
> 1 *fábrica* (workshop) for making chocolate.
>
> 1 *fábrica* (workshop) for tanning leather.[58]

Importantly, the report demonstrates that *indústria* referred exclusively to the process of rendering raw materials into higher value commodities.

Araujo Brusque em 1 de setembro de 1862 (Pará: Tip. de Frederico Carlos Rhossard, 1862); *Relatorio apresentado à Assembléa Legislativa da provincia do Pará na segunda sessão da XIII legislatura pelo excellentissimo senhor presidente da provincia, doutor Francisco Carlos de Araujo Brusque, em 1 de novembro de 1863* (Pará: Tip. de Frederico Carlos Rhossard, 1863); *Relatorio do secretario da provincia* (Pará: Tip. de Frederico Rhossard, 1864); and *Relatorio dos negocios da provincia do Pará* (Pará, Tip. de Frederico Rhossard, 1864); and *Relatorio dos negocios da provincia do Pará seguido de uma viagem ao Tocantins até a cachoeira das Guaribas e às bahias do rio Anapú, pelo secretario da provincia, Domingo Soares Ferreira Penna, da exploração e exame do mesmo rio até acima das ultimas cachoeiras depois de suajuncção com o Araguaya, pelo capitão-tenente da armada* (Pará: Tip. de Frederico Rhossard, 1864).

[58] *Relatorio apresentado à Assemblea Legislativa da provincia do Para... em 1de setembro de 1862* (Para: Tip. de Frederico Carlos Rhossard, 1862), p. 57.

It further evidences the presence of mechanized production in the capital city, listing sixteen steam-driven sugar, alcohol, and lumber-processing mills. The 1,165 establishments for processing manioc flour, a staple of the local diet, were probably small-scale operations that employed rustic tools, simple manual techniques, slaves, and as few as one worker, though they too were included under the heading *indústria*. Brusque's report clearly demonstrated that processing food for local or regional consumption, the manufacture of construction materials and pottery, and the traditional export crop of sugar comprised the main industries in Belém, most of which were produced with animal or manual labor. In addition, Brusque identified several native species potentially useful for textile and oil production.

The Pará reports underscore several important points. First, industry was quantified in the number of workers (presumably both slave and free) and the type of machinery employed (especially steam engines). The volume and monetary value of the finished products sold was absent due to a lack of available data. Second, the term *indústria* described items fabricated both by hand (manioc flour) and steam-powered machines (sugar and lumber). The majority of Paraense economic production clearly was not yet mechanized nor complex enough for a rational division of labor, but the term nonetheless conveyed the economic sense outlined by Sir James Steuart.

In Rio Grande do Sul, provincial president, Espiridião Eloy de Barros Pimental, a judge and native of the northeastern state of Alagôas, also discussed *indústria*. He lamented the lack of manufacturing enterprises in Brazil where the "primary industry, agriculture" was still woefully backward. He noted that if labor and capital were already insufficient to meet the demands of Brazilian agriculture or to invest in costly machinery and other agricultural improvements, what hope was there for capital-intensive mechanized industry?[59] Pimental complained about the lack of data on existing industrial establishments though he described several factories and workshops that processed mate and vegetable oil. He also praised shipyards in Porto Alegre, Rio Grande, and Pelotas that turned out "national ships" despite stiff competition from overseas shipbuilders. Additionally, Pimental provided a detailed description of a sample of canned beef sent to Porto Alegre from a manufactory in Buenos Aires. The

---

[59] *Relatorio apresentado pelo presidente da provincia de S. Pedro do Rio Grande do Sul, dr. Espiridião Eloy de Barros Pimental, na 1.a sessão da 11.a legislatura da Assembléa Provincial* (Porto Alegre: Tip. do Correio do Sul, 1864), p. 61.

new process promised to provide a way to market Brazilian meat products in Europe, an attempt to remedy the unpopularity of *charque* (salted beef) overseas, the province's main export commodity. *Charque* was purchased primarily by slaveholders whose captives had little choice in their diet. Pimental highlighted the entrepreneurial efforts of Dr. Manoel Pereira da Silva Ubatuba, who planned to introduce a beef-canning manufactory in Rio Grande do Sul, which he later successfully accomplished.[60] Pimental also suggested a list of remedies for obstacles to economic development reminiscent of twentieth-century import substitution:

I persist in my previously stated opinion that indirect policies are more rational and useful than direct methods of supporting industry [i.e. through state loans]. It seems to me that the best way for our manufactures to gain vigor and outcompete foreign products is to make credit available in a variety of forms; provide elementary and professional education; implement a well-conceived system of tariffs on imports; give preference to the purchase of national products deemed superior or equal to imports for use in the different branches of public service; and animate and improve production so that our exports meet the demands of new markets in addition to the markets where they are presently accepted. The inexpensive and abundant raw materials produced by our domestic agriculture gives our producers in certain manufacturing [sectors] a definite advantage on the peaceful battleground of industry.[61]

Pimental further observed that free markets benefited the "civilized nations" of the North Atlantic, but were disastrous for less developed nations like Brazil that could not hope to compete with superior and cheaper imported manufactures.[62] This last observation bears a resemblance to the tenets of twentieth-century Dependency Theory.[63] Whereas Brusque's analysis focused on the quantification of existing commodity production and the location of raw materials from Brazilian forests that could be made into new commodities (i.e., Amazonian tree fibers for use in papermaking and textiles), Pimental emphasized the need for new technology and government policies designed to encourage industrial growth and improvement.[64]

---

[60] *Relatorio apresentado pelo presidente da provincia de S. Pedro do Rio Grande do Sul, dr. Espiridião Eloy de Barros Pimental, na 2.a sessão da 10.a legislatura da Assembléa Provincial* (Porto Alegre: Tip. do Correio do Sul, 1863), p. 65.

[61] *Relatorio apresentado* ... 1864, p. 62.   [62] *Ibid.*

[63] Fernando Henrique Cardoso and Enzo Faletto, *Dependency and Development in Latin America*, Marjory Mattingly Urquidi, trans., (Berkeley: University of California Press, 1979).

[64] *Relatorio apresentado à Assembléa Legislativa da provincia do Pará na segunda sessão da XIII legislatura pelo excellentissimo senhor presidente da provincia, doutor Francisco*

As these examples demonstrate, the term *indústria* explicitly referred to economic and mechanized production by the 1860s even if manual and slave labor still predominated in Brazilian workshops and manufactories. The increasing association of industry with machines in two very different provincial economies tied Brazil to a greater transatlantic phenomenon. If Brazil's economy was not yet industrial in a manufacturing sense, strategies for making it so, based on the nation's abundant tropical resources and agricultural potential, were definitely on the minds of influential Brazilians. Both provincial presidents called for modernized methods for processing important commodities like sugar and rubber in Pará and preserved beef in Rio Grande do Sul with the aim of improving the reputation of Brazilian products abroad. Brusque's vision for the development of new Amazonian products from plant oils and textile fibers also demonstrated that government officials sought ways to diversify the economy beyond Brazil's traditional cash crops.

By the 1880s in Brazil, *indústria* had evolved into the fully modern economic definition of "a particular form or branch of productive labor" as evidenced in the report for Rio's sixth National Exhibition organized by the newly formed Industrial Association of Rio de Janeiro in 1881. Hinting that many of the displays at the previous exhibitions of 1861, 1866, 1873, 1875, and 1878 were mere curiosities and not truly marketable products, organizers crowed that the 1881 exhibition displays were almost all decidedly *industrial*.[65] Two examples illustrate the distinction made by the organizers. The first involved a petition by the Women's Commission for the inclusion of women's handicrafts and artwork for exhibition awards. The items in question included the artistic creations of society women made at their leisure: embroidered linens, doilies, lacework, paintings, and paper, cloth, and feather flowers. The jury admired the works of the women – "[the products were] lovely, beautiful, admirable, splendid" – but refused to consider them for official awards because they were "... not industrial."[66] Jury members asserted that only products created in the "humble workshops of labor," as did

Carlos de Araujo Brusque, em 1.o de novembro de 1863 (Pará: Tip. de Frederico Carlos Rhossard, 1863), pp. 43–62.

[65] *Archivos da Exposição da Industria Nacional: actas, pareceres e decisões do jury geral da Exposição da Industria Nacional realizada no Rio de Janeiro in 1881* (Rio de Janeiro: Tip. Nacional, 1882), p. XIX.

[66] *Archivos da Exposição da Industria Nacional* p. XX; also cited in José Werneck da Silva, "As Arenas Pacíficas do Progresso" (Ph.D. dissertation, Universidade Federal Fluminense, Rio de Janeiro, 1992), Vol. 2, p. 39.

many "of our country-women who [thusly] earn their daily bread . . . and educate their children" were of a genuine "industrial character."[67] In an example that stands out for its reference to female labor, the organizers made a clear distinction between "mere ability" and "industry" as an economic process that resulted in a marketable product.[68]

A second example of the transformation in the meaning of industry involved exhibits of Brazilian wood. Displays of timber and wood were an important subcategory at nineteenth-century international exhibitions, along with displays of industrial, technological, and consumer products. Brazil could not compete with the more advanced industrializing nations in technological development, but the tropical nation was widely admired for its diverse natural resources and its tree species in particular. Brazilian exhibition organizers cultivated a modern image of Brazil based on the potential for development of its forests, minerals, and fields. Organizers also hoped to inspire domestic production by presenting new and unknown resources from remote provinces to entrepreneurs, engineers, and craftsmen at national exhibitions in Rio de Janeiro. Consequently, the empire's national and international exhibitions displayed hundreds of samples of plant extracts, fibers, and wood in raw and finished form accompanied by lengthy catalog descriptions. One goal was to disseminate information about the various uses of Brazilian wood in naval and civil construction as Andre Reboucas's three-volume tome on trees demonstrated, a topic that will be explored further in Chapter 3.[69]

At the 1881 exhibition, a collection of wood sent by a Commander Pimenta Burns from the northern state of Pará drew sharp criticism from organizers because its presentation was deemed amateurish and of little use to *industriais* (industrialists):

---

[67] One such "workshop of labor" was described in the 1856 travel account of a British traveler who marveled at the young female workers who produced feather jewelry and floral arrangements on the Rua do Ouvidor Street:

> In the back part of the shop was a long bar, behind which numerous young girls were employed in making up the flowers, twisting, cutting, and gumming away vigorously. There were heaps of feathers before them . . . It is really surprising how such delicate materials can be managed so skillfully, especially as the flowers are not dyed . . . but separate feathers are gummed together to produce each effect.

Edward Wilberforce, *Brazil viewed through a naval glass: with notes on slavery and the slave trade* (London: Longman, Brown, Green, and Longmans, 1856), p. 52.

[68] *Archivos da Exposição da Industria Nacional*, pp. XIX–XX.

[69] André Rebouças, *Ensaio de indice geral das madeiras do Brazil*, 3 vols. (Rio de Janeiro: Tip. Nacional, 1877).

This collection . . . doesn't satisfy the requirements of an industrial exhibition . . . it was not prepared for such a purpose, and was brought out from the collector's cabinet as a simple indication of the variety of resources available in the Amazon Valley . . . [70]

In contrast, a display of lumber from Espirito Santo and Rio de Janeiro provinces submitted by Carlos Moreaux caught the organizers' attention because it clearly indicated how men of industry might make use of each species:

Although this display was incomparably less varied than those of the other exhibitors, it deserves more recognition. The wood was presented in ample-sized stumps and well-formed planks, both lightly worked and partially varnished, permitting the man of industry to make very useful observations on the potential application he could derive from each species of tree.[71]

Moreaux's properly industrial example demonstrated the exhibition organizers' desire to highlight the commercial application of Brazilian resources. In contrast to the scientific or merely curious display of an amateur collector, the latter exhibit captured the mystique of commodity creation described by Karl Marx:

It is absolutely clear that, by his activity, man changes the forms of the materials of nature in such a way as to make them useful to him. The form of wood, for instance, is altered if a table is made out of it. Nevertheless the table continues to be wood, an ordinary, sensuous thing. But as soon as it emerges as a commodity, it changes into a thing, which transcends sensuousness. It not only stands with its feet on the ground, but, in relation to all other commodities, it stands on its head, and evolves out of his wooden brain grotesque ideas far more wonderful than if it were to begin dancing of its own free will.[72]

Brazil's new class of *industriais* were not interested in identifying, cataloging, or even necessarily understanding the biological characteristics of a given tree species. They wanted to see the potential for a new product or commodity in each tree sample. How might a tree trunk be transformed into "ideas far more wonderful than if it were to begin dancing of its own free will"? The exhibition's industrialists viewed Brazilian forests as

[70] *Archivos da Exposição da Industria Nacional*, p. XLVIII.
[71] *Ibid.*
[72] Karl Marx, *Capital: A Critique of Political Economy*, Vol. I (London: Penguin Books, 1976), pp. 163–4; see also Livia Lazzaro Rezende's discussion of the commodification of forest resources as a unique expression of Brazilian modernity, "The Raw and the Manufactured: Brazilian Modernity and National Identity as Projected in International Exhibitions (1862–1922)," (Ph.D. dissertation, Royal College of Art, 2010), pp. 113–15.

a valuable resource for industrial arts and a potential for wealth accumulation.

Across the late eighteenth- and nineteenth-century Atlantic world, industry was a word in gestation; it recorded tangible transformations as the rise of mechanized production and capital investment demanded new ways of thinking about and describing economic relationships and modes of production. Brazilians employed the word widely, using it to describe specific branches of productive labor in agriculture, manufacturing, and commerce. The term also referred to the economy as a whole, demonstrating that the economic sense of industry (the value added by the labor process) firmly surpassed its premodern sense of diligence, skill, or ability by the end of the nineteenth century.

Aperfeiçoar

Aperfeiçoar (to perfect) is another term that provides insight into the way Brazilians engaged with the transitioning economic, social, and material realities of the nineteenth century. Frequently invoked in discussions of the economy and technological development, the word appeared in public letters, provincial reports, exhibition speeches, *O Auxiliador*, and patent applications. The 1831 edition of the Moraes Dictionary defined *aperfeiçoar* as "to finish or complete with perfection, to perfect, polish, or to arrive at perfection." *Aperfeiçoar* was thusly aligned with the overarching Enlightenment belief in the forward march of material and moral progress.[73] The term also revealed the cautious nature of Brazilian modernization.

Aperfeiçoar closely resembled its French cognate *perfectionner*, and the more etymologically distant but semantically close English equivalent, *to improve*. In the eighteenth century, Diderot's *Encyclopedie* defined *perfectionner* thusly: "to correct of faults, to advance to a state of perfection, to improve oneself, to perfect a work *(ouvrage)*."[74] *Perfectionner* contained two central concepts: the improvement of an individual through education (the acquisition of knowledge, manners, and morals), and the beneficial physical transformation of material objects into new and desirable forms. Transforming the tangible/outer world and the

[73] Antônio de Moraes Silva, *Diccionario da Lingua Portugueza*, 4th ed., s.v., "aperfeiçoar."
[74] *Encyclopédie, ou dictionnaire raisonné des sciences, des arts et des métiers, etc.*, Vol. 12, Denis Diderot and Jean le Rond d'Alembert, eds., University of Chicago: ARTFL Encyclopédie Project (Spring 2013 Edition), Robert Morrissey, ed., http://encyclopedie.uchicago.edu/, s.v. "perfectionner."

intangible/inner world converged in *perfectionner*. What are seen today as separate processes of material and moral development went hand-in-hand in the writings of Enlightenment thinkers like the Marquis of Condorcet who argued that technology facilitated the moral improvement of both the individual and society.[75] *Perfectionner*, defined as a process that resulted in an improved moral or material state, illustrated an important aspect of late-eighteenth and nineteenth-century conceptions of progress.

To perfect, the English version of *perfectionner*, shared the same general semantic sense as its Romance cognates. The term *improvement*, however, came closer to expressing the notion of material and moral progress of *perfectionner*. In eighteenth- and nineteenth-century England, *improve* also possessed an explicitly economic sense that was absent in the definition of the French and Portuguese terms.[76] Nineteenth-century British agricultural improvement was explicitly economic; plows, reapers, and steam-powered machines (as will be explored further in Chapter 5) were designed to increase crop yields with the aim of boosting a farm's profitability. Improved practices also resulted in a secondary economic value that accrued in the land itself. Fences, workshops, barns, silos, and machinery further added to a farm's productivity in addition to the value of the land, thereby facilitating availability of loans for additional improvements based on increased equity. In terms of moral improvement, British mutual improvement societies provided adult education in the form of evening lectures and meetings ranging from basic literacy and arithmetic to religion and science with the aim of elevating an individual's material knowledge, employability, and character. Through these processes of improvement, the economic, material, and moral circumstances of the human condition were elevated.[77]

By the end of the nineteenth century, three definitions arose in Brazil for *aperfeiçoar*: following the previously mentioned French and English examples, the first two senses referenced moral and material

[75] Marquis of Condorcet, "The Future of Man," in *French Utopias: An Anthology of Ideal Societies*, Frank E. Manuel and Fritzie P. Manuel, eds. and trans., (New York: The Free Press, 1966), p. 194. The civilizing effects of technology on primitive societies was also enfolded into nineteenth-century British colonial discourse in India and Africa, Michael Adas, *Machines as the Measure of Men: Science, Technology, and Ideologies of Western Dominance* (Ithaca: Cornell University Press, 1989), pp. 229–30.

[76] *The Oxford English Dictionary*, s.v. "improve."

[77] English mutual improvement societies were also a response to the reduction in educational opportunities for the working classes during the Industrial Revolution, M. I. Watson, "Mutual Improvement Societies in Nineteenth-Century Lancashire," *Journal of Educational Administration and History*, Vol. 21, No. 2, 1989, pp. 8–9.

improvement. Already an important term at the end of the colonial period, an excerpt from *O Auxiliador* from the 1830s demonstrated a third sense of *aperfeiçoar*, the explicit link to technological development that expressed a belief in the power of science to conquer the secrets of the natural world and harness its resources for the benefit of humankind:

We are already studying and discovering the immense riches that God, the creator, bestowed upon us. Additionally, we have begun to take advantage of the immense fertility of our Brazilian lands. In recognition of the importance of introducing perfected machines [*máquinas aperfeiçoadas*] and new processes of cultivation [the Sociedade Auxiliadora da Indústria Nacional] was created with the purpose of displaying objects of great interest to this end... [78]

Two ads for agricultural equipment provide further examples of the association of *aperfeiçoar* with technology in the 1850s and 1860s. The first described a perfected corn dehusker invented and sold by Nathaniel Sands, the North American proprietor of an import house in Rio that specialized in US agricultural instruments. In this example, *aperfeiçoar* referenced both technological progress and modifications designed specifically for Brazilian conditions. Not only did the dehusker "out-produce the labor of 20 slaves," further improvements included "durability, simplicity, resistance to breakage, and easy transportability."[79] The description touched on two important themes of Brazilian modernization. The first was locating alternatives to slave labor, and the second was overcoming the physical challenges to transporting and using machinery in remote locations, themes that will be addressed further in Chapters 4 and 5. A second ad for a "perfected [grain] mill," and a "hay cutter" advertised by importer Manoel Abranches, further demonstrated the association of *aperfeiçoar* with technology. The hay cutter improved the nutritional value of hay, the ad declared, but more importantly "[the model is used] in stables across Europe where [it is] considered the most perfected of [its] type (Fig. 2.6)."[80] By 1881, a dictionary entry sealed the association of *aperfeiçoar* with technological progress, defining it as: "to perfect an invention or machine."[81]

The desire to replace slave labor with machinery illustrates deeper cultural meanings of *aperfeiçoar*. Though slavery was still a robust

[78] *O Auxiliador*, January 1878, p. 18.
[79] "Perfected Corn Milling Machine by Inventor Sands," *JC*, February 12, 1853.
[80] "Machinas de Lavoura," *JC*, January 9, 1860.
[81] F. J. Caldas Aulete, *Diccionario Contemporario da Lingua Portugueza* (Lisboa: Imprensa Nacional, 1881), s.v. "aperfeiçoar."

MACHINAS DE LAVOURA.

MOINHO APERFEIÇOADO.

Recebem-se uns novos moinhos aperfeiçoados para moer milho para dar-se aos animaes.

Tambem proprios para reduzir o milho a farinha, sendo neste genero o mais perfeito que até o presente se tem importado.

CORTADOR DE CAPIM.

As presentes machinas servem para reduzir o capim ao córte que se queira para dar-se a os animaes, de mistura com farelo ou milho; serve-se da mais nutrição e não desperdicio.

São usadas igualmente em todas as cavallariças da Europa, e tidas como as classe das mais aperfeiçoadas em seu genero.

Ha outras muitas machinas e instrumentos de lavoura, para as quaes se pede a attenção de todos os Srs. fazendeiros.

MANOEL OLEGARIO ABRANCHES
10 Rua da Alfandega 10

DEFRONTE DO BANÇO DO BRAZIL.

FIGURE 2.6. "Agricultural Machines." *Source: Jornal do Commercio*, January 9, 1860. Courtesy of the Acervo da Fundação Biblioteca Nacional, Brazil.

institution by mid-century, *fazendeiros* and would-be modernizers increasingly sought alternatives, especially by the 1870s.[82] Fear of labor scarcity and its potential to harm the export economy accompanied anxiety about race and concern about the "uncivilizing" influence of Africans in the Brazilian countryside. *Máquinas aperfeiçoadas* (perfected machines) promised a peaceful transition from slavery to free labor without overturning the social order, as the following excerpt from O *Auxiliador* illustrates:

Having considered the direct and material importance of the employment of [plows], let us now look at it from another point of view. This perspective is more extensive to be sure, in that it is a relation of the indirect influences, that is, the moral and social influences, on our particular circumstances. [These instruments] will show that with the improvement of our agriculture, the number of agricultural laborers will diminish and correspondingly the importation of Africans will decrease further; and with this diminution the spontaneous taming (*adoçamento*) of the customs of our rural populations will emanate in a gradual manner... [83]

The substitution of backward – and potentially dangerous – African slaves with agricultural technology promised reliability, profitability, and regularity, with no uncontrollable social upheavals. Unlike the cultural and racial superiority central to the US mantra of Manifest Destiny, perfected technology, not people, stood at the center of this version of Brazilian progress.[84] Yet, while *aperfeiçoar* conveyed the forward march of human civilization in an expansive and abstract sense, on a deeper level it was a very cautious term. It suggested an *improvement* over that which already existed, but did not advocate a *revolutionary* change. In an age of revolutions and rebellions, the close-ended nature of this choice is telling. From the 1820s to the 1840s, the Brazilian state struggled to contain slave and regional revolts. The ongoing fear of a slave rebellion colored

---

[82] Thomas H. Holloway, "Immigration and Abolition: The Transition from Slave to Free Labor in the São Paulo Coffee Zone," Dauril Alden and Warren Dean, eds., *Essays Concerning the Socio-Economic History of Brazil and Portuguese India* (Gainesville: University Presses of Florida, 1977), pp. 5–10; and *Immigrants on the Land: Coffee and Society in São Paulo, 1886–1934* (Chapel Hill: University of North Carolina Press, 1980), pp. 35–6; and Jeffrey Needell, *A Tropical Belle Epoque: Elite Culture and Society in turn-of-the-century Rio de Janeiro* (Cambridge: Cambridge University Press, 1987), p. 7.

[83] "Instrumentos aratorios," O *Auxiliador*, November 1850, p. 210. The article was published shortly after the abolition of the Brazilian slave trade on September 4, 1850.

[84] Amy S. Greenberg, *Manifest Manhood and the Antebellum American Empire* (Cambridge: Cambridge University Press, 2005), pp. 19–21; and Albert K. Weinberg, *Manifest Destiny: A Study of Nationalist Expansionism in American History* (Chicago: Quadrangle Press, 1963), p. 163, pp. 211–12 and pp. 307–8.

the thoughts of Brazilian elites, as the midwife to Princess Isabel's children, conveyed in 1871, "Let us not deceive ourselves. All slaves possess only one sentiment, one firm idea, which is... the desire for vengeance against the free population...."[85] She proposed that slaves be gradually civilized through education to prepare them for a free but still subordinate role in society wherein their former masters became enlightened tutors.[86] Technological improvements provided a path for achieving transformation without dangerous social change.

The Brazilian understanding of progress embedded within *aperfeiçoar* also differed sharply from the bombast of Manifest Destiny that envisioned a profound reshaping and expansion of the US nation that was, ostensibly at least, based on individual freedom. In contrast, *aperfeiçoar* resulted in progress, but through taming older customs, not by uprooting them. In the previous examples, technology and education acted as a gentler, more controllable catalyst for the transition from backwardness to *aperfeiçoamento*.

Sociedade Auxiliadora member José Pereira Rego's speech for the organization's fortieth anniversary celebration in 1867 offers a final example of the shades of meaning underlying *aperfeiçoar*.[87] Rego called for the establishment of a network of industrial societies across the Brazilian nation to disseminate information about machinery and scientific agricultural methods in addition to providing a live forum of exchange for both agriculturalists and manufacturers. The industrial societies would act as "calculated revolutions" expressed through provincial and national exhibitions where members of the lower classes were to be "moralized"

---

[85] M. J. M. Durocher, *Idéias por coordenar á respeito da emancipação* (Rio de Janeiro: Tip. Diario do Rio de Janeiro, 1871), p. 8. Durocher was a colorful figure by nineteenth-century Brazilian standards. Well regarded for her work as a midwife (she was the only woman accepted as a member of the Academia Nacional de Medicina in the nineteenth century), she dressed in a feminine skirt, masculine coat jacket, tie, and top hat when she tended to her patients, Schuma Schumaher and Érico Vital Brazil, eds., *Dicionário Mulheres do Brasil de 1500 até a atualidade*, 2nd ed. (Rio de Janeiro: Jorge Zahar, 2000), s.v., "Maria Josephina Matilde Durocher." For a treatment of post-abolition fear of Afro-Brazilians see Celia Maria Marinho de Azevedo, *Onda Negra, Medo Branco: o negro no imaginário das elites século XIX* (São Paulo: Annablume, Editora, 2004).

[86] Durocher, p. 13.

[87] José Pereira Rego Filho graduated from Rio de Janeiro's School of Medicine, and was a member of both the Sociedade Auxiliadora's machinery committee, and the Industrial Association in Rio de Janeiro. He was an organizer and promoter of Brazil's participation in the 1882 exhibition in Argentina.

(turned into good workers) via exhibition materials.[88] A further aim was to demonstrate existing advances in Brazilian industry, as well as to provide real-life examples of progress and improvement (*progresso and aperfeiçoamento*) to backward Brazilian producers.[89] Rego's "calculated revolutions" was a carefully chosen phrase. The goal was not to radically alter the social fabric of society, nor unleash the more uncontrollable forces of industrial and commercial development, but instead to judiciously orient and improve Brazilian economic production. In sum, these examples point to a distinction between the legacies of Enlightenment thought among the former European colonies of the Americas. As Daniela Bleichmar has observed in the case of late eighteenth-century Spanish botanical expeditions to the New World, the Spanish crown understood Enlightenment science as a way to restore the former productivity of its American colonies, not as a way to break from the past.[90] This sense of improving but not revolutionizing also surfaces in the Portuguese *aperfeiçoar*.

Conclusion

The examination of the evolving vocabulary of modernization provides a deeper understanding of how nineteenth-century Brazilians responded to and constructed new ideas about *indústria, aperfeiçoamento*, and the overarching idea of progress itself. This approach provides a contrast to the statistical analysis employed in economic and business history and demonstrates how context and culture were shaped by and also shaped the absorption of ideas about modernization in Brazil.

Brazilian elites were keenly aware of innovations in Europe and the United States, but they were more cautious about the social transformations that these technologies might engender. They did not want to instigate revolution or implement changes they could not control. Their cautiousness, to be sure, was in part based on a scarcity of capital and other difficulties specific to their physical realities, as other chapters will explore. Fear of the majority non-European population also profoundly shaped the social risks they were willing to take as they modernized.

---

[88] José Pereira Rego Filho, "Relatorio dos trabalhos da Sociedade do anno corrente," *O Auxiliador*, November 1867, p. 459.

[89] Rego, pp. 458–9.

[90] Daniela Bleichmar, *Visible Empire: Botanical Expeditions and Visual Culture in the Hispanic Enlightenment* (Chicago: University of Chicago Press, 2011), p. 12 and ch. 2.

The term *aperfeiçoar* in particular provides a Brazilian inflection of the nineteenth-century belief in the advancement of human civilization through progress. During the period of the Brazilian Empire, this progress was not to be an open-ended path to liberation. It should not surprise us that many Brazilian elites were not trying to "liberate" their society, but to *improve* upon it, to make it more efficient and profitable. They desired to be more European, to be sure, but selectively so. We may naturally view some of their decisions as an attempt to prolong slavery and to maintain a self-serving social structure that, in the words of statesman José Bonifácio, was only for the gain of "riches and more riches" for a select few.[91] But the ethical judgments emanating from that observation cannot precede a clear-eyed attempt to understand the choices they believed lay before them; present-day prosperity, too, contains its own forms of exploitation, oppression, and expropriation. The terms discussed here reveal, beneath the surface, the cultural and social constraints acting on Brazilian elites as they engaged with the transformations of their time.

[91] José Bonifácio de Andrada e Silva, "Representação à Assemblea Geral Constituinte e Legislativa do Imperio do Brasil Sobre a Escravatura" (Paris: Tip. de Firmin Didot, 1825) in *Obras Científicas e Sociais de José Bonifácio de Andrada e Silva, coligadas e reproduzidas por Edgard de Cerqueira Falcão*, Vol. II (São Paulo: Revista dos Tribunais, 1963), p. 131.

3

Industrial Forests

*We undervalue that which we have, while we yearn for that which is foreign.
We fail to make use of our many [native] species of silkworm . . . while we
spend 300 contos per year to import silkworms from China to no avail.
We have endless varieties of bees, yet we . . . import them from Europe . . .
We purchase coal on which we have fecklessly spent hundreds of contos to
the advantage of European charlatans who profit from our ignorance . . . All
that we don't have, we want, while we neglect to appreciate that which God
gave to us. We fail to utilize our precious Turfa that is so plentiful in the city
of São Paulo, and here in Ingá, in Rio de Janeiro . . . why do exert ourselves
so uselessly?*[1]

In 1870, Antônio Salustiano Antunes, a Portuguese engineer in Bahia,
proposed a remedy for Brazil's dependence on costly imports of foreign coal: the oily, coconut-like seed of the *piaçabeira* palm. He asserted
that the *coquilho* (as the seeds were called) represented an unused and
heretofore neglected product of Brazil's "industrial forests" and were, in
fact, "a powerful combustible and a rival to coal." Antunes' plan for the
piaçabeira involved the cultivation of palm groves next to train stations
and along railway tracks where they were to provide a self-reproducing
and, he emphasized, an inexhaustible source of fuel for Brazilian locomotives. And this was just the beginning. Antunes further envisioned the
large-scale cultivation of the palms in "open air mines" that would meet
the energy needs of all manner of industries.[2] The engineer did not propose the *coquilho* as a replacement for coal, rather he championed it as

---

[1] "Os Camellos no Ceará," *Publicações a Pedido*, JC, May 3, 1862.
[2] Antônio Salustiano Antunes, "Correspendencia," *O Auxiliador*, November 1870,
pp. 460–1.

an auxiliary that would enrich Brazil's "industrial arsenal" and provide the nation with an inexpensive alternative. All that Brazilians needed was "a bit of patriotism and volition," the engineer asserted, in order to take advantage of what Providence had so generously bestowed upon them.[3]

At first glance, Antunes' proposal appears outlandish. Yet in the early twentieth century agronomist Edmundo Navarro de Andrade successfully acclimatized eucalyptus trees for the Companha Paulista, a railroad company in São Paulo. Planted on fazendas near stations and alongside railroad tracks, eucalyptus groves supplied wood for locomotive fuel and railroad construction.[4] Present-day experiments with biofuels further prove the possibility of using plant combustibles for engines large and small.[5] The most successful of these, sugar cane *alcool*, powers Brazilian automobiles, small engines, and even airplanes.

Whether a crackpot or merely ahead of his time, Antunes' example serves as an introduction to a little-studied topic in Brazilian historiography during the late colonial period and nineteenth century: the attempts of Brazilian scientists and entrepreneurs to locate and develop domestic resources for combustibles and commodities. Scholars have examined European and North American investigations of Brazil's resources, but few works have addressed the efforts of Brazilians themselves.[6] Despite the dominance of sugar and coffee in their nation's nineteenth-century

[3] Antônio Salustiano Antunes, "O Coquilho das Piassabeiras como Combustível," *O Agricultor Progressista*, October 3, 1881, p. 3.

[4] Augusto Jeronimo Martini, "O Plantador de Eucaliptos: A Questão da Preservação Florestal no Brasil e o Resgate Documental do Legado de Edmundo Navarro de Andrade," (Master's thesis, Universidade de São Paulo, 2004), pp. 66–7, and 69.

[5] "Biofuel, Partly From Nuts, Is Tested on an Airline Flight," *New York Times*, February 25, 2008.

[6] See Stephen Bell, "Aimé Bonpland e a avaliação de recursos em Santa Cruz, 1848–50," *Estudos Ibero-Americanos*, PUCRS, XXI: 2 (1995), pp. 63–79, and *A Life in Shadow: Aimé Bonpland in Southern South America, 1817–1858* (Stanford: Stanford University Press, 2010); Warren Dean, "Deforestation in Southeastern Brazil," in Richard P. Tucker and J. F. Richards, eds., *Global Deforestation and the Nineteenth-Century World Economy* (Durham, NC: Duke University Press, 1983), pp. 50–67; and *Brazil and the Struggle for Rubber: a study in Environmental History* (Cambridge: Cambridge University Press, 1987); Marcus Vinicius de Freita, *Hartt: Expedições pelo Brasil Imperial* (São Paulo: Metalivros, 2001), and *Charles Frederick Hartt, um naturalista no império de Pedro II* (Belo Horizonte, MG: Editora da UFMG, 2002); Greg Grandin, *Fordlandia: The Rise and Fall of Henry Ford's Forgotten Jungle City* (New York: Picador, 2009), pp. 305–15; Mary Louise Pratt, *Imperial eyes: travel writing and transculturation* (New York: Routledge, 1992); and Nancy Stepan, *Beginnings of Brazilian Science: Oswaldo Cruz, Medical Research and Policy, 1890–1920* (New York: Science History Publications, 1976), pp. 26–7, and *Picturing Tropical Nature* (Ithaca, NY: Cornell University Press, 2001), chaps. 2 and 3.

export economy, many Brazilians recognized the economic potential of their native flora and strove to diversify agricultural production by developing new agro-industrial commodities. Accordingly, botanical experimenters like Antunes identified wood for civil construction and ship-building; fibers for textiles, cordage, and paper; medicinal plants; waxes and resins for candles and varnishes; and substitutes for sugar, coffee, and tea. The call to valorize national resources and replace imported raw materials with domestically sourced alternatives, was, at its heart, a nineteenth-century version of import substitution that its advocates hoped would lead to economic self-sufficiency in Brazil.[7] Antunes was a member of a small but earnest circle of entrepreneurs who advocated for the development of domestic commodities, an enterprise that was most vocally supported by the Sociedade Auxiliadora.[8] In addition to the influence of the Physiocrats and Adam Smith described in Chapter 2, the less well-known economic thought of Swedish naturalist Carl Linnaeus played an important role in the society's vision of economic development.

This chapter begins with a description of the impact of the eighteenth-century Enlightenment-influenced Pombaline reforms on nineteenth-century discussions of economic development, particularly in the Sociedade Auxiliadora.[9] Second, this chapter examines the economic nationalism woven into the society's projects, an influence that owes its provenance, in part, to Linnaeus' political economy of national self-sufficiency. Beyond ordering the natural world into kingdoms, phylums, and orders, Linnaeus saw scientific classification as a tool for identifying natural resources for national economic development. Linnaeus' taxonomy was, therefore, explicitly crafted to "perfect the self-sufficiency of the nation and the physical and social state of its inhabitants."[10] Linnaeus

---

[7] See Werner Baer, "Import Substitution and Industrialization in Latin America: Experiences and Interpretations," *Latin American Research Review*, 7:1 (1972), pp. 95–122.

[8] André Luiz Alípio de Andrade, "Variações sobre um tema: a Sociedade Auxiliadora da Indústria Nacional e o debate sobre o fim do tráfico de escravos (1845–1850)," (Master's thesis, Universidade Estadual de Campinas, Brazil, 2002), pp. 18–21, pp. 9–10 and chap. 1. See also Regina Patrícia Corrêa Barreto "Sociedade Auxiliadora da Indústria Nacional: o templo carioca de palas atena" (Ph.D. dissertation, Universidade Federal do Rio de Janeiro, 2009), pp. 94–106; and José Agosto Pádua, *Um Sopro de destruição: pensamento político e crítica ambiental no Brasil escravista (1786–1888)* (Rio de Janeiro: Jorge Zahar, 2003), pp. 15–17.

[9] Agricultural reforms were central to Luso-Brazilian Enlightenment thought, J. H. Galloway, "Agricultural Reform and the Enlightenment in Late Colonial Brazil," *Agricultural History*, 53:4 (1979), pp. 778–9.

[10] Emma Spary, "Political, Natural, and Bodily Economies," in N. Jardine, J. A. Secord, and E. C. Spary, eds., *Cultures of Natural History* (Cambridge: Cambridge University Press, 1996), pp. 178–9. See also Lisbet Koerner, *Linnaeus: Nature and Nation*

hoped to end his nation's dependence on foreign rivals for tropical commodities by identifying native replacements and acclimatizing non-native species to Sweden's environment. Originally introduced into the Portuguese colonial world by Domenico Vandelli, an Italian naturalist, professor at Coimbra University, director of the Lisbon Botanical Gardens, and correspondent of Linnaeus, the Swede's political economy of national autarky appears in the writings of the Sociedade Auxiliadora.[11] Third, this chapter describes the economic projects of Brazilian scientists, entrepreneurs, and engineers (most of whom were associated with the Sociedade Auxiliadora) who have until recently remained at the margins of historiography despite their importance in debates about economic, technological, and scientific development in nineteenth-century Brazil. All of the actors described herein promoted their projects under the banner of national economic self-sufficiency. More was therefore at stake than merely personal profit, or so they intimated. As the engineer Antunes demonstrated, they envisioned Brazil's "industrial forests" as central to the construction of an independent, economically vibrant nation.

The Forest as Factory

Antunes' groves of *piaçabeira* palms counter the European image of the materially rich, but "dark and menacing tropics" so vividly described by historian Nancy Stepan.[12] Far from a dangerous wilderness, Antunes crowed, his *piaçabeiras* were "industrial plants...and promoters of progress."[13] "Industrial" invoked a sense of order, productivity, and reliability that belied contemporary European representations of the tropics as disorderly, predatory, and chaotic. Furthermore, as Chapter 2 demonstrated, *indústria* emphasized the economic potential of the nation's flora.[14] Antunes' industrious palms were therefore more than a discreet

(Cambridge, MA: Harvard University Press, 1999), p. 6 and pp. 102–9; Staffan Müller-Wille, "Nature as Marketplace: The Political Economy of Linnaean Botany," *History of Political Economy*, 35, Annual Supplement (2003), p. 154; and Paula de Vos, "Natural History and the Pursuit of Empire in Eighteenth-Century Spain," *Eighteenth-Century Studies*, 40:2, (2007), p. 212.

[11] Pádua, pp. 14–15.
[12] Stepan, *Picturing Tropical Nature*, chaps. 1 and 2.
[13] *O Agricultor Progressista*, October 3, 1881, p. 2.
[14] Geraldo de Beauclair Mendes de Oliveira, *Raízes da Indústria no Brasil* (Rio de Janeiro: Studio F & S, 1992), pp. 15–16; and José Luiz Werneck da Silva, "Isto é o que me parece: a Sociedade Auxiliadora da Indústria Nacional (1827–1904) na formação social brasileira. a conjuntura de 1881–1877," (Master's thesis, Universidade Federal Fluminense, Niterói, 1979), vol. I, p. 8.

botanical species going about the daily business of metabolizing sun-
light into chemical energy; they were, in essence, botanical factories
that awaited innovators with the proper "spirit of entrepreneurship"
to develop their natural productivity toward economically and socially
profitable ends.

In championing the *piaçabeira*, the engineer from Bahia made claim
to a discourse and way of perceiving the natural world deeply influenced by European scientist and explorer Alexander von Humboldt.
Enfolded within Humboldt's description of the sublime elemental forces
of South America was the economic value of its flora, fauna, and mineral resources.[15] As the nineteenth century progressed, these visions of
economic development were amplified and carried deep into the interior of the continent by increasing numbers of mostly European travelers
described in the work of Mary Louise Pratt as the "capitalist vanguard."
Dispensing with Humboldt's emotional engagement with the landscape,
this wave of explorers turned a sharp, calculating eye to the economic
potential of South American natural resources and quickly set about
collecting, analyzing, and naming whatever species or material seemed
promising.[16] Humboldt's traveling partner, naturalist Aimé Bonpland,
and English geologist and mining engineer turned botanist, John Miers,
serve as examples of Pratt's vanguard. Bonpland remained in South America where he studied and promoted native species in European scientific
circles. Miers published several works on South American plants based
on his travels in Argentina, Chile, and Brazil in the 1820s and 1830s.[17]
After returning to England, Miers maintained connections with Bonpland
and Brazilian institutions. He published an 1861 article on *Ilex paraguariensis* or mate (a tree native to the Río de la Plata region and southern
Brazil) based on specimens sent to him by Bonpland.[18] Miers also wrote
a report for the Brazilian government on the nation's botanical display at
the 1862 Exhibition in London and later corresponded with the Sociedade

---

[15] The introduction of Peruvian guano to European scientific circles, for example, is
attributed to Humboldt, Jimmy M. Skaggs, *The Great Guano Rush: Entrepreneurs
and American Overseas Expansion* (New York: St. Martin's Press, 1994), p. 4.

[16] Pratt, pp. 146–55.

[17] John Miers, *Travels in Chile and La Plata: including accounts respecting the geography,
geology, statistics, government, finances, agriculture, manners and customs, and the
mining operations in Chile: collected during a residence of several years in these* countries
(London: Baldwin, Cradock, and Joy, 1826); and *Illustrations of South American Plants*
(London: Baillière, 1849).

[18] Bell, *A Life in Shadow*, p. 206 and footnote 204, p. 289.

Auxiliadora about the commercial potential of Brazilian species.[19] While Brazilian scientists and entrepreneurs were influenced by and benefited from European research transmitted through transatlantic networks, as Miers and Bonpland illustrate, Europeans also benefited from Brazilian scientific networks. Bonpland, for instance, sent his mate specimens to Miers via the Botanical Garden in Rio de Janeiro. For scholars such as Pratt scientific exploration was a purely European enterprise synonymous with colonial exploitation. Yet Brazilians too appropriated this European vision, molding it into a ideology of national economic self-sufficiency. As this chapter demonstrates, Brazilians actively sought to develop forest resources in service of the economy and nation.

Commodifying the Forest: Colonial Precedents

Though Brazil's incorporation into the Portuguese colonial empire began, as is well known, with the extraction of native dyewood along the coastal regions in the early 1500s, by 1600 the colony became the site of intensive plantation agriculture based on one introduced species in particular: sugar cane. By the mid-seventeenth century, various *drogas do sertão* (native plant and animal materials collected in the wild) from the Amazon came to supplement the Portuguese trade in cultivated crops.[20] While colonial sugar planters, missionaries, and other observers described the potential of Brazilian fibers and oils to replace European imports, the Portuguese government made no sustained attempt to explore, catalog, or systemically exploit new species for commercial use until the late 1700s.[21]

[19] Francisco Ignacio de Carvalho Moreira, *Relatorio sobre a Exposição Internacional de 1862* (London: Thomas Brettell, 1863), pp. 43–122; and Nicolau Joaquim Moreira, *Historical Notes Concerning the Vegetable Fibres exhibited by Severino L. da Costa Leite* (New York: O Novo Mundo, 1876), pp. 1–4.

[20] Heather Flynn Roller, "Colonial Collecting Expeditions and the Pursuit of Opportunities in the Amazonian *Sertão*, c. 1750–1800," *The Americas*, 66:4 (2010), pp. 437–45.

[21] Colonial observers included sugar planters Ambrósio Fernandes Brandão (c. 1555–?) and Gabriel Soares de Sousa (c. 1540–91). Both advocated for the study and economic development of Brazilian species. Ambrósio Fernandes Brandão (attributed), *Dialogues of the Great Things of Brazil (Diálogos das Grandezas do Brasil)*, Frederick Holden Hall, William F. Harrison, and Dorothy Winters Welker, trans., (Albuquerque: University of New Mexico Press, 1987); Gabriel Soares de Sousa, *Tratado Descritivo do Brasil em 1587*, Francisco Adolfo de Varnhagen, ed., (Recife: Fundação Joaquim Nabuco and Editora Massangana, 2000). On the exchange of plant species among Europe, Brazil, Africa, and Asia during the colonial period, see A. J. R. Russell-Wood, *The Portuguese Empire, 1415–1808: A World on the Move* (Baltimore: Johns Hopkins University Press, 1998), pp. 152–82.

An important exception was the Portuguese adoption (initially pioneered by Jesuit missionaries) of indigenous Brazilian treatments derived from native flora. Recent scholarship has documented the long-standing and truly global dissemination of Brazilian remedies from the New World to Europe, Africa, and Asia. Brazil's nineteenth-century modernizers therefore followed a Luso-Brazilian tradition of investigation and experimentation established in the early colonial period and expanded in the late eighteenth century.[22]

The first consistent and widespread attempt to diversify the Brazilian economy and develop its native species was undertaken toward the end of the colonial period under the ascendance of the Marquis of Pombal (Sebastião José de Carvalho e Melo, 1699–1782). In line with his reformer counterparts in Bourbon Spain, Pombal hoped to diversify and increase Brazilian production in support of the mercantilist goals of Portugal. In Brazil, the leadership and initiative of the Marquis of Lavradio (Luís de Almeida Portugal Soares de Alarcão d'Eça e Melo Silva Mascarenhas, 1729–90), whom Pombal made viceroy in 1769, resulted in experiments with newly discovered Brazilian species.[23] He solicited reports from provincial militia commanders on potentially useful native plants with the order to disseminate seeds and information about the cultivation of promising species to local farmers and planters. During this period, ship cordage developed from *guaxima*, an acclimated African species that grew wild in Rio de Janeiro met with some success in Brazil, but production foundered due to a lack of support from Portugal.[24]

Outside of the colony, the government's interest in commodity diversification was further evidenced by Brazilian-born Hipólito José da Costa Pereira's visit to the United States in 1799. Although couched as a diplomatic exchange, the trip was nothing less than an act of economic

---

[22] Profits from the local sale of an indigenous medicine made from Brazilian plants provided the lion's share of the Colégio dos Jesuitas' annual income in Bahia, Timothy Walker, "Acquisition and Circulation of Medical Knowledge within the Early Modern Portuguese Colonial Empire," in Daniela Bleichmar, Paula de Vos, Kristin Huffine, and Kevin Sheehan, eds., *Science in the Spanish and Portuguese Empires* (Stanford: Stanford University Press, 2009), p. 266. See also, Walker, "The Medicines Trade in the Portuguese Atlantic World: Dissemination of Plant Remedies and Healing Knowledge from Brazil, c. 1580–1830," *Mobilising Medicine: Trade & Healing in the Early Modern Atlantic World*, special issue, *The Social History of Medicine* 26:3 (2013), pp. 406–7.

[23] Kenneth Maxwell, *Pombal: Paradox of the Enlightenment* (Cambridge: Cambridge University Press, 1995), p. 118.

[24] Dauril Alden, *Royal government in colonial Brazil; with special reference to the administration of the Marquis of Lavradio, viceroy, 1769–1779* (Berkeley: University of California Press, 1968), p. 359 and pp. 370–1.

espionage underwritten by the Portuguese crown. Hipólito investigated US production of tobacco, whale oil, maple sugar, hemp, and lumber, the last two of strategic importance for shipbuilding.[25] His report was intended to provide new inspiration for Brazilian production, though ultimately his observations and the botanical samples he sent back to Portugal came to naught.[26]

The efforts of Lavradio, Hipólito da Costa, and other reformers and expeditioners took place within the context of the aforementioned Luso-Brazilian Enlightenment centered at Coimbra University where Pombal's reform of 1772 ushered in an era of scientific interest in Brazilian resources.[27] Coimbra luminaries like Vandelli instructed a generation of Brazilian-born politicians, intellectuals, and scientists, including botanist and expedition leader Alexandre Rodrigues Ferreira (1756–1815), botanist Manuel Arruda da Câmara (1752–1811), and engineer and statesman José Bonifácio.[28] José Murilo de Carvalho observes that it was this generation of Brazilian-born scientists who realized the "first scientific activity" in Brazil, and not Europeans as was the case in other colonial empires.[29] The works of this cohort of Coimbra-trained scientists were regularly cited in nineteenth-century publications on economic botany; their work thus served as a conduit between the late colonial Luso-Brazilian Enlightenment and the nineteenth century.[30]

---

[25] Manoel Ferreira Lagos, ed., "Hipólito José da Costa Pereira, manuscrito," *Revista do Instituto Histórico Geographico Brasileiro*, Tomo XXI, 2a edição, 1858, p. 317. See also Neil Safier, "A Courier between Empires: Hipólito da Costa and the Atlantic World," in Bernard Bailyn ed., *Soundings in Atlantic History* (Cambridge, MA: Harvard University Press, 2009), pp. 265–93, and "Spies, Dyes, and Leaves: Agro-Intermediaries, Luso-Brazilian Couriers, and the Printed Worlds They Sowed," in Simon Schaffer, Lissa Roberts, Kapil Raj, and James Delbourgo, eds., *The Brokered World: Go-Betweens and Global Intelligence, 1770–1830* (Uppsala: Watson Publishing International, 2009), pp. 239–69.

[26] Lagos, "Hipólito José da Costa Pereira," pp. 327–28.

[27] The *Academia de Ciência* was likewise founded in 1789.

[28] Pádua, *Um Sopro*, pp. 15–16. Ferreira lead an expedition into the Amazon and Mato Grosso from 1783–92.

[29] *Ibid.*; José Murilo de Carvalho, *A Escola de Minas de Ouro Preto: o peso da glória* (Rio de Janeiro: FINEP, and São Paulo: Editora Nacional, 1978), pp. 7–8.

[30] The Coimbra-trained botanist Manuel Arruda da Câmara published some of the first scientific treatments of Brazilian commercial species, *Dissertação sobre as plantas do Brazil, que podem dar linhos próprios e suprir falta do cânhamo, indagas de ordem do príncipe regente, nosso senhor* (Rio de Janeiro: Impressão Regia, 1810). See also Joaquim de Almeido Pinto, *Diccionario de Botanica Brasileira ou Compendio dos Vegetaes do Brasil. Tanto Indigenas Como Acclimados* (Rio de Janeiro: Tip. Perserverança, 1873); and *Documentos Officiaes da 3a Exposição Nacional inaugurada na cidade do Rio de Janeiro em 01 de Janeiro de 1873* (Rio de Janeiro: Tip. Nacional, 1875), pp. 108–10.

In addition to his advocacy of Linnean economic botany as a way to broaden the colonial economy, Vandelli decried the ongoing use of slash-and-burn agriculture, a chief factor in forest destruction in Brazil. Vandelli's concern was influenced by Linnaeus' developing ecological thought as the latter witnessed the decimation of Swedish forests. Linnaeus lamented the loss of potentially useful but undiscovered species through this destructive process. José Pádua has traced the influence of Linnaeus' ecological views from Vandelli to some of the most important Brazilian politicians, scientists, and agricultural reformers of the nineteenth century, of whom the following were also prominent members of the Sociedade Auxiliadora: judge, naturalist, and student of Vandelli, Baltazar da Silva Lisboa (1761–1840), scientists Frederico Burlamaque, Joaquim Nicolau Moreira (1824–94), and the Baron of Capanema, and engineer André Rebouças.[31] Society members' advocation of forest protection was not a demand for preservation for its own sake, nor was it based on a sentimental concept of nature. Indeed, this chapter argues that the society's stance on forest protection was firmly linked to and derived from a Linnaean vision of economic development. The Sociedade Auxiliadora viewed forest protection, like Linnaeus, as an essential component in the search for new agro-industrial commodities – and ultimately national economic self-sufficiency. Their writings demonstrate the conviction that nowhere was this vision of economic nationalism more appropriate than the lush tropical forests of Brazil.

José Bonifácio, Vandelli's most famous student, best encapsulates the Linnean influence on nineteenth-century modernizers, and the Sociedade Auxiliadora in particular. The statesman was a vociferous critic of slash-and-burn agriculture, linking it to the barbarity of slavery in his famous 1825 treatise calling for abolition.[32] Bonifácio advocated for the technological modernization of Brazilian agriculture with the triple aim of improving productivity, ending slavery, and conserving forests for more diverse and, in present-day parlance, sustainable economic pursuits. The politician's position was echoed regularly in *O Auxiliador*.[33] What started as imperial policy meant to revitalize the mercantilist relationship between

---

[31] Pádua, *Um Sopro*, pp. 15–17.

[32] José Bonifácio de Andrada e Silva, "Representação à Assembléa Geral Constituinte e Legislativa do Império do Brasil Sobre a Escravatura," (Paris: Tip. de Firmin Didot, 1825) in *Obras Científicas e Sociais de José Bonifácio de Andrada e Silva, coligadas e reproduzidas por Edgard de Cerqueira Falcão*, Vol. II, (São Paulo: Revista dos Tribunais, 1963), pp. 133–6.

[33] Pádua, *Um Sopro*, pp. 174–9.

Portugal and Brazil was transformed after independence into a project of national economic development. The Sociedade Auxiliadora became an important site for discussions of agricultural improvement, mechanical innovation, and the economic development of forest resources, extending Vandelli's Linnaean vision well into the nineteenth century.

Cataloging the Nation: National Exhibitions, the Industrialization of Scientific Knowledge, and the Search for Agro-Industrial Commodities

Sociedade Auxiliadora members and contributors to *O Auxiliador* regularly lamented the lack of interest in potentially economically useful forest species. In part, such complaints resembled the observations of European travelers that South Americans had done little to capitalize upon their abundant natural resources.[34] But these attitudes also reflected a forceful advocacy of the development of domestic resources based on patriotic grounds, a clear reflection of Linnaean economic self-sufficiency. Remedying this lack of scientific and economic initiative was one of the driving forces behind a series of national exhibitions sponsored by the Ministry of Agriculture and the Sociedade Auxiliadora in Rio de Janeiro in 1861, 1866, 1873, 1875, and 1878.

Organized as rehearsals for Brazil's participation in international exhibitions in London in 1862, Paris in 1867, Vienna in 1873, and Philadelphia in 1876, the national exhibitions were intended as educational celebrations of the empire's resources, products, and technology.[35] Frederico Burlamaque, a military-trained scientist, self-described agronomist, and editor of *OAuxiliador*, declared the first National Exhibition of 1861 an opportunity to display technology, domestic resources, and industrial

---

[34] Pratt, pp. 147–8.

[35] Noah Elkin, "Promoting a New Brazil," p. 15. Due to the Parayguayn war, the 1878 exhibition was smaller in scale than previous years; subsequently no catalog was published due to the disruption of the war. For works on international exhibitions outside of Brazil, see Paul Greenhalgh, *Ephemeral Vistas: The Expositions Universelles, Great Exhibitions, and World's Fairs, 1851–1939* (Manchester, UK: Manchester University Press, 1988); Peter H. Hoffenberg, *An Empire on Display: English, Indian, and Australian Exhibitions from the Crystal Palace to the Great War* (Berkeley: University of California Press, 2001); Werner Plum, *World Exhibitions in the Nineteenth Century: Pageants of Social and Cultural Change*, Lux Furtmuller, trans., (Bonn-Bad Godesberg: Freidrich-Ebert-Stiftung, 1977); Rydell, Robert, *All the World's a Fair: Visions of Empire at American International Expositions, 1876–1916* (Chicago: University of Chicago Press, 1984); and Tenorio-Trillo, Mauricio, *Mexico at the World's Fairs: Crafting a Modern Nation* (Berkeley: University of California Press, 1996).

products in a didactic manner to the Brazilian public. Notwithstanding the fact that the exhibition was restricted to an audience of the more affluent residents of Rio de Janeiro city and province, the event was an important first attempt to nationalize information about Brazilian resources.

The catalogs and reports on Brazil's national exhibitions provide a rich, if irregular, glimpse into agricultural production, technological innovation, and the consolidation of both lay and scientific knowledge about the empire's resources. The catalogs for the 1861 exhibition, for instance, were organized by province and category and varied in the depth and breadth of their botanical descriptions, sometimes appearing short and cryptic – "resin of the *tupinambur* root – a powerful purgative: one eighth is a sufficient dosage for adults" – to quite detailed, as evidenced by a paragraph describing the *Piassaba* palm (another name for the species championed by Antunes) outlining its habitat, botanical characteristics, economic uses, and sale price in regional markets.[36] The latter example evidenced a lively network of knowledge-sharing and regional trade in products derived from domestic species. Brazilian catalog categories, systems of classification, and botanical descriptions also conformed to an established international format.[37]

Using the categories outlined in exhibition catalogs, Figures 3.1, 3.2, and 3.3 illustrate the types of items displayed in Rio. Each chart reflects the number of individual exhibitors by category and not necessarily the total number of items displayed. A few observations stand out. The higher number of exhibits for "medicines, pharmaceuticals, and chemicals" in the 1861 exhibition (25 percent of the total number of exhibitors) compared to the 1875 exhibition (6 percent of the total) is most likely due to the fact that Pará and Amazônas, two provinces with ready access to the Amazon forest, sent the largest number of total items after Rio de Janeiro in 1861. Both of these provinces were home to a vibrant regional and international trade in wild-harvested *drogas do sertão* as reflected in their displays. In comparison, nearby São Paulo sent only four items in 1861. Minas Gerais and Bahia, both important agricultural provinces, sent a

---

[36] *Catalogos dos productos naturaes e industriaes remettidos das provincias do Imperio do Brasil que figurárão na Exposição Nacional inaugurada na Côrte no Rio de Janeiro no dia 2 de Dezembro de 1861* (Rio de Janeiro: Tip. Nacional, 1862), pp. 73 and 140.

[37] See for example, *Official Descriptive and Illustrated Catalogue of the Great Exhibition, 1851* (London: Spicer Bros., 1851); *Official Catalogue of the International Exhibition of 1876*, rev. ed., (Philadelphia, PA: John R. Nagle & Co., 1876); and *Official Catalogue of the British Section* (London: Eyre and Spottiswoode, 1876).

1861 CATALOG

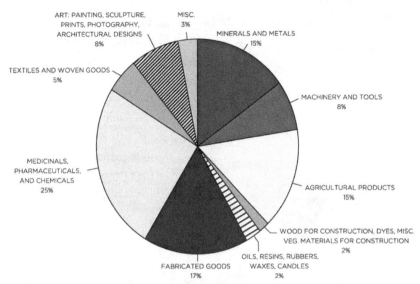

FIGURE 3.1. Table of exhibition materials by category at the 1861 National Exhibition (see caption for Fig. 3.3 for information on source material).

total of 291 items, a number that was certainly not representative of the economic output of these regions nor of their importance in the national economy. A larger number of provinces participated in the 1875 exhibition, including São Paulo, Bahia, Rio Grande do Sul, and Minas Gerais. The higher number of agricultural exhibitors (39 percent in 1875 compared to 15 percent in 1861) is probably in part related to the maturation of the coffee economy in Rio de Janeiro and São Paulo, both of which sent numerous display items for this category in later exhibitions.

Exhibition displays evidenced the effort to project a unified national image of Brazil through its neatly cataloged natural resources, industrial products, and technology.[38] More importantly, the exhibits rendered local knowledge about species and resources "legible" on national and international stages through increasingly scientific descriptions.[39] In part, this was an exercise in centralization; contemporaries complained that the

[38] Elkin, "Promoting a New Brazil," p. 15.
[39] The term is borrowed from James C. Scott, *Seeing Like a State: how certain schemes to improve the human condition have failed* (New Haven, CT: Yale University Press, 1998), see chaps. 1 and 2. See also, Elkin, "Promoting a New Brazil," pp. 45–6.

1866 CATALOG

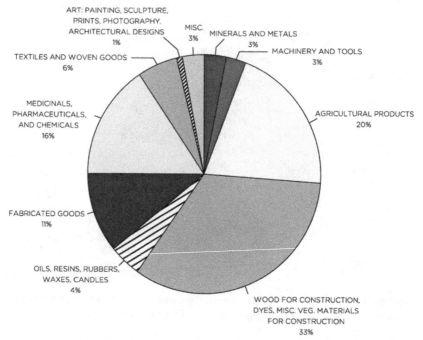

FIGURE 3.2. Table of exhibition materials by category at the 1866 National Exhibition (see caption for Fig. 3.3 for information on source material).

multitude of names for the same tree and plant species (or, conversely, one name for multiple species) across and even within provinces confused efforts to systematically identify and exploit forest resources.[40] Stuart McCook observes a similar process for the Spanish Caribbean beginning in the 1870s where the "plant sciences" were used to "consolidate [the nation's] ... political and economic power."[41] Standardizing botanical information in exhibition catalogs served two purposes: first it employed the precise language of scientific measurement in identifying a

[40] Ladislau Netto, "Botanica Industrial," *O Auxiliador*, August 1879, p. 176. Conversely, a French scientist who hoped to popularize botanical knowledge within Brazil complained that the Latin names for Brazilian species impeded more than they facilitated the dissemination of botanical knowledge, Bell, *A Life in Shadow*, p. 161.

[41] Stuart McCook, *States of Nature: Science, Agriculture, and Environment in the Spanish Caribbean, 1760–1940* (Austin: University of Texas Press, 2002), p. 2; see also ch. 2.

1875 CATALOG

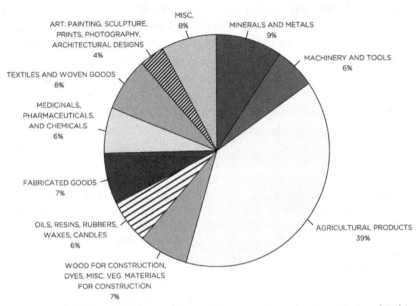

FIGURE 3.3. Table of exhibition materials by category at the 1875 National Exhibition. Totals for Figures 3.1 through 3.3 are based on the total numbers of exhibitors, not individual items. The category for *Wood* in 1861 listed only three exhibitors, but included 371 wood samples in total, making it one of the larger categories in terms of exhibited samples. The category *Fabricated Goods* includes products made by hand and machine. No catalog was published for the 1878 exhibition. Compiled from *Catalogo dos Productos Naturaes e Industriaes que Figurarão na Exposição Nacional* (Rio de Janeiro: Tip. o Diaro do Rio de Janeiro, 1862); *Catalogo da Segunda Exposição Nacional de 1866* (Rio de Janeiro: Tip. Perserverança, 1866); and *Catalogo da Exposição em 1875* (Rio de Janeiro: Tip. Carioca, 1875). Table Design: Alana Baldwin and Christina Frantom.

plant's qualities, thereby presenting a species by its usable components to national and global audiences; second it consolidated the abundant local names for a given species under one scientific label. This process also invoked the authority of science in presenting information collected from indigenous peoples. The restructuring of local knowledge under scientific classification is apparent in the catalogs; descriptions for trees in the 1861 exhibition, for example, were almost all listed under their regional, usually indigenous, names. By 1875, scientific names appeared alongside vernacular names in a majority of descriptions.[42] Within the empire, it was hoped that this information would encourage domestic development; abroad it would project the image of a modern nation: cataloged, analysed, organized, and ripe for economic development. Evidence that the catalogs were used as repositories of scientific knowledge beyond exhibition halls is supplied by the Portuguese commentary on plant species carefully written in the margins of the catalog for items sent to the 1867 Paris Exhibition (Fig. 3.4). The notes include additional information on the listed species as well as phonetic spellings of plant names.[43]

Despite the enthusiastic descriptions of Brazilian natural resources in catalogs and the self-congratulatory tone of exhibition reports, the national exhibitions also had their critics. A wry reviewer of the exhibit for the province of Paraná in 1875 commented:

One of the richest exhibits is certainly the display of... wood from Paraná. The exhibition is exceptional in this regard, yet the display of such products does nothing but reveal the egotism of that province. Naturally, he who examines such... samples will want to buy them. But herein lies the difficulty – these are only for looking at – the lumber cannot leave the province because there are no roads on which they can be transported.... [44]

This observation underscored a major obstacle to establishing a national market of industrial inputs no matter how well cataloged the species of a region might be: the generally poor state of transportation between and within provinces, an obstacle to development that will be further explored in Chapter 5. As the previous observer pointed out, the great diversity of materials on display could not easily be developed into national or even regional commerce without improved transportation networks. The fact that most Brazilian forests (with the exception of the pine forests of Paraná) were comprised of hundreds of different species spread over great distances in rugged tropical terrain further challenged the

---

[42] *Catalogo dos Productos Naturaes e Industriaes que Figurárão na Exposição Nacional* (Rio de Janeiro: Tip. o Diaro do Rio de Janeiro, 1862); *Catalogos dos Productos Naturaes e Industriaes Remettidos das Provincias do Imperio do Brasil que Figurárão na Exposição Nacional* (Rio de Janeiro: Tip. do Diario do Rio de Janeiro, 1862); *Catalogo da Segunda Exposição Nacional de 1866* (Rio de Janeiro: Tip. Perserverança, 1866); and *Catalogo da Exposição Nacional em 1875* (Rio de Janeiro: Tip. Carioca, 1875).

[43] *Catalogo dos Objectos Enviados para a Exposição Universal de Paris em 1867* (Rio de Janeiro: 1867?), pp. 33–41, bound with *Brazil na Exposição de 1867* (Rio de Janeiro: 1867?), Division of Rare and Manuscript Collections, Cornell University Library.

[44] "A Exposição Nacional," *O Mosquito*, December 4, 1875, No. 325, p. 4.

Sucupíra. (Bowdichia virgilioides, Mart.) *Sâpúpíra*

Madeira extrahida da arvore conhecida vulgarmente com igual nome mui frequente nas matas da província do Amazonas e de outras províncias ao sul desta. A arvore é de grande porte, e mesmo colossal; seu tronco mede de 80 a 100 palmos (17^m,60 a 22^m,00) de alto, e 8 a 10 (1^m,77 a 2^m,20) na maior circumferencia. Seu cerne é dos mais resistentes e de longa duração; quer empregado em obras enterradas; quer immersas ou expostas ao tempo.

Tapurú-úba.
Tururí.
Tanimbuqueira. *Tanimúc ýa*

221 Manoel Nicoláo de Mello.
Muirapiranga.

222 Repartição das Obras Publicas. *anhuýa*
Âmago de Sucupíra.
Pau-lacre.

Nome commum da arvore conhecida na província do Amazonas com igual denominação. O cerne da madeira é bastante resistente. É empregada em obras internas. O tronco da arvore mede 20 a 30 palmos (4^m,40 a 6^m,60) de alto, e 2 a 4 de grossura (0^m,44 a 0^m,88) na maior circumferencia. Produz a resina que lhe dá o nome.

223 Thury & Irmãos.
Gen papeiro. (Genipa Brasiliensis.) *Yěnépaúa*

Madeira extrahida da arvore conhecida vulgarmente com o nome de genipapeiro, arvore cujo fructo tem alguma applicação na medicina para curativo interno das hernias, e que abunda nas matas da província do Amazonas, tendo o seu tronco de 30 a 50 palmos (6^m,60 a 11^m) de alto, e 4 a 5 (0^m,88 a 1^m,32) na sua maior circumferencia. O peso específico desta madeira e a maciêsa do seu cerne proporcionão-lhe o maior emprego que tem, tanto nas obras de coroneiro, como na marcenaria, sendo nas construcções só empregada economicamente em obras internas; por isso que exposta ao tempo o seu tecido não é de longa duração.

Jacaré-úba. (Calophyllum brasiliense.) *Yacaré ýa*
Macaca-úba.

Madeira extrahida da arvore conhecida vulgarmente com este nome. É frequente nas matas da província do Amazonas com quatro qualidades diversas; mas todas de igual valor, quanto ao emprego; que são: a macaca-úba commum; a da mata; a da varzea, e a da terra firme,

transportation of lumber. Yet such material constraints did little to dampen the enthusiasm of the Sociedade Auxiliadora.

Oils, Wood, and Wax

Frederico Burlamaque's detailed report on the first National Exhibition of 1861 vigorously praised the hundreds of displays as "Brazil's first inventory of natural resources and industry," an event that "[opened] a new pathway to prosperity" for the nation. Part botanical report (as outlined earlier the majority of plant specimens displayed came from the northern provinces of Pará and Amazonas and were thus new to observers in Rio de Janeiro), part economic treatise, and part social critique, Burlamaque bitterly complained about the lack of Brazilian initiative in exploiting domestic resources for the national economy. He decried the seeming indifference of his compatriots to transform plant oils from the Amazon into industrial products as particularly deficient:

What an extensive commerce the [northern] provinces could provide, if only these [raw] materials were exploited with the same vigor that nature produces them . . .

The collection of . . . oils on display is large and diverse: there are oils for culinary uses, for illumination, for the fabrication of soap, for medicines, and painting. Nonetheless, the capital of the Empire, which is only 300 maritime leagues [*sic*] from the mouth of the Amazon, is illuminated with foreign oil . . . and it consumes soap made from the tallow of cattle from the Río de la Plata. . . . [45]

Burlamaque pointed to western Africa, which he claimed faced the same problems of underdevelopment and labor shortages as northern Brazil, but nonetheless supplied European factories with palm oil for the fabrication of soap and candles. Burlamaque asserted that Brazil could easily replace imports with domestically produced oils, soap, and candles as well as provision European manufacturers with a new complement of raw materials, thereby diversifying the nation's agricultural exports.[46]

There was a precedent for the success that Burlamaque envisioned for Amazonian oils. The 1850 provincial report for the northeastern province

---

[45] Antonio Luiz Fernando da Cunha, *Relatorio Geral da Exposição Nacional de 1861 e Relatorios dos Jurys Especiaes* (Rio de Janeiro: Tip. do Diario do Rio de Janeiro, 1862), p. 27. According to Burlamaque, 2,099 of the total of 9,962 objects exhibited in 1861 came from Pará and Amazônas. Only Rio de Janeiro supplied a higher number of products with a total of 5,928, *ibid.*, p. 21.

[46] *Ibid.*, p. 28. Burlamaque was especially critical of the monoculture of coffee, p. 32.

of Alagoas lauded the Fábrica de Oleos Purificados e de Manipular Arroz (Purified Oil Factory and Rice Mill), a medium-scale operation owned by a local family. The establishment refined castor oil for medicinal use and illumination, a substitute for linseed oil extracted from unspecified "certain nuts," and coconut oil appropriate for all manner of cooking, perfumes, and the most "delicate works of watch-making or cutlery." Production of the oils already "consumed all the raw material available in the area," which, according to the report, had doubled in price since the factory's construction. The report highlighted the potential for developing new oils based on the many native coquilhos abundant in the province. Sharing Burlamaque's patriotic assessment of the superiority of Brazilian oils, the author praised the factory's products as less expensive replacements for the "poor quality whale oil introduced by the North Americans." The author further proclaimed that the factory provisioned markets in Alagoas Pernambuco, and as far away as Rio de Janeiro and Rio Grande do Sul, "depriving the [foreign merchant] a large part of his profit." On one hand, the enthusiastic description here must be considered with skepticism. The report's praise of the national origin of the oils and its superiority over imports justified the request for a state loan for the impressive amount of 50 contos (UK£5,988) to underwrite ongoing costs of labor and raw material.[47] Nonetheless, the author's appeal to economic self-sufficiency, which he asserted would ensure a domestic supply of medicinal castor seed oil for the treatment of yellow fever victims, strongly echoed the economic nationalism of the Sociedade Auxiliadora.[48]

Oil was not the only product derived from native flora that received high praise in exhibition catalogs. Numerous indigenous tree species supplied a dizzying variety of fruit, medicine, resins, fibers, and lumber, sometimes all from a single tree.[49] For example, *Jurema branca* (*acacia*

---

[47] Conversion value for 1850 from Nathaniel H. Leff, *Underdevelopment and Development in Brazil, Vol. I: Economic Structure and Change, 1822–1947* (London: George Allen & Unwin, 1982), p. 246.

[48] José Bento da Cunha e Figueiredo, *Falla dirigida à Assembléa Legislativa da provincia das Alagoas na abertura da primeira sessão ordinaria da oitava legislatura, pelo exm. presidente da mesma provincia, em cinco de maio de 1850* (Maceió: J. S. da S. Maia, 1850), pp. 37–8.

[49] Medicinal plants were also important in period publications, see Sociedade Auxiliadora member Nicolou Joaquim Moreira's *Diccionario de Plantas Medicinaes Brasileiras contendo o nome da planta, seu genero, especie, familia e o botanico que o classificou; o logar onde é mais commun, as virtudes que se lhe atribue, e as doses e formas da sua aplicação* (Rio de Janeiro: Tip. de Correio Mercantil, 1862). German immigrant

jurema), a species from the northeastern province of Rio Grande do Norte, was esteemed for its suitability in civil construction and furniture while the bark provided a treatment for dandruff.[50] Echoing colonial observers, Burlamaque lamented the importation of foreign lumber when Brazilian trees were abundant and far superior in variety and quantity.[51] He hoped the rich displays of native wood would encourage Brazilian engineers, shipbuilders, and craftsmen to incorporate them into their constructions.[52]

One notable tree showcased at each of the national exhibitions was the carnaúba palm (Fig. 3.5). No other national species presented such a diverse sampling of products and applications. The trunk supplied wood for corrals, buildings, musical instruments, and pumps. Its ash contained potassium for fabricating soap and a "salt as of yet unstudied," while the roots provided a "substitute for sarsaparilla." Through undisclosed processes, the palm was transformed into "wine," "vinegar," and a "saccharine substance." The carnaúba's fruit made a nourishing flour. The tree's toasted seeds were proposed as a replacement for coffee "which is said to be pleasant and could supply a substitute for the original fruit from Arabia." The palm's leaves were readily transformed into hats, baskets, and fans. But the most commercially successful application by far was a wax made into candles shipped across Brazil.[53]

Though many of the uses of the versatile carnaúba outlined here were probably commercially impractical, the palm's description demonstrated the enthusiasm and creativity with which exhibition organizers promoted national species. Indeed, carnaúba had several Brazilian champions,

---

and pharmacist Theodore Peckholt studied the medicinal use of 6,000 Brazilian plants. Peckholt published his research in national and international journals and contributed botanical samples for Brazil's exhibition displays. Brazilian-born pharmaceutical pioneer Ezequiel Corréa dos Santos was the first to isolate the active alkoloid in the *pau-pereira* tree, a species used by indigenous peoples to treat malaria, Nadja Paraense dos Santos, Angelo C. Pinto, and Ricardo Bicca de Alencastro, "Theodoro Peckholt: Naturalista e Farmacêutico do Brasil Imperial," *Química Nova*, 21:5 (1998), p. 669; and Nadja Paraense dos Santos, "Passando da Doutrina à prática: Ezequiel Corrêa dos Santos e a Farmácia Nacional," *Química Nova*, 30:4 (2007), p. 1042.

[50]   *Catalogo da Segunda Exposição Nacional 1866*, p. 383.
[51]   Shawn William Miller, *Fruitless trees: Portuguese conservation and Brazil's colonial timber* (Stanford: Stanford University Press, 2000), p. 82; Cunha, *Relatorio Geral . . . 1861*, p. 27.
[52]   Cunha, *Relatorio Geral . . . 1861*, p. 75.
[53]   *Catalogo da Segunda Exposição de 1866*, pp. 488–90.

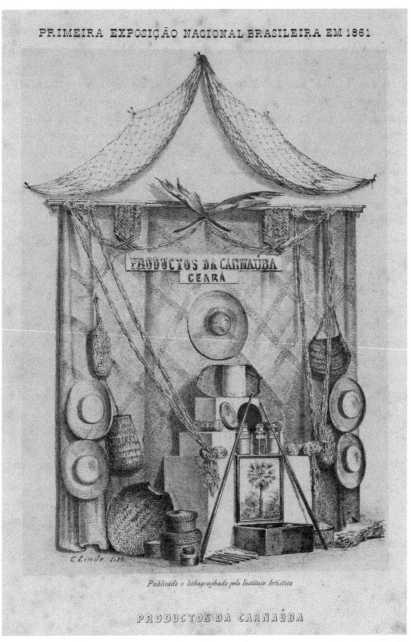

FIGURE 3.5. "Products of the Carnaúba palm." *Source: Recordações da Exposição Nacional de 1861* (Rio de Janeiro: Tip. Universal de Laemmert, 1862). Courtesy of the Acervo da Fundação Biblioteca Nacional, Brazil.

including Manuel Arruda da Câmara who was the first to describe the species to the Portuguese crown in 1796. In 1836, the governor of Piauí launched a thirty-year campaign to market carnaúba in France, which included sending a sample for analysis to the Sorbonne and a display of the wax for the 1867 exhibition in Paris. The Baron of Mauá (the industrialist responsible for Brazil's first railroad) also recognized the economic potential of the carnaúba and published a short-lived journal on industrial wax in the late 1840s. European botanists affirmed the suitability of carnaúba for candle-making, though it was ultimately most commercially successful as a floor polish.[54]

Above and beyond wax and oils, the previous examples also underscore the importance of trees for manufacturing and construction. The nineteenth century is called the age of iron and coal, but wood was just as indispensable as it fulfilled many of the functions of plastic in our present culture.[55] In addition to carnaúba, the Baron of Mauá recognized the industrial potential of Brazilian wood and displayed a decorative mosaic made from 43 different Amazonian tree species at the 1861 national exhibition and again at the 1862 exhibition in London (Fig. 3.6).[56] None doubted the aesthetic appeal of such displays, yet the question remained how to transform the polished sections of an artfully arranged mosaic into information that could spur industrial development. In 1877, the engineer André Rebouças attempted to do just that with his three-volume publication on industrial tree species *Ensaio de índice geral das madeiras do Brazil (General Index of Brazilian Wood)*. He succinctly described more than 1,300 species used for dyes, medicine, and textiles, though application in civil construction was the focus. The presentation of information took the following form as exemplified by this description of the *camaçarí* tree:

1. Local names – Camaçarí; Camaçary; Camassari
2. Botanical Classification – *Carapa pyramidata. Familia das Meliaceas.*
3. Characteristics of duramen [heartwood] – Of a clear rose color; compact tissue; easily visible longitudinal pores

[54] Jörn Seemann, "From Candle Wax to E 903: Commodity Geographies of the Carnaúba Palm (*Coperinicia cerifera*) from Northeastern Brazil," unpublished paper, *Brazilian Studies Association Conference*, 2008, New Orleans, pp. 5–7.

[55] Michael Williams, "Industrial Impacts of the Forests on the United States: 1860–1920," *Journal of Forest History*, 31:3 (1987), p. 1.

[56] *Catalogo dos Productos Naturaes e Industriaes que Figuràrão na Exposição Nacional . . . 1861*, pp. 41–2.

PRIMEIRA EXPOSIÇÃO NACIONAL BRASILEIRA EM 1861

O BRASIL NA EXPOSIÇÃO INTERNACIONAL DE LONDRES

FIGURE 3.6. The Brazilian display at the 1862 Exhibition in London. Wood mosiacs are displayed on the back wall, while plant extracts, medicines, and botanical specimens are arranged in bottles, cases, and a terrarium. *Source: Recordações da Exposição Nacional de 1861* (Rio de Janeiro: Tip. Universal de Laemmert, 1862). Courtesy of the Acervo da Fundação Biblioteca Nacional, Brazil.

4. Assessment – Employed in civil construction. Short-lived under exposure to the elements; twenty years is the expected duration under such conditions.
5. Specific weight – 0.755
6. Dimensions of Trunk – .4 to .6 meters. Reaches a height of 12 to 14 meters.
7. Habitat – Can be found in Alagoas, Bahia, and neighboring provinces.
8. Additional Properties – Produces a milky liquid that is used as a bait for capturing small birds.[57]

---

57 André Rebouças, *Ensaio de indice geral das madeiras do Brazil*, vol. 1 (Rio de Janeiro: Tip. Nacional, 1877), p. 220.

Culled from the research of German botanist Karl von Martius (1794–1868), Brazilian botanists Francisco Freire Allemão de Cisneiros (1897–74) and José Saldanha da Gama (1839–1905), and extensive indigenous knowledge, the *Ensaio de indice geral* was meant to provide a "helpful reference for Brazilian Engineers" as well as a description of the nation's trees for the upcoming Universal Exhibition in Paris in 1878.[58] The index most likely owed its inspiration to Rebouças' observations at the 1862 London exhibition, which he attended with his brother and fellow engineer Antônio Pereira Rebouças. In exhibition reports prepared for the Brazilian government, the Rebouças brothers asserted that Brazilian lumber was far superior to imported wood for civil and naval construction. André and Antônio called for the analysis of Brazilian trees with the aim of developing a national lumber industry. Brazilian wood was, in Antônio's estimation, even better suited to the nation's tropical climate than imported iron for components in railroad tracks.[59]

Rebouças' students at the Polytechnic School in Rio de Janeiro calculated the specific weight for many of the species described in the *Ensaio de indice geral*. The index also reflected decades of accumulated practical knowledge; descriptions of each species' applicability in construction and shipbuilding almost certainly drew from the long-standing shipwright's trade in Brazil.[60] Late colonial shipbuilders in Bahia were noted for their expertise in employing a variety of Brazilian woods in a single ship, a practice that differed greatly from Europe where ships were often constructed from a single species. The use of multiple species in ship construction required considerable skill and experience to ensure a vessel's soundness over many decades at sea.[61] Rebouças' index also

---

[58] Rebouças, *Ensaio*, preface.

[59] Antônio Pereira Rebouças, "Classe IV: Material de Estradas de Ferro," pp. 214 and 218, and André Rebouças, 'Classe VII: Construções Civis: Diques e Apparelhos para a Reparação dos Navios,' in Francisco Ignacio de Carvalho Moreira, ed., *Relatorio Sobre a Exposição Internacional de 1862* (London: Thomas Brettell, 1863), p. 370. After their return from the 1862 Exhibition, André and Antônio organized an ultimately unsuccessful pine lumbering company in Paraná; Richard Graham, *Britain and the Onset of Modernization in Brazil*, pp. 194–5.

[60] Miller, *Fruitless Trees*, p. 207; and Diogo de Carvalho Cabral, "Floresta, política e trabalho: a exploração das madeiras-de-lei no Recôncovo da Guanabara (1760–1820)," *Revista Brasileira de História*, 28:55 (2008), pp. 219–20. Sociedade Auxiliadora Member Baltasar da Silva Lisboa published an earlier volume on Brazilian wood, *Riqueza do Brasil em madeiras de construção e carpintaria* (Rio de Janeiro: n/p, 1823).

[61] In the late colonial period Colonel Theodósio da Silva Raboxo assessed the density and relative strength of Bahian wood for use in shipbuilding, Miller, pp. 204–7.

underscored the nineteenth-century convergence of engineering, botany, and the emergence of laboratory analysis for determining the practical application of plant species in industrial production.[62] In an age before synthetics, botanists (or engineers with a deep understanding of the same) were important intermediaries between the natural world and industrial production. For the Rebouças brothers, using science to measure and document "the most important natural resource bestowed upon [Brazil] by the Creator" was of paramount importance for achieving economic self-sufficiency.[63]

Textiles and Paper

The search for indigenous textile fibers and the neglect of local sources moved more than one researcher to hyperbole. In 1851, Cearense Braz da Costa Rubim roundly praised the fibers of the acclimated *coqueiro da Bahia*, asserting its superiority for ship cordage and mattresses "suitable for the Brazilian climate," in addition to "a thousand other uses... if only [Brazilians] would look with more sagacity on our natural riches." Despite the palm's economic usefulness, he lamented "...there are immense forests of *coqueiros* that are born, grow, and die without any human influence upon their lives."[64] Like Antunes' *piaçabeira*, Rubim asserted that the *coqueiro da Bahia* was by nature an industrious plant that required only the spirit of entrepreneurship to harness its natural productivity for the national economy.

Twenty years later a dedicated individual from Minas Gerais, Severino Lourenço da Costa Leite, championed the indigenous *cipó lactescente* (milky vine) as a replacement for cotton and flax in textile manufacturing.[65] Leite also hoped to find alternatives to coffee, a monoculture crop that he predicted was on the verge of ecological and economic disaster as agricultural land became increasingly depleted by its cultivation.[66]

---

[62] See Suzanne Zeller, "Darwin meets the Engineers: Scientizing the Forest at McGill University, 1890–1910," *Environmental History*, 6:3 (2001), pp. 428–50.

[63] Rebouças, *Ensaio de indice geral*, preface.

[64] Braz da Costa Rubim, "Ensaio sobre a historia das Plantas uteis do Brasil," *O Auxiliador*, January 1851, p. 289. In India, the same coconut fibers (*coir*) have been used for centuries to produce mattresses and rope, among many other products.

[65] Severino Lourenço da Costa Leite, "Botanica Industrial: Breve Noticias sobre o Cipó Lactescente," *O Auxiliador*, January 1878, p. 26.

[66] For a description of the forest destruction caused by the expansion of coffee plantations in nineteenth-century Brazil, see Warren Dean, *With Broadax and Firebrand*, pp. 180–90, and Stanley Stein, *Vassouras A Brazilian Coffee County, 1850–1900: The Roles of*

Cipó lactescente provided a viable alternative, he argued, because it could be grown year after year with minimal improvement to the soil in contrast to the establishment of new coffee plantations in virgin forest, a major contributor to forest destruction.[67] A special report on Leite's *cipó* sponsored by Imperial Instituto Fluminense de Agricultura for the Ministry of Agriculture underscored this point. The fact that the vine depended on large trees for cultivation (it could grow to a height of 100 feet) would preserve virgin forest "without the sad and lamentable need to destroy it, and to damage the earth for other cultivations perhaps not as profitable and certainly more demanding [in terms of labor]. . . . "[68] The ecological sensibility reflected here was a new iteration of the long-standing criticism of slash-and-burn agriculture by the Sociedade Auxiliadora and may have also reflected concern for the declining fertility of the Paraíba valley, a major producer of coffee in this period.[69]

The Sociedade Auxiliadora conducted experiments with cipó lactescente with the aim of providing scientific evidence for the usefulness of the fiber in a report published in English for the 1876 International Exhibition in Philadelphia. Samples were also sent to John Miers in England who suggested to the Sociedade Auxiliadora that the manufacturers of Manchester would be interested in purchasing the *cipó* fiber if sufficient quantities could be cultivated.[70] Unfortunately, producing *cipó lactescente* fiber for large-scale industrial use proved challenging as extraction was difficult to mechanize, and thus the material was ultimately not commercially successful.[71]

The discovery of domestically sourced material for papermaking, an industry dependent on plant fiber, was early deemed a matter of national priority. A paper factory established in Bahia in the 1840s employed locally harvested banana tree fiber; the provincial presidential report

---

Planter and Slave in a Plantation Society (Princeton, NJ: Princeton University Press, 1958 and 1985), pp. 219–25. *O Auxiliador* deeply criticized the environmental destruction caused by slash-and-burn agriculture, and society member the Baron of Capanema published a vigorous critique of forest destruction in 1855, Pádua, *Um Sopro*, pp. 174–9 and pp. 244–6.

[67] Leite, "Botanica Industrial," p. 26.

[68] José Fernandes da Costa Pereira Junior, "Novas Plantas Textis," *Relatorio apresentado à Assembléa Geral Legislativa na Segunda Sessão de Decima Quarta Legislativa pelo Ministro e Secretario de Estado dos Negocios de Agricultura, Commercio, e Obras Publicas* (Rio de Janeiro: Tip. Commercial, 1873), *annexo C*, p. 2.

[69] Stein, pp. 214–25.   [70] Moreira, *Historical Notes*, pp. 3–4 and 8–14.

[71] W. Michler and Antônio José Sampaio, "Industrial Textil," *O Auxiliador*, June 1884, p. 130.

from 1843 speculated that the factory would stimulate banana cultivation in Bahia and encourage the discovery of additional "fibrous trees
which are unappreciated and unknown amongst us, even though they
are indigenous."[72] The Baron of Capanema's paper factory (described in
Chapter 2) was highlighted in the 1853 report for Rio de Janeiro. Located
in the mountains outside of Petrópolis, it was powered by a nearby water-
fall and used the latest in French machinery.[73] Though the factory initially
employed imported raw material, Capanema soon developed a process
for making paper from domestic species including the *folha do gravatá* (a
cactus-like plant with long, tongue-shaped leaves), bromeliad fibers, and
the banana tree.[74] The turn to local resources was precipitated by the difficulty and expense of procuring linen and cotton rags from Europe (then
the predominant material for making paper) and the absence of a local
market for rag-collecting in nearby Rio de Janeiro, "despite an abundance
of material." It also reflected Capanema's commitment to using Brazilian
resources for domestic industry.[75]

The Orianda Factory produced high-quality paper throughout the
1850s, before ultimately closing in 1861, due to financial mismanage-
ment and Capanema's frequent absences as a government envoy. Before
its demise, the factory supplied paper for several Rio newspapers: the
Diário do Rio de Janeiro, *Correio da Tarde*, and the *Correio Mercantil*,
in addition to the *Correio Mercantil* in Porto Alegre.[76] A surviving example from the Orianda Factory exists in the form of a map of Brazil from
1857. The fine print proudly declares its national provenance, underscoring the Sociedade Auxiliadora's vision in a powerful metaphor for
economic nationalism: a map of the nation printed on domestically produced paper from Brazilian raw material.[77]

The Sociedade Auxiliadora's review of a patent application in 1878 by
engineers Samuel Severiano Figueira de Aguiar and Francisco Carlos da

---

[72] *Falla que recitou o presidente da provincia da Bahia, o conselheiro Joaquim José Pinheiro de Vasconcellos, n'abertura da Assembléa Legislativa da mesma provincia em 2 de fevereiro de 1843* (Bahia: Tip. de J. A. Portella e Companhia, 1942 [*sic*]), p. 12, also cited in Geraldo de Beuclair Mendes de Oliveira, *A Construcção Inacabada*, p. 177.

[73] Sebastião Ferreira Soares, *Historico da Fabrica de Papel de Orianda ou a defesa do Dr. Guilherme Shüch de Capanema* (Rio de Janeiro: Tip. Universal de Laemmart, 1860), pp. 27–8.

[74] Capanema patented the process in 1857, "Decreto 2053, 16 de Dezembro, 1857," www.senado.gov.br/sf/.

[75] Soares, p. 29.   [76] *Ibid.*, p. 37.

[77] *Nova Carta Corographica do Imperio do Brazil* (Rio de Janeiro: Lithographia Imperial de Eduardo Rensburg, 1857), *Arquivo Histórico do Exército*, Mapa 13.01.2649.

Silva for the "establishment of a paper factory . . . in São Paulo province" prompted a heated discussion among the members of the Committee on Industrial Manufacturing.[78] The committee declared the factory deserving of enthusiastic support, including government subsidies, but declined to grant the petitioners a patent of protection. While the proposed factory used the latest in European papermaking techniques, it did not demonstrate any innovation in developing Brazilian materials. Committee members also protested the assertion in a recent report by Professor Ernesto Guignet of the Polytechnic School in Rio de Janeiro that Brazilian paper production suffered from a lack of raw material.[79] Nine patents granted for papermaking techniques between 1857 and 1878 proved the possibilities for domestic production, they argued. Among the raw materials described in the patents were Capanema's "indigenous vegetal fibers native to the country," sugar cane *bagasse*, corn, bamboo, unspecified "native fibers," and "Brazilian vegetal fibers." To drive their point home, the committee awarded a patent to the *cipó lactescente*'s champion, Severino Lourenço da Costa Leite, for his paper fabricated from "various tree species commonly referred to as *figueira brava* (wild fig)."[80] In addition to paper, Leite claimed that the outer bark of the versatile *figueira brava* could be fabricated into clothing for "rural workers or any other type of labourer," as described in the florid prose of a report on the 1875 national exhibition.[81]

Though these patents demonstrated creativity, initiative, and a solid interest in developing paper production in Brazil, members of the Sociedade Auxiliadora recognized that the creation of a national industry was difficult in the face of competition from foreign imports and the chronic shortage of start-up capital. A lack of domestic material was not the problem, they insisted; rather, cheap foreign imports hindered the

---

[78] The application was for a "patent of introduction," or short-term monopoly of ten to twenty years in which the engineers would have the exclusive right to import and use the paper machinery, "Ordem do Dia," *O Auxiliador*, October 1878, p. 223.

[79] *Ibid.*, p. 222; Ernesto Guignet, "Relatorio sobre uma viagem á [*sic*] provincia de Minas Geraes dirigido à S. Ex. O Sr. ministro do Imperio, pelo Sr. Ernesto Guignet, professor da escola Polytechnia," *Revista Agricola do Imperial Instituto Fluminense de Agricultura*, September 1877, p. 100.

[80] "Ordem do Dia," pp. 222–3. An additional patent not mentioned in society minutes was granted to Eugênio Muller for a process for the fabrication of yarn, thread, and paper from banana trees, "Decreto no. 3415, 15 de Março, 1865," www.senado.gov.br/sf/.

[81] José de Saldanha da Gama, *Estudos sobre a Quarta Exposição Nacional de 1875* (Rio de Janeiro: Tip. Central de Brown and Evaristo, 1876), pp. 90–1.

development of domestic production.[82] Would-be manufacturers of any stripe faced numerous challenges in launching industrial enterprises during this period. Barbara Weinstein's work on the Amazonian province of Pará provides an example of another failed papermaking factory. Founded in 1892, the Fábrica de Papel in Pará employed " ... native woods and regional materials such as banana leaves, straw and vegetable fibers... " in addition to *bagasse* in the production of wrapping and printing paper.[83] In spite of positive publicity and partial ownership by a Paraense businessman, the *fábrica* suffered from a lack of capital. The factory also ran into difficulties procuring regular supplies of raw material, despite ownership of a sugar mill designed to supply the necessary *bagasse*.[84]

A small vile of acid displayed by Italian immigrant Luiz Terragno at the 1875 exhibition in Rio provides an additional example of the challenges faced by Brazilian entrepreneurs in the absence of networks of research labs and accessible capital. Terragno, a photographer resident in the southern province of Rio Grande do Sul, submitted a small vile of the toxic acid extracted from manioc root at the National Exhibition of 1875. One species of manioc – an indigenous tuber and a staple of the Brazilian diet – contains naturally occurring cyanide that must be removed before consumption. It was this poisonous by-product that Terragno asserted had enormous potential for speeding the exposure time for taking photographs. This was a significant selling point as nineteenth-century photography techniques required long exposures in order to capture sufficient visual information for developing images, a process that limited subject matter to static scenes.[85]

The entrepreneur sent a sample of the manioc acid (he named it *sulfo-mandiocate of iron*) with a colleague for analysis in Paris, but his hopes were thwarted by the outbreak of the Franco-Prussian War. He also lacked the necessary capital for further experimentation in Brazil and called upon the exhibition participants to recognize the potential "applications of [manioc acid] in the arts, industry, [and] medicine... "

[82] "Ordem do Dia," p. 223.

[83] Barbara Weinstein, *The Amazon Rubber Boom: 1850–1920* (Stanford: Stanford UniversityPress, 1983), p. 93.

[84] *Ibid.*, p. 94.

[85] *Catalogo... 1875*, pp. 571–2. Cited also in Maria Inez Turazzi, *Poses e Trejeitos: a fotografia e as exposições na era do espectáculo (1839–1889)* (Rio de Janeiro: Funarte, Editora Rocco Ltda., 1995), p. 144.

Sulfo-mandiocate of iron, he argued, would profitably utilize a heretofore discarded by-product of an existing agricultural industry.[86]

Terragno's example demonstrates a spirit of entrepreneurship and tradition of scientific research then developing in Brazil, but also underscores innovators and entrepreneurs' continued dependence on more developed scientific centers in Europe for scientific analysis and – perhaps more importantly – validation of potential industrial commodities. By the 1870s, botanical research labs existed at the Escola Politécnica, the Imperial Instituto Fluminense de Agricultura and the Museu Nacional in Rio, and the Escola de Minas in Ouro Preto, Minas Gerais, among others, but these were clustered in urban areas far from potential entrepreneurs in far-flung provincial regions.[87] Analysis therefore often depended on assessments by European scientists and industrialists, which, as Terragno's example suggests, could be time-consuming and suspect to disruptions in communication. Additionally, pejorative perceptions of Latin American science made European validation all the more necessary in the attempt to overcome lack of knowledge about and distrust of new tropical commodities in North Atlantic markets.[88]

Could *sulfo-mandiocate of iron* have been developed into a successful photographic chemical or other industrial application? It is hard to discern from this short description; perhaps it was not feasible to produce the substance in quantities large enough to develop into a marketable product, or it was not as effective as the photographer claimed. On the other hand, with the right institutional support it might have developed into a new chemical for processing photographs. In either case, Terragno

---

[86] *Catalogo... 1875*, pp. 571–2.
[87] Carlos Glasl, "Relatório do Jardim Botânico e da Fazenda Normal da data do ultimo até o fim de Abril de 1873," *Revista Agricola do Imperial Instituto Fluminense de Agricultura*, December, 1873, p. 41. German Immigrant Theodoro Peckholt operated a private lab at his pharmacy in Rio were he analyzed the chemical properties of more than 6,000 Brazilian plants; Nadja Paraense dos Santos, Angelo C. Pinto, and Ricardo Bicca de Alencas, "Theodoro Peckholt: Naturalista e Farmacêutico do Brasil Imperial," *Química Nova*, 21:5, 1998, pp. 668–9.
[88] Louis Couty, a French physiologist hired by Pedro II to fill the Chair of Industrial Biology at the Polytechnic school in Rio, facilitated a series of experiments with mate at the Collège de France in the 1880s, "O Mate," *Revista Agricola do Imperial Instituto Fluminense de Agricultura*, March 1883, p. 41. See also Louis Couty, *A erva-mate e o charque* (Pelotas: Seiva, 1880, 2000). In Peru, French pharmacist Alfredo Bignon identified and legitimated cocaine as a respectable substance for scientific and pharmaceutical use in the 1880s; see Paul Gootenberg, "A Forgotten Case of 'Scientific Excellence on the Periphery': The Nationalist Cocaine Science of Alfredo Bignon, 1884–1887," *Comparative Studies in Society and History* 49:1 (2007), pp. 202–32.

underscores the creativity with which those in Brazil studied potentially economically useful botanical products.

Mate

If domestic sources of textile fibers and oils were viewed as essential to developing the national economy and diversifying exports, another indigenous species, mate, the aforementioned "herb" native to southern Brazil and the River Plate region, was heralded as a potentially lucrative export and replacement for other hot, caffeinated beverages in foreign markets. By the 1850s, Brazil exported mate to Argentina, Uruguay, Paraguay, and Chile, nations that also produced the herb, but modernizers hoped to expand the trade to the North Atlantic. In a practice adopted from indigenous peoples, the slightly bitter leaves and stems of *Ilex paraguariensis* are steeped in a gourd and then sipped through a bamboo or metal straw. The resulting hot beverage provides a stimulating caffeinated drink that though pungent is milder in flavor than coffee. For this reason Brazilians envisioned mate as an ideal replacement for tea and coffee, both of which were consumed across Europe and North America but cultivated in the tropics.

While mate was a popular colonial beverage among the lower classes and elites in eighteenth-century Río de la Plata and Andean communities, it was French botanist and colleague of Alexander von Humboldt, Aimé Bonpland (1773–1858), who circulated specimens of mate in the European scientific community in the 1800s.[89] Members of the Sociedade Auxiliadora, Imperial Instituto Fluminense de Agricultura, and the Associação Brasileira de Acclimação (Brazilian Acclimatization Association, founded in 1873) in Rio de Janeiro also promoted mate at international exhibitions in Europe and the United States.[90] By presenting mate as a less expensive alternative to coffee and tea for thrift-conscious industrial workers and military officials looking for frugal ways to provision their troops, Brazilians demonstrated that they understood the necessity of marketing in order to entice European consumers to try their product. Yet despite high hopes, entrepreneurs faced multiple obstacles in

---

[89] The Jesuits were the first European cultivators of mate, Ross W. Jamieson, "The Essence of Commodification: Caffeine Dependencies in the Early Modern World," *Journal of Social History*, 35:2 (2001), p. 276; Stephen Bell, "Aimé Bonpland," pp. 67 and 75. See also Bell, *A Life in Shadow*, p. 206.

[90] André Rebouças, *Acondicionamento da Herva-Mate* (Rio de Janeiro: Tip. Carioca, 1875), p. 1.

introducing mate abroad. As Ross Jamieson observes, coffee, tea, and chocolate were already well-established consumer products in Europe and North America by the 1600s, leaving little room for the introduction of another exotic, caffeinated beverage in the 1800s. Furthermore, unlike cacao and coffee plants, the deceptively delicate mate tree proved difficult to transplant and cultivate in traditional plantation style; after the fall of the Jesuit missions in the eighteenth century (where mate was produced during the colonial period), harvesting in Brazil relied primarily on wild groves, which sometimes resulted in irregular supply.[91] Finally, the plant seems to have aroused suspicion about its salubriousness due to its association with "miserable and poorly nourished" populations in faraway tropical and subtropical regions. In the twentieth-century United States, banana distributers used aggressive marketing to improve the fruit's negative image due to its association with dark-complexioned races and dangerous tropical forests.[92] According to Brazilian observers, the racial stigma of mate proved difficult to combat despite vigorous lobbying by the imperial government in French scientific circles in the 1880s.[93]

While the government promoted mate in the esteemed halls of French scientific institutions, André Rebouças, ever the Renaissance man, blamed the generally poor reputation of Brazilian products abroad, and mate in particular, on a lack of product presentation.[94] Why, he lamented, did producers send mate to market wrapped in rough leather hides that were suitable for the wild pampas of Uruguay and Argentina, but appeared crude to sophisticated consumers in the Europe and the United States?:

Much the same as people, industrial and agricultural products have their ceremonial costumes and *toilettes*: one does not go to a ball in the same clothes they would wear for the countryside; likewise a product should not be presented at an industrial festival with the same rustic packaging as that for the consumption of semi-barbarous populations...[95]

---

[91] Ross W. Jamieson, "The Essence of Commodification," pp. 276–7.
[92] John Soluri, *Banana Cultures: Agricultural Consumption, & Environmental Change in Honduras & the United States* (Austin, TX: University of Texas Press, 2005), pp. 34–6 and 58–60.
[93] "O Mate," p. 43. In nineteenth-century Peru, the association of coca leaves with the indigenous population "left coca racially debased in the eyes of Creole elites...," Gootenberg, p. 205, Soluri, pp. 58–62.
[94] Couty, "O Mate," p. 41.
[95] André Rebouças, *Acondicionamento da Herva-Mate* (Rio de Janeiro 1875), p. 2.

Rebouças further entreated producers to pay attention to what "nature... is instructing [us]" and use the pine from forests that grew alongside mate groves to fabricate attractive boxes for packaging the herb. If mate packaging more closely resembled that of tea, he argued, foreign consumers could be persuaded to try it. Additionally, Rebouças argued that Brazilian pine resin would provide an excellent finishing varnish for the boxes to protect the delicate contents from humidity on the way to market, an important consideration in tropical Brazil.[96]

This examination of Brazilian attempts to introduce mate to foreign markets leads to two conclusions. First, Rebouças' observation that the Brazilian landscape itself presented a lesson in how to develop the national economy reflected a Linnaean sensibility. Second, efforts to promote mate consumption abroad demonstrated that Brazilians fully participated in transatlantic channels for legitimizing botanical species as commodities in both scientific and consumer venues. In the case of mate, Brazilians were clearly active (if not necessarily successful) agents in promoting a potentially lucrative botanical species.[97]

Turfa Wars

As the example of engineer Antônio Antunes demonstrated at the beginning of this chapter, the exploration and development of combustible fuels occupied the attention of Brazilian innovators throughout the period. In this vein, Brazilians were full participants in the nineteenth-century race to locate and extract sources of energy for burgeoning industrial, transportation, and household needs. Though coal was the most sought-after fuel, Brazilians explored other possibilities in an effort to secure domestically produced sources of energy.

---

[96] *Ibid.*

[97] For selected works on mate see Luiz Carlos Barbosa Lessa, *História do chimarrão*, 3 ed., (Porto Alegre: Sulina, 1986); Temístocles Linhares, *História econômica do mate* (Rio de Janeiro: José Olympio Editora, 1969); and Arlene Renk, *A luta da erva: um ofício étnico da nação brasileira no oeste catarinense*, 2. ed. (Chapecó: Argos, 2006). Early twentieth-century promotional materials on mate include Commissão pela Expansão Ecônomica, *Il Mate del Brasile* (Roma: Tip. Enrico Voghera, 1910) and *Le thé maté du Brésil: analyse chimique* (n/p: Mission Brésillienne du Propagande, 1908). See also Vanderlei Ribeiro, *Dicionário da terra*, Márcia Motta, ed. (Rio de Janeiro: Civilisação Brasileira, 2005), s.v. "Instituto Nacional do Mate." The herb eventually became a niche export to the Old World, if not to the markets that Rebouças envisioned. Today mate is cultivated and consumed in Syria and Lebanon where it was introduced by returning Middle Eastern immigrants in the twentieth century. My thanks to scholar Roberto Khatlab for this observation.

One promising combustible, *turfa* (turf or peat), was celebrated by Brazilian observers. In 1849, an article published in the *Jornal do Commercio* praised a sample of turfa, extracted in Ingá across the bay from Rio. Citing the successful application of peat-fuel in France and Holland, the article called for the exploitation of the combustible in Brazil, especially in light of the failure to locate easily accessible coal deposits by the 1840s.[98] Twenty-six years later, the Baron of Vila-Franca displayed an example of turfa extracted from the margins of the river *Quissamã* in Rio de Janeiro province at the 1875 exhibition. Vila-Franca experimented with using peat for "working iron" on the *fazenda* of Santa Francisca to apparently favorable but unspecified results.[99] Turfa deposits in Bahia were also described in the 1866 exhibition catalog:

Large-scale exploration of the deposits of turfa is highly desirable. Many of the deposits are located next to waterways that make it easy to transport. Undoubtedly any person who undertakes extraction of *turfa* will be more than rewarded for his efforts as it is proportionally less expensive than that of coal and certain to be in high demand. [Turfa] will, most assuredly, become another important branch of industry and commerce to be developed in this country.[100]

In 1850 the Baron of Capanema experimented with gas extracted from *turfa* for use in street illumination.[101] In 1865, William Gilbert Ginty received a patent for "his process for preparing turfa as a substitute for all or part of native as well as prepared vegetal combustibles and minerals."[102] But it was an article in the *Jornal do Commercio* that fully illustrated the material's commercial potential. In January of 1880, Joaquim Alves de Souza, a machinist and resident of Rio de Janeiro, demonstrated his system for using turfa to make gas for illumination at the offices of the Dom Pedro II Railroad. Souza also described useful by-products, including turpentine, "combustible bricks," and "coke" that comprised a "satisfactory and economical fuel." The machinist and his business partner asserted that turfa would provide a less expensive alternative to existing sources of illumination fuel because of its abundance and availability across Brazil.[103]

Souza's demonstration provoked an angry response in the next day's *Jornal do Commercio* from the inventor Antônio Lucio de Medeiros who

[98] "Turfa no Ingá, em Nitherohy," *JC*, December 6, 1849, pp. 1–2.
[99] Gama, *Estudos*, p. 68.   [100] *Catalogo da Segunda Exposição, 1866*, pp. 81–2.
[101] "Noticia Sobre a Illuminação a Gaz," *O Auxiliador*, December 1850, pp. 275–6.
[102] "Decreto no. 3485, 21 de Junho, 1865," www.senado.gov.br/sf/.
[103] "Gaz de Turfa," *Gazetilha, JC*, January 19, 1880, p. 1.

accused the machinist of copying his system for processing turfa into gas. Not only had Medeiros patented a peat-gas system seven years earlier, he asserted, his apparatuses had been in use since 1875 at the "establishments of the Ministry of the Navy" situated on the *Ilha das Cobras* in Guanabara Bay. Indeed, a patent for "mechanical fire" (*fogões mecânicos*) called the 'Double Economy' was given to Medeiros in January of 1873, with an extension of ten years granted in September of 1874 (Fig. 3.7).[104] A month-long, vitriolic exchange between the two inventors ensued in the pages of the *Jornal do Commercio*. Unfortunately, the disagreement between Medeiros and Souza falls silent in the sources, leaving tantalizing clues but no definitive answers as to the outcome of the patent dispute or the extent to which turfa was successfully employed in Brazilian industry.

Could turfa, as its supporters claimed, have met growing industrial and domestic needs for combustibles in Brazil? In the nineteenth century peat was successfully used in Europe and the United States to produce gas for illumination, power farm machinery, warm houses, heat cooking stoves, fuel forges, and run steam engines of all kinds, up to and including locomotives.[105] By the 1860s, the material was used as a combustible in France, Ireland, Italy, and the United States, especially in regions facing firewood shortages due to forest depletion or where coal was scarce.[106] Peat was also showcased at international exhibitions. French peat displayed at the 1851 Great Exhibition in London, for example, excited attention for its inexpensiveness and suitability for running "stationary steam engines and locomotives."[107] The Swedish catalog of the 1876 Philadelphia Exhibition described a burgeoning peat-manufacturing industry facilitated by new machines that produced easily transported "peat balls," presumably for heating, domestic use, and light industry.[108]

Though it is impossible to know how much Medeiros and Souza might have been aware of or influenced by peat technology developing abroad, they provide strong evidence for a lively community of inventors and

---

[104] "Decreto no. 5199, 11 de Janeiro, 1873," www.senado.gov.br/sf/; and "Decreto no. 5752, 23 de Setembro, 1874," www.senado.gov.br/sf/.

[105] T. H. Leavitt, *Facts about Peat as an Article of Fuel* (Boston, MA: Lee and Shepard, 1867), pp. 16–17, and 82.

[106] *Ibid.*, pp. 73–173.   [107] *Ibid.*, p. 82.

[108] *Swedish Catalogue* (Philadelphia, PA: Hallowell and Co., 1876), pp. 192–3. Peat remained an important twentieth-century combustible in Ireland, Kevin C. Kearns, "Development of the Irish Peat Fuel Industry," *The American Journal of Economics and Sociology*, 37:2 (1978), pp. 179–93.

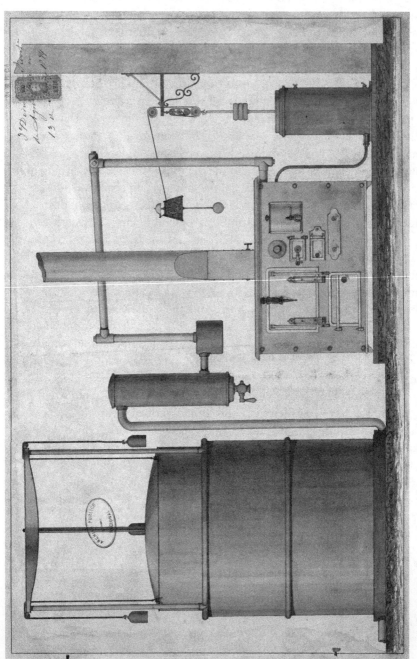

FIGURE 3.7. The patent design for the "Double Economy" system for converting peat into gas for illumination by Antônio Lucio de Medeiros. *Source:* Privilégios Industriais do Império, *Decreto* 5752 23/9/1874 Mapoteca 18 G2. Courtesy of the Arquivo Nacional, Brazil.

researchers in the capital city of the empire, and, moreover, demonstrate that Brazilians possessed a spirit of scientific inquiry and the technological know-how to apply domestic resources to practical and profitable use. Importantly, Brazilian peat entrepreneurs also emphasized the national provenance of their turfa. For them peat presented more than a commercial opportunity for personal enrichment, they declared with apparent sincerity; the combustible also promised to aid national economic self-sufficiency. As the anonymous letter-writer at the beginning of this chapter despaired, why did Brazilians continue to waste money on imported coal, when God had so generously blessed them with peat?[109]

Conclusion

This chapter has described a vibrant, if small, nexus of inventors, scientists, botanists, and engineers who hoped to create Brazilian economic self-sufficiency through the development of domestically produced agro-industrial commodities and combustibles. The actors described here drew from a tradition of scientific investigation established during the Pombaline reforms and transmitted through the Sociedade Auxiliadora. Brazil's thousands of "industrial" species and seemingly exhaustless tropical fecundity appeared the perfect setting for a Linnaean vision of economic self-sufficiency. For the visionaries of the Sociedade Auxiliadora, no other country seemed better positioned to provision its own economy and that of the world with new agro-industrial commodities.

Significantly, the majority of the entrepreneurs described in this chapter were affiliated with the Sociedade Auxiliadora either as members or as contributors to *O Auxiliador*. As scholar Patrícia Corrêa Barreto argues, the society provided an important venue for disseminating scientific information and promoting scientific activity within Brazil, even if its contours and methods differed from institutions in Europe.[110] The Sociedade Auxiliadora provided a crucial national forum for bringing together botanical entrepreneurs through *O Auxiliador*, exhibitions, and the Imperial Instituto Fluminense de Agricultura. This chapter therefore counters the notion that Brazilians of Pedro II's reign – a period primarily associated with technological backwardness and a slave-dependent export economy – were mere consumers of technology and scientific information imported from the North Atlantic industrializing nations. On the contrary, nineteenth-century modernizers inherited a Luso-Brazilian tradition

---

[109] "Os Camellos no Ceará," May 3, 1862.
[110] See Chapter 1, footnote 48.

that drew upon the knowledge and observations of native peoples, Brazilians, and Europeans alike. Their efforts represented a project of national economic development that sat at the intersection of science, technology, botany, environmental conservation, and agricultural improvement.

Why, then, were so many of these projects ultimately unsuccessful? Transportation was (and remains) a major hindrance to establishing commercial contact between the Brazilian provinces as *O Mosquito* caustically noted in the case of timber samples from Paraná. Even today many Amazonian products are unknown outside of the northern provinces where they are produced. Ironically, despite the eighteenth- and nineteenth-century image of the Brazilian wilderness as an Eden bursting with botanical riches, tropical commodities also suffered from a lack of familiarity in North Atlantic markets at best and pejorative associations of tropical environments and nonwhite populations at worst. This was compounded by a lack of Brazilian marketing savvy when it came to packaging. The lower cost of European imports was also blamed for handicapping Brazilian entrepreneurs. Would-be paper producers, for example, faced challenges in procuring inexpensive quantities of locally sourced raw materials, a problem that was exacerbated by difficulties of transportation that increased the sale price further. Processing the final product was also often difficult to mechanize as in the case of Leite's *cipó* fibers or the carnaúba palm. All of these were significant obstacles that prevented Brazilian botanical entrepreneurs from fully realizing their projects.

On a final note, the experiments, observations, and declarations proffered by the likes of the members of the Sociedade Auxiliadora suggest that nineteenth-century Brazilians were influenced by a hybrid of economic ideologies that went beyond the dominant philosophies of the time. Carl Linnaeus strongly influenced the ecological thought of important nineteenth-century Brazilians, which in turn shaped ideas about political economy. The Sociedade Auxiliadora developed a vision of ecological, scientific, and economic modernization that both appropriated European ideologies and expressed a uniquely Brazilian perspective based on the nation's immense natural resources. The key to preserving the nation's forests for the study and development of new commodities rested on agricultural improvement, a topic to which we now turn.

4

The Most Useful of Instruments

Plows and Agricultural Innovation

> *Master:*   *Whom among you will provide the name of the instrument*
> *That enjoys the highest esteem...*
> *It is a relative of the sword, yet it causes a thousand wounds*
> *without leading to death, nay, without shedding blood*
> *It brings forth all the benefactions of life!*
> *Its power, without guile or pain,*
> *Ennobles, enriches, renders existence sweet and balanced*
> *It has founded vast empires;*
> *And erected the most ancient cities;*
> *It has never led to war, nor disturbed peace*
> *And brings happiness to all who trust in it?*
>
> *Students:*   The Plough.[1]

In 1860, antislavery proponent and educator Antônio Marques Rodrigues published an impassioned, multi-page *apedido* (misleadingly) titled, "A Few Words about Brazilian Agriculture," in which he celebrated the establishment of a new agricultural school in his home province of Maranhão. Operated under the auspices of the provincial government with a French agronomist as director, the school featured the latest in agricultural technology including a selection of imported plows. For the Maranhense, plowing comprised the most important component of the school's curriculum, and the plow represented more than a mere farming instrument. Rodrigues considered the plow crucial for reforming, restructuring, and modernizing Brazilian agricultural practices and rural society itself. This chapter uses Rodrigues' lengthy missive as a lens through which to understand the visions and strategies of improvers who

---

[1] "Agricultura Mechanica," *O Auxiliador*, December 1861, p. 457.

saw the dissemination of agricultural technology along with immigration and agricultural education as an essential component of modernization. For Rodrigues and the modernizers of the Sociedade Auxiliadora, the plow was the key to improving crop production, increasing agricultural revenue, ending slavery, preserving forests for longer-lasting economic development, and transforming rural society through stable and legalized landholding that would end violent conflicts over land. The group most in need of reformation, Rodrigues and society members charged, were Brazil's *rotineiros*, the backward agriculturalists who relied on and perpetuated the cycle of slash-and-burn cultivation that resulted in the abandonment of depleted land and the further destruction of valuable virgin forest. For reformers, plows were an ideal *aperfeiçoamento*. The instrument was imagined as a way to peacefully transform rural society, again underscoring the deeper concerns for cautious social reform that underlie modernizing projects in nineteenth-century Brazil.

This chapter will also examine the reasons for the *rotineiros'* reluctance to adopt plows and other innovations. Among the obstacles to introducing agricultural technology were high import tariffs on machinery, merchant and patent fees, the difficulty of transporting heavy equipment through rugged territory, a lack of infrastructure for repairs and maintenance, and the necessities of Brazilian cultivation for which many imported instruments were ill suited, as we shall see shortly.[2] Furthermore, the *fazendeiros'* resistance to plows in particular followed local economic logic in which slash-and-burn cultivation simply generated faster and more profitable results. Fields recently cleared of forest were so fertile that plants required "almost no labor" to produce impressive crop yields, as French planter Vigneron Jousselandiére [*sic*] confidently declared in his 1860 treatise on plantation management.[3] Though power relationships based on slaveholding and patronage between the rural wealthy and poor were also a factor in agriculturalists' reluctance to adopt the plow, the fact that plowing was often, counterintuitively, more labor intensive in Brazil made it unattractive to *fazendeiros*.

Despite the failure to disseminate plows during the period of this study, Brazilians successfully developed agricultural innovations when it was

---

[2] Eulalia Maria Lahmeyer Lobo, *História Político-Administrativo da Agricultura Brasileira, 1808–1889* (n/p: 1979), p. 80.

[3] S. V. Vigneron Jousselandiére, *Novo manual pratico da agricultura intertropical: seguido do calendario do agricultor de todos os mezes do anno e de conselhos de medicina, tudo fruito de 37 annos de experiencia de um lavrador pratico do Brasil* (Rio de Janeiro: E. & H. Laemmert, 1860), p. 32.

practical and expedient to do so. The final section of this chapter examines the invention of agricultural machinery – primarily in the coffee sector – that met Brazilian needs. As Luís Ribeiro observes, coffee machinery proliferated on plantations in the 1870s and 1880s, contributing to the ongoing growth of coffee exports even as the number of slave laborers declined.[4] The productivity of the expanding coffee frontier in Rio de Janeiro, São Paulo, and Minas Gerais propelled Brazil to the position of global leader in coffee exports by the second half of the nineteenth century, a development that was facilitated by Brazilian technological innovation.[5] Imported coffee-processing machines competed with Brazilian inventions in the 1850s and 1860s, but by the turn of the twentieth century, Brazilian manufacturers dominated the production of coffee equipment and also emerged as global suppliers of processing machinery.[6] Where plows failed, coffee processors flourished.

To Plow or Not to Plow

From a twenty-first-century perspective, the plow seems an unlikely hero in our narrative. Present-day popular imaginings of nineteenth-century innovation conjure more spectacular examples of technology: the railroad, the telephone, and the steamship, for example. But in the 1800s the plow was more than an instrument for shaping fields; it was a symbol of civilization, particularly for agricultural and frontier nations like the United States and Brazil. A US observer extolled the virtues of a plow on display at the 1876 Philadelphia Exhibition, "Instead of tearing open the bosom of mother earth with the root of a tree...the green covering rolls away with the perfection and grace of art itself, from the polished moulding-board [*sic*] of a Pittsburgh Steel Plow."[7] As this example brings to light, plows were a potent metaphor for progress; foremost, they provided the foundation of the settled agriculture that distinguished "primitive" hunter-gatherers from progressive modern societies

---

4 Luíz Cláudio M. Ribeiro, *Ofício Criador: invento e patente de máquina de beneficiar café no Brasil (1870–1910)*, (Master's thesis, Universidade de São Paulo, 1995), pp. 180–5.
5 Mario Samper and Radin Fernando, "Historical Statistics of Coffee Production and Trade from 1700 to 1960," in William Gervase Clarence-Smith and Steven Topik, eds., *The Global Coffee Economy in Africa, Asia, and Latin America, 1500–1989* (Cambridge: Cambridge University Press, 2003), pp. 422, and 432–3.
6 Hildete Pereira de Melo, "Coffee and the Rio de Janeiro Economy," in Clarence-Smith and Topik, eds., *The Global Coffee Economy*, pp. 375–7.
7 Thomas Bentley, *The Illustrated History of the Centennial Exhibition, Philadelphia, 1876* (New York: John Filmer, 1876), p. 23.

as John Gast's famous 1872 painting *Westward Ho! (American Progress)* illustrates.[8] A group of pioneers with oxen pulling a plow appears in the first plane of the painting, signaling their foundational role in the material and moral restructuring of the North American continent. It was for this reason that Brazilian modernizers saw the plow as more than a technological innovation; it had the potential to civilize the backward, "nomadic," slash-and-burn agriculture established during the colonial period. In contrast to the United States where plows represented the core of a technological arsenal that Europeanized the wilderness and displaced nomadic indigenous peoples, in Brazil it was the *rotineiros – fazendeiros, agregados*, and slaves alike – who were to be civilized through the symmetry of plowed fields. In nineteenth-century Brazil, plows were not envisioned as a tool for terra forming the wilderness as they were in the US, rather they were envisioned as essential for reforming agriculturalists, ending slave labor, and preserving forest resources for sustainable economic uses.

The call to introduce plows in Brazil comprised an important component of economic revitalization during the Pombaline reforms of the late colonial period, although the instrument ultimately met with little success.[9] After independence in 1822, it was statesman José Bonifácio who brought the question of plows, improved agriculture, and the end of slavery to the fore. Bonifácio, followed by the Sociedade Auxiliadora after him, decried the cycle of environmental destruction that resulted from slash-and-burn cultivation.[10] The target of Bonifácio's criticism was twofold: the swidden agriculture that laid waste to Brazilian forests, and slavery, which he viewed as an uncivilized practice that perpetuated backward agriculture:

... when that abominable method of farming is at an end, by which we go on, in rapid progression, cutting down forests and laying the surface bare to the powerful action of the sun; once the improvements in European agriculture are introduced among us, no doubt, with only a few laborers and by the aid of ploughs and other useful implements, the cultivation of our soil will advance rapidly, our estates will become more organized and attractive, and the land, by being better worked, will be rendered more productive. Nature, wise and provident, in every

---

[8] Richard Grusin, *Nature, Technology, and the Creation of America's National Parks* (Cambridge: Cambridge University Press, 2004), pp. 71–2.

[9] Warren Dean, *With Broadax and Firebrand: The Destruction of the Brazilian Atlantic Forest* (Berkeley: University of California Press, 1995), p. 101; J. H. Galloway, "Agricultural Reform and the Enlightenment in Late Colonial Brazil," *Agricultural History*, 53:4 (1979), pp. 778–9.

[10] Bonifácio was also influenced by Physiocratic ideology, Nícia Vilela Luz, *A Luta Pela Industrialização do Brasil* (São Paulo: Difusão Européia do Livro, 1961), pp. 15–16.

part of the globe, affords the means necessary for the ends of civil society, and no country requires forced and foreign labourers to become cultivated and rich.[11]

Bonifácio's call to replace the destructive practices of Brazilian agriculture with the plow echoed forcibly in the pages of *O Auxiliador*.[12] Yet *rotineiros* proved frustratingly resistant, society members complained, to the adoption of new machinery from the simplest plows to the latest in steam-powered apparatuses, fertilizers, irrigation systems, and other improvements. For Rodrigues, the "nomadic" character of Brazilian agriculture was its most backward feature; within one or two generations cultivation moved into new areas as established plantations lost their fertility, devouring ever larger sections of virgin forest. The task of burning and clearing the forest was undertaken by slaves, hired hands, or free rural farmers who comprised the vanguard of settlement in new regions. Free poor settlers, referred to as *posseiros* (squatters), cleared small plots in unclaimed or public lands hidden by thick forest in an effort to gain land independently away from maurading livestock that damaged crops and the yoke of paternalism imposed upon them in settled regions. As larger and more powerful landholders expanded into the forest, *posseiros* were forced to become *agregados* (sharecroppers), or to abandon their plots for more remote locations, pushing the process of forest destruction and depletion further into the interior.[13]

Whether completed by *posseiros*, slaves, or hired clearers, the ash produced by burning the dense foliage provided a rich fertilizer for crops, with coffee becoming the predominant cultivar in the expanding agricultural lands of the southeastern provinces by the 1840s. At the same time and in spite of its fertility, the debris of the forest created obstacles that made mechanized cultivation difficult; manual laborers using hoes were still the most efficient method for planting new crops among charred stumps and branches, especially in the hillsides that *fazendeiros* preferred

---

[11] José Bonifácio de Andrada e Silva, "Memoir addressed to the General Constituent and Legislative Assembly of the Empire of Brazil on Slavery!," William Walton, trans., (London: A. Redford and W. Robins, 1825) in *Obras Científicas e Sociais de José Bonifácio de Andrada e Silva, coligadas e reproduzidas por Edgard de Cerqueira Falcão*, Vol. II (São Paulo: Revista dos Tribunais, 1963), p. 183. Bonifácio was also an advocate of the plow as an improvement over slave labor, " ... 20 working slaves require 20 hoes, the expense of which could be replaced with only one plow," p. 185.

[12] José Augusto Pádua, *Um Sopro de Destruição: pensamento político e crítica ambiental no Brasil escravista (1786–1888)* (Rio de Janeiro: Jorge Zahar, 2002), pp. 174–7, and 244–6.

[13] Mario Grynszpyn, in Márcia Motta, ed, *Diccionário da Terra* (Rio de Janeiro: Civilização Brasileira, 2005), s.v. "Posseiro."

for coffee plantations in order to better supervise slaves. Under this system agriculturalists needed continual sources of virgin forest in order to remain economically successful past the productive life of a given section of land.

Another problem with slash-and-burn agriculture, argued Rodrigues and members of the Sociedade Auxiliadora, was that *fazendeiros* also depended on reserves of virgin forest to supply wood for running sugar mills, construction projects, and other plantation needs. The heavy demands placed on forest resources for all aspects of plantation agriculture resulted in a voracious frontier that consumed a seemingly endless supply of forest and slaves. As *fazendeiros* searched for new sources of virgin forest, and the cycle of violent confrontation between rival claimants, burning, planting, and depletion repeated, the negative impact on social relationships and the environment amplified. The low market value of land that resulted from this cycle, and the destruction of forests that modernizers argued could be exploited for more sustainable economic uses, as Chapter 3 illustrated, were at the root of the social problems generated by slash-and-burn cultivation. The plow, modernizers declared, was the perfect remedy.[14]

The low value of agricultural land and the ongoing rural violence it produced were the most egregious result of burning the forest, according to Rodrigues. One of the biggest benefits of plowing regimes, he argued, was growth in the monetary value of land. Under the current system of slash-and-burn cultivation the value of cultivated land decreased within a few generations as soils lost their fertility, rendering it useless as collateral for financing improvements such as agricultural machinery, irrigation systems, or buildings. Citing a plantation in Louisiana that employed the latest water pumps, steam-powered sugar mills, and plows even while it still depended on slave labor, Rodrigues argued that the same technology applied in Brazil would build up equity in land (as occurred in the United States) in a virtuous and self-sustaining cycle of economic growth that would ultimately result in social improvement and settled agriculture.[15]

Here Rodrigues alluded to ongoing confrontations between *fazendeiros* who settled claims to contested rural land through coercion and violence. The Maranhense published his *apedido* ten years after the

[14] See Pádua for a further examination of the social problems attributed to swidden agriculture, *Um Sopro*, ch. 5.

[15] Antônio Marques Rodrigues, "Duas palavras sobre a nossa agricultura," *Publicações a Pedido, JC*, December 23, 1860.

enactment of the *Lei de Terras* (1850), the state's attempt to regularize land registries and reform the *sesmaria* land grant system inherited from the colonial period. Despite the new law, rural violence over land continued, and in some cases increased. Rodrigues lamented that the ongoing abandonment of land spurred further violence, which in his view was the root reason for the destabilization of rural society and an obstacle to economic growth over the long term.[16] It is important to note, as Márcia Motta observes, that land conflicts were not only about access to territory. Some of the fiercest conflicts between powerful *fazendeiros* were held over access to what was in the end insignificant parcels of land; the real issue at stake was control over the rural inhabitants of the region. Land did not increase in economic value over time, but controlling large swaths of territory had enormous social and political value that lead to other sources of wealth.[17] For this reason Rodrigues charged that land registries were an essential component in legitimizing property rights and ending rural violence. Vague and often undocumented delineations of property worked to the advantage of the powers that be as they dominated both access to land and control of the rural poor.[18] Plowing would solve all of these problems, Rodrigues asserted, as it was only settled agriculture that promoted a much needed emotional connection to the land with the potential to transform (though he did not say it directly) the violent passions unleashed in rural conflicts: "[The plow]... results in peaceful customs, good habits, honored traditions, from which the most pure filial affections voluntarily take root, grow, and flourish in the home..."[19] Rodrigues' prose is evocative of Domingo Sarmiento's critique of the wandering Argentine gauchos who provided the military might for caudillo President Manual Rosas. He saw the gauchos as the chief impediment to establishing settled communities of more industrious peoples on the Pampas.[20] In both cases the negative view of rural "nomadism" underscored the nineteenth-century association of settled agriculture with civilization. With the advent of plows, Rodrigues declared in a subtle challenge to the status quo, "... land registries will appear...," definitively ending the violence against both forest and humans.[21] Beyond the potential

---

[16] Dean, pp. 147–9.
[17] Dean, p. 148; Motta, *Nas Fronteiras do Poder: conflito e direito à terra no Brasil do século XIX* (Rio de Janeiro: Vício de Leitura: 1998), pp. 38–9.
[18] Rodrigues, "Duas palavras..."   [19] *Ibid.*
[20] Domingo Sarmiento, *Facundo: Or, Civilization and Barbarism*, Mary Mann, trans., Ilan Stavans, ed., (New York: Penguin, 1998), pp. 19–22.
[21] Rodrigues, "Duas Palavras..."

for economic growth, Brazilian reformers like Rodrigues envisioned plows as a way to quietly reform powerful rural interests.

Caetano da Rocha Pacova, an agronomist and proponent of improved agriculture also from Maranhão, argued that plows would hasten the shift to free labor in his 1859 treatise on agricultural education. Pacova asserted that the plow was crucial for rehabilitating depleted agricultural land, the location of which, he pointedly observed, was already conveniently located near cities and waterways. Again, plows were the key innovation, rendering work more profitable for agriculturalists and thusly more attractive to free laborers:

[Let us t]ransform the basis of labor; sink the plow into these so-called "exhausted" lands – almost all of which are located close to cities and towns, on the banks of our navigable rivers; add life and variation to our cultivation through manuring and crop rotation; provide perfected instruments that produce more and tire the worker less; then we will find ourselves in the position to offer our laborers good salaries, [and] abundant and healthy food; free labor, whether Brazilian or immigrant, will become a reality; only with this system will the free laborer achieve a level of well-being which has not been possible in the virgin forests to which they have been directed.[22]

Rocha Pacova's assessment of the social inequities of slash-and-burn agriculture, like his fellow Maranhense Rodrigues, was also inspired by the low market value of depleted land. The frenetic energy unleashed by slash-and-burn agriculture created wealth for a privileged few over short periods of twenty to thirty years, but again did not build value in the land itself.[23] Moreover, the link between slavery and the low value (or inexistence) of wage labor illustrates that far more was at stake for modernizers than the superficial transformation of agricultural techniques. For Pacova, the plow was the answer to Brazil's larger problems of slavery, soil erosion, abandoned land, and scarcity of wage labor. Though Pacova and Rodrigues were careful to soften their suggestions with words like civilization and improvement, for both, the plow clearly had the potential to engender a "calculated revolution" in Brazil.[24]

---

[22] Caetano da Rocha Pacova, *Apontamentos sobre a Necessidade de Uma Escola de Agricultura, Theoria e Pratica* (Rio de Janeiro: Tip. de N.L. Vianna e Filhos, 1859), pp. 12–13.

[23] Pádua further discusses the observations of Pacova and the Baron of Capanema on the social consequences of slash-and-burn agriculture, *Um Sopro*, pp. 244–50.

[24] This was Sociedade Auxiliadora member José Pereira Rego's term from Chapter 2, "Relatorio dos trabalhos da Sociedade do anno corrente," *O Auxiliador*, November 1867, p. 459.

Mechanical Marvels

By the 1840s, Sociedade Auxiliadora members began calling for the establishment of agricultural schools in order to more efficiently reeducate agriculturalists and disseminate information on improved cultivation and machinery, a principal aim of which was to replace slaves with labor-saving machinery. Frederico Burlamaque, an opponent of slavery, enthusiastic researcher of technology from abroad, and an advocate for domestic agricultural innovation, as outlined in previous chapters, was also a proponent of agricultural technology as the pathway to modernize Brazil. In his 1837 publication described in Chapter 1, *Memória analítica acerca do comércio de escravos e acerca dos males da escravidão doméstica* (Analytical Treatise on the Harmful Effects of the Slave Trade and Domestic Slavery), Burlamaque declared that the replacement of slaves with machines, "far from being a great ill, will on the contrary lead to new prosperity through stimulating production on the *fazenda* and further developing industry."[25] Here, Burlamaque alluded to the recent abolition of the Slave Trade in an 1831 treaty with Great Britain. Though in practice the treaty was inconsistently enforced by the Brazilian government and did little to abate the arrival of new slaves (the illegal importation of slaves into Brazil continued and indeed, increased in the 1840s, primarily to meet demand in the coffee sector), the call for the end of slavery was a repeated, if sometimes understated, theme in Burlamaque's writings and *O Auxiliador*.[26]

Burlamaque argued that agricultural technology was an important tool for diminishing the number of enslaved Africans in Brazil and pointed to an example of an enterprising *fazendeiro* in São Paulo who had created a simple pestle and lever mechanism for de-hulling coffee beans called a *"monjollos"* (*monjolo*) that replaced the labor of twelve slaves. Pointedly, he observed that machinery need not be expensive nor especially sophisticated to be effective, an observation intended to reassure planters unwilling or unable to make large capital investments in machinery without proof of its usefulness.[27] Thirty years later, Confederate

---

[25] Frederico Burlamaque, *Memoria analytica a'cerca do commercio de escravos e a'cerca dos malles da escravidão domestica* (Rio de Janeiro: Tip Commercial Fluminense, 1837), p. 115.

[26] Robert Conrad, *The Destruction of Brazilian Slavery, 1850–1888* (Berkeley: University of California Press, 1972), pp. 22–3.

[27] Burlamaque, *Memoria analytica*, p. 116. For a further description of the *monjolo* see Stanley Stein's classic study, *Vassouras: A Brazilian Coffee County, 1850–1900: The*

observer John Gaston had a more disparaging view of the *monjolo*, though he too admitted that its simplicity made it accessible to those without the means to purchase better quality machines:

...though much more efficient means have been devised, of accomplishing all that can be done by the Monjolo, yet its ready adaptation, with a very small stream of water, renders it useful in the hands of many, who cannot employ other labor-saving appliances. It pounds coffee,...hominy, farina, and would beat dough finely.[28]

These examples demonstrate that Brazilian agriculturalists adopted labor-saving devices when it was practical to do so.

Burlamaque's *Manual de Máquinas, Instrumentos e Motores Agrícolas* (Manual of Agricultural Machines, Motors, and Instruments), published twenty-two years after his treatise calling for the end of slavery, reveals his ongoing dedication to technological solutions for backward Brazilian agriculture.[29] Using the same critical tone toward *rotineiros* as he would later take in his posthumously published 1870 educational manual *Catechismo de Agricultura* (Catechism of agriculture), Burlamaque revealed his ongoing exasperation with the state of Brazilian cultivation:

Our first intention was to give this manual the title of 'Mechanical Agriculture'; we desisted because this...requires information that presupposes certain accepted knowledge that the majority of our readers do not possess. Therefore the writer, like the orator, must use language that the listener will understand or suffer the risk of neither being heard nor read.[30]

The manual contained more than two hundred pages of descriptive text and illustrated plates, demonstrating Burlamaque's wide-ranging knowledge about advances in agricultural machinery in other parts of the globe, including the US, Europe, and China. Collected from agricultural treatises, international exhibition catalogs, and foreign journals, Burlamaque described machines and instruments ranging from shovels and pitchforks to the most sophisticated steam machines of the day. He also placed

Roles of Planter and Slave in a Plantation Society (Princeton: Princeton University Press, 1958, 1985), pp. 36–7.

[28] John McFadden Gaston, *Hunting a Home in Brazil. The Agricultural Resources and Other Characteristics of the Country. Also, The Manners and Customs of the Inhabitants* (Philadelphia: King & Baird, Printers, 1867), pp. 82–3.

[29] Frederico Leopoldo Cezar Burlamaque, *Manual de Maquinas, Instrumentos e Motores Agricolas* (Rio de Janeiro: Tip. N.L. Vianna & Filhos, 1859).

[30] Burlamaque, *Manual de Maquinas*, p. 3.

special emphasis on plows, which comprised the largest category of illustrations (39 out of 186 diagrams or 21 percent of the total). The manual further illustrates that Brazilians closely followed the development of new technologies abroad, and they actively participated in networks of information sharing.

Burlamaque extolled the virtues of one of the agricultural marvels of the day: self-propelled, mechanical "steam-horses" first developed in Great Britain. Multi-taskers par excellence, they sowed, harvested, hauled, and processed crops. Enthralled by the range of tasks the machines could perform, Burlamaque enthused, "You can see for yourself the incredible convenience of these machines, especially in countries with labor shortages. The time is coming when they will be indispensable for agriculture in all nations, from the tropics to the... Pampas."[31]

One steam-horse in particular, a sprawling contrivance with multiple applications constructed by an English inventor appeared in the *Manual de Máquinas* (1859), the *Revista Agrícola* (1870), and again in the *Catechismo de Agricultura* (1870) (Fig. 4.1).[32] The machine consisted of a complicated convergence of tubes, wheels, levers, six plows, and a coal-fired engine. It required two operators to steer with additional workers to direct its six plows. The main wheels were enormous – taller than a person – and turned on a "continuous track" of movable wooden boards that were attached to the wheels and provided traction. The plows moved "in turn with the axle in such a way that they all rotated at the same time," propelling the machine over the earth "like a steamship in water." Loud, slow-moving, and trailing a thick veil of coal smoke, the invention more likely crawled through fields like a belching devil.[33] Nonetheless, the machine captivated audiences on both sides of the Atlantic, providing a window into the novelty and marvel that the new inventions of the nineteenth century inspired in onlookers, even on paper and from afar. One senses Burlamaque's awe – and perhaps envy – when considering what such inventions might accomplish in Brazil's fertile soils. And he was not alone. The US press also praised the steam-horse's labor-saving

---

[31] Burlamaque, *Manual de Maquinas*, note, p. 51.

[32] Burlamaque, *Manual de Maquinas*, pp. 51–2; *Revista Agricola do Imperial Instituto Fluminense de Agricultura*, April 1870, pp. 55–8; *Manual de Maquinas*, Plate 13; and *Catechismo de Agricultura* (Rio de Janeiro: Tip. Deseseis de Julho), Endplate, fig. 20.

[33] Burlamaque, *Manual de Maquinas*, p. 52. The machine's "continuing tract" was a precursor for the traction system on tanks and caterpillar machinery.

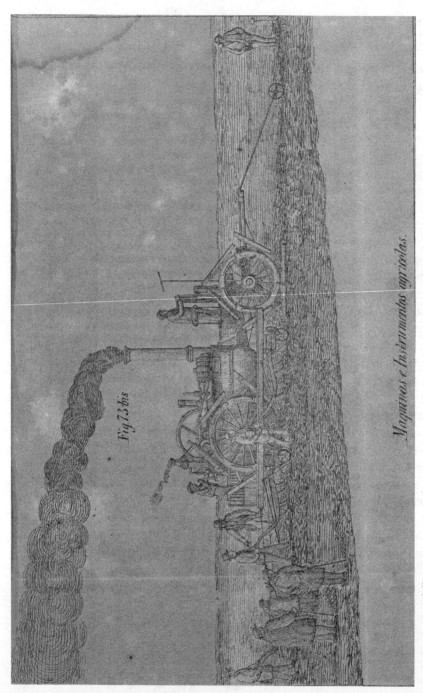

Maquinas e Instrumentos agricolas.

FIGURE 4.1. Boydell's steam-powered tractor. *Source:* Frederico Burlamaque *Manual de Maquinas, Instrumentos e Motores Agricolas* (Rio de Janeiro: Tip. N.L. Vianna & Filhos, 1859), Plate 13. Courtesy of the Acervo da Fundação Biblioteca Nacional, Brazil.

potential, remarking that it was especially suited for the "level lands" of Illinois – an important point that we will return to shortly.[34]

Notwithstanding its impressive list of applications, the steam-horse most likely received a skeptical reception from Brazilian agriculturalists who encountered its description in Burlmaque's manual. Aside from its expense, it would have been difficult if not impossible to transport to remote locations and utterly useless among the stubble and debris of deforested and hilly fields. Indeed, though it looked impressive in print, the machine's innovative wheels proved fragile and impractical in all but the most level of ground. English agriculturalists complained that the machines' eight tons (!) compacted the earth underneath its tracks, which rendered the soil impossible to cultivate and defeated its main purpose. Furthermore, "the machine was wont to tip over sideways when passing over ruts or stones."[35] Even in Great Britain, where steam-horses were the most successful, the machine was fraught with complications.[36] It might have been a noteworthy representation of the possibility of technology, and a powerful metaphor for progress that dazzled the members of the Sociedade Auxiliadora, but its practical application was sorely matched to Brazilian needs.

The steam-horse is an extreme example, but nonetheless illustrates that a major obstacle to adopting agricultural innovations in Brazil centered on the difficulty and expense of transporting large and heavy items to remote *fazendas*. As will be discussed in Chapter 5, before the construction of railroad lines, ox carts and the even more ubiquitous mule trains provided the principal mode of transportation into the hinterland for supplies large and small, as Gaston observed upon encountering a train of a thousand mules returning from the port of Santos to the interior of São Paulo in 1864:

... [the mules were] laden with various kinds of merchandise for the consumption of the people of the interior; or in some instances with pieces of machinery for the improvement of their industrial appliances. In one instance, a mule was carrying two immense boxes which literally covered it from head to tail.[37]

Until railroads facilitated shipping, the *serra* (the coastal escarpment that separated the port of Santos from coffee-producing regions in the

---

[34] "Steam Plows," *Harper's Weekly*, September 12, 1857, p. 589, as cited in Clark C. Spence, *God Speed the Plow: The Coming of Steam Cultivation to Great Britain* (Urbana: University of Illinois Press, 1960), p. 34.

[35] *Ibid.*, p. 37. [36] *Ibid.*, p. 37 and 161. [37] Gaston, *Hunting a Home*, p. 53.

interior) proved a formidable barrier to the rapid dissemination of agricultural machinery; only the wealthiest had the means to pay for the expense. A cotton gin manufactured in the US, for instance, was transported by oxen to the *fazenda* of José Vergueiro in Rio de Janeiro province though, tellingly, it had been modified to produce smaller cotton bales that could be moved to market by mule.[38] Portability and durability were indeed selling points as illustrated in an advertisement from 1860 for an imported coffee and rice processor: "[This] machine, the most perfected of its kind, . . . is difficult to damage and easy to transport."[39] In the face of such challenges, agriculturalists wanted proof of results before purchasing new, untried, and unwieldy equipment. In 1853, a *fazendeiro* requested that the Sociedade Auxiliadora confirm that an imported "elliptical corn mill" could indeed grind kernels and cob together, and inquired whether it could be powered by water, "The cost of the [mill] obliges me to fully consider [its usefulness] before purchasing it," he remarked.[40]

Notwithstanding the Sociedade Auxiladora's long-standing criticism of *rotineiros*, the society's annual report for 1869 recognized the impracticability of many European agricultural innovations in Brazil, as exemplified by a collection of miniature models of German machines displayed in a special gallery at the União e Indústria agricultural school located in Juíz de Fora, Minas Gerais. Unlike Brazil, German fields had been cultivated for centuries, and "no longer offered resistance" to agricultural instruments, nor did they possess the "same quantity of stumps and

---

[38] Gaston, p. 103.

[39] "Annuncios," *JC*, January 16, 1860. Portability and reliability of agricultural machinery remain important considerations for Brazilian agriculture, as the website of one of the world's largest manufacturer of coffee processing equipment claims. Located in São Paulo state, the company sells coffee processing equipment in Brazil and to the developing world:

Pinhalense equipment has been especially developed for the conditions that usually prevail in the developing world . . . Pinhalense plants and equipment are easy to operate and maintain. They are made to last, even in the absence of adequate servicing.

Pinhalense produces a full range of equipment in all of its lines: coffee, cocoa, tea, nuts, seeds and grains. Many machines are offered in several sizes in order to be compatible with farm use, small-to-medium installations and large-scale processing plants. Almost all pieces of equipment may be diesel or gasoline driven for mobility and use in remote areas.

Pinhalense corporate website is www.pinhalense.com.br/site/eng/index.htm. My thanks to Leo Goldfeld for this reference.

[40] *O Agricultor Brazileiro*, Vol. I, December 1853, p. 15.

stones... eroded land, or swamps." European technology worked best in the well-used fields where it was developed and did not transfer well to Brazil's rugged geography and recently cleared agricultural frontier. The models were useful for "inspiring the spirit, enlivening the intellect, and facilitating the modification" of machinery that would better meet the needs of Brazilian cultivators, the report's author proclaimed.[41] Even the Confederate Gaston, who roundly discommended the absence of plows on the *fazendas* he visited, provides evidence for the difficulty of using the instruments:

This [recently cleared] land had the timber felled and dried, when fire was applied and burnt over the whole, destroying all the leaves and small limbs, and yet leaving the larger limbs and trunks upon the ground. In the midst of this network, it was expected to set out the coffee trees, and between them to plant corn and beans with the expectation of getting a full crop of the latter articles. Of course no ploughing is practicable, and all the work is done with the hoe.... [42]

Jousselandiére also observed that in "newly cleared fields it is only possible to employ the hoe due to the [the remants of] tree stumps, roots, [and] stones," some of which could be up to nine feet in circumference with even larger root systems.[43] Hardwood species in particular proved difficult to cut and extract, rendering stumps a serious obstacle to mechanized cultivation. Equipment and machines for removing roots were featured in *O Auxiliador* and the *Revista Agrícola*, though it remains unclear that they were experimented with or successfully adopted.

The agronomist Pacova cast a more sympathetic eye on the *rotineiros'* reluctance to adopt untried technologies: "... [Brazilian] cultivators recognize that backward techniques are their downfall, but none have been able to cast off this Tunic of Nessus... "[44] Agriculturalists' reluctance to embrace mechanical innovations resulted from the very real difficulties of adapting imported instruments and machinery to local conditions:

---

[41] *O Auxiliador*, "Escola Agricola da Companhia União e Indústria," September 1870, pp. 474–5. Adapting machinery to local conditions remained a challenge for developing nations, Yovanna Pineda, "Financing Manufacturing Innovation in Argentina, 1890–1930," *Business History Review*, 83:3 (Autumn 2009), p. 558.

[42] Gaston, pp. 86–7; Jousselandiére, p. 48.

[43] "What force would be necessary to remove or uproot... a sapucaí, a copal, a ourucurana, a sapupema of a circumference of nine feet, whose tap roots sink into the earth to the depth of fifteen or twenty feet, and whose lateral roots spread for great distances?" Jousselandiére, p. 42.

[44] The "tunic of Nessus" was the poisoned shirt that weakened Hercules and led to his demise.

We know of many laudable attempts to introduce...instruments of cultivation...that are successfully employed in Europe and North America. But, in general, these attempts have lacked a precise study of the specific circumstances of our rural establishments. [This lack] has resulted in the little profit that has been accomplished...

Instruments of excellent service have been ordered many times, experimented with, condemned, and shortly thereafter abandoned. There are many reasons for this; the incapacity or bad faith of the individual who selected it, ignorance on the part of the person who put it together or used it, and the difficulty if not impossibility, in certain locations, of repairing the slightest malfunction of the instrument. Those of us who know the truth...do not agree with those who only have disdain for the backwardness of our agriculture...No. There are real difficulties that should be studied, as well as the ways in which to overcome them...[45]

As these examples illustrate, obstacles to agricultural improvement extended beyond the physical barriers of steep *serras* and rough fields to the difficulties of maintaining, repairing, and customizing imported machines in remote locations without facilities for repairs and maintenance. Large *fazendas* were self-sufficient enterprises complete with slave-operated smithies and carpenter shops that maintained and constructed plantation necessities, resources that were not available to less affluent agriculturalists.[46] An 1870 patent by a Brazilian inventor for a coffee-drying system comprised entirely of wood received high praise from the Sociedade Auxiliadora's committee on machinery. The simple design employed readily available Brazilian lumber that could be constructed on-site in *fazenda* workshops, overcoming challenges to transportation, maintenance, and repair. Another solution was offered in the 1870s by the Rio-based Lidgerwood company, a manufacturer of coffee machinery that advertised a team of "expert engineers" ready to travel to the interior to service machinery.[47]

---

[45] Pacova, p. 7.

[46] Herbert Smith described a plantation in the 1870s in Rio de Janeiro province:

> A large plantation...is a little world in itself; there are smithies and workshops, machines for preparing mandicoa, a saw-mill, a corn-mill, a sugar-can mill, and a still...At one end of the inclosure there is a brick-kiln, and near by a pottery, where most of the pots [for the nursery] were prepared. The machinery is moved, partly by a turbine wheel, but principally by a large steam-engine..., Herbert H. Smith, "Coffee Culture in Brazil," *Scribner's Monthly: an Illustrated Magazine for the People*, Volume XIX, November 1879 to April 1880, pp. 232–3.

[47] "Milford and Lidgerwood," *Almanak Administrativo, Mercantil, e Industrial* (Rio de Janeiro: Tip. Laemmert, 1876), p. 52.

An additional defense of *rotineiros* that underscored the difficulties of transportation and the high cost of machinery appeared in Rio Grande do Sul in 1861:

Our farmers have been accused of possessing an obstinate spirit of backwardness. Yet even if this is true in part, the accusation is not entirely justified. Only large landowners have the resources to undertake the expensive and adventurous experiments from which new discoveries arise. Our farmers are not in the same [financial] position, nor do they possess knowledge [about farming practices] in other countries. Because of the difficulty of communication, and the large distances that separate them from centers of civilization, they continue with the usual processes that are commonly practiced, accompanied by new immigrants. This is the principle explanation for the backwardness of our agriculture.[48]

The report for the following year also lamented the fact that German immigrants adopted native agricultural practices rather than introducing improved European technologies, a fact attributed in part to the arrival of immigrants with no prior knowledge of farming. Instead of "Europeanizing" Brazil, they became "Brazilianized." In the end, existing Brazilian techniques proved more effective and cost-efficient than transporting costly and untried machinery to the interior.[49]

The criticisms of Gaston, Burlamaque, and other would-be reformers were also countered by practicing cultivators. Contrary to accusations of backwardness, many of the so-called *rotineiros* were well aware of new technologies. An 1878 agricultural treatise acknowledged that plows would render cultivation more efficient and productive, but declared that they were impossible to use until roots and debris were sufficiently decomposed, a process that could take many years.[50] Jousselandiére proclaimed that plowing and fertilizer did little to rejuvenate "exhausted" fields and was hardly "worth the trouble," and instead counseled that abandoned fields be turned over to pasture for livestock.[51] Additionally, a former

---

[48] *Relatório com que o conselheiro Joaquim Antão Fernandes Leão entregou a presidencia da provincia de S. Pedro do Rio Grande do Sul ao exm. sr. vice-presidente, commendador Patricio Correa da Camara* (Porto Alegre, Tip. do Jornal–A Ordem, 1861), p. 48.

[49] Jeffrey Lesser discusses the Brazilianization of immigrant identity and economic culture, *Negotiating National Identity* (Durham, NC: Duke University Press, 1999), pp. 7–9; See also Jean Roche, "La Colonisation Allemande et le Rio Grande do Sul," (Ph.D. dissertation, Faculté des Lettres de L'Université de Paris, Institute des Hautes Études de L' Amérique Latin, 1959), pp. 232–3.

[50] Francisco Peixoto de Lacerda Werneck, *Memória sobre a fundação de uma fazenda na província do Rio de Janeiro (Edição original de 1847 e edição modificada e acrescida de 1878)* (Rio de Janeiro: Fundação Casa de Rui Barbosa, 1985), pp. 227–8.

[51] Jousselandiére, p. 33.

cereal farmer complained in 1885 that he switched crops because he was unable to produce wheat as cheaply as foreign agriculturalists due to the higher costs of transportation, fertilizer, and the difficulty of adopting agricultural machinery in Brazil:

Sirs, I will tell you now why I have not continued cultivating wheat.

1. It is not possible to compete with foreign production without using the same arsenal of instruments developed for wheat cultivation, such as sowers, mowers, bailers, and steam-powered threshers.
2. Such instruments are only advantageous when employed on large, well-worked tracts of land... [yet] only with great difficulty are we able to conquer our agricultural land from... old and second-growth forests and from the hilly nature of our soil.
3. Fertilizing wheat fields with lime is a necessity of rational cultivation, especially for virgin land. My land is deficient in lime, yet it is so expensive as to be beyond the reach of agricultural application.
4. We are also lacking improved mills for wheat and oats, and the freight on the D. Pedro II railroad for the respective flours produced therein costs *thirty times* [emphasis in the original] the freight on the railroad between Chicago and New York.[52]

Because of these conditions, Brazil was at a disadvantage when competing with temperate crops cultivated in the new agricultural lands of the US Midwest and the Argentine Pampas.[53] The level and obstacle-free landscape in these regions was ideal for the large-scale mechanical cultivation of cereal staples such as wheat, corn, and oats.[54] Furthermore, the rapidly growing and less expensively constructed network of railroad

---

[52] "Correspondencia," *Revista Agricola do Imperial Instituto Fluminense de Agricultura*, December 1885, p. 237.

[53] William Cronan describes the "grid" pattern of new agricultural lands in Illinois in the 1830s and 1840s, "Rectangular fields meant that farmers and horses could cut long, straight swaths whether they pulled plows, harrows, or newfangled tools like reapers. Because farm fields were large, uniform, and relatively free of rocks or other obstructions, prairie farmers enjoyed economies of scale which left them better able to adopt new agricultural machinery than many of their eastern counterparts..." *Nature's Metropolis: Chicago and the Great West* (New York: W. W. Norton & Co., 1991), p. 102; Steam-powered plows were introduced into Argentina by 1868 where they successfully tilled the rich sod of the Pampas. Clark C. Spence, *God Speed the Plow: the coming of steam cultivation to Great Britain* (Urbana, IL: University of Illinois Press, 1960), p. 158.

[54] Argentina experienced an agricultural revolution in the 1870s facilitated by imported machinery; they emerged as a major exporter of wheat by the end of the nineteenth century, Pineda, pp. 545, 546–7, and 561–2; and David Rock, *Argentina 1516–1987:*

lines in the US and Argentina linked cities, internal markets, and ports, ensuring profits for producers in quickly expanding agricultural areas. Transitioning tropical forest to agriculturally productive land was more time-consuming. Jousselandiére advised that new fields be started two to three years before cultivation to allow dense layers of wood and brush to decay after burning.[55] In contrast, polished steel plow blades churned the rich soil of the pampas and the thick prairie sod of the Midwest into arable fields in as short as one season. These circumstances contributed to the expansion and dependence on the coffee sector in Brazil, a tropical commodity for which Brazil was at a competitive advantage.

Geographical obstacles to the adoption of technological innovation were not the only issue in modernizing agriculture. An 1871 report on cultivation in Bahia hinted at the cultural and social values that worked against the plow:

Cultivation, in general, is very poorly executed. The plow is used more to "etch out lines" in the earth than it is used to [properly] turn the soil.

On this point, the old-fashioned hoes perform better, and it is for this reason that many cultivators and landowners extol this old instrument, while failing to give credit to the [plow]...

The land is fertile and inexhaustible, they say... fertilizer is a wasteful and unnecessary expense, the earth itself is the best builder of roads, and the preparation of the land with the plow and its accessories is a luxury of the gardener who is more interested in aesthetics than the [the final product]. Against such attitudes it is absolutely impossible to implement a workable reform, and those planters who attempt it... eventually give up in the face of their neighbor's sarcasm. They even fall victim to malicious acts that sabotage, if not render useless, the work already accomplished.[56]

If we take at face value the author's charge of *fazendeiros'* general hostility to new technology, it appears that social practices played a part in the failure to disseminate the plow. Perhaps the expense of new equipment bred resentment among fellow agriculturalists, especially those with less means to purchase expensive imported instruments. There was also a fear that machines would disrupt established work regimes and that slaves would remain idle. Sociedade Auxiliadora members argued that plows resulted

---

From Spanish Colonization to Alfonsín (Berkeley: University of California Press, 1985, 1987), p. 136.

[55] Jousselandiére, p. 30.

[56] "A Situação Agricola da Provincia da Bahia, em 1870," *Revista Agricola do Imperial Instituto Fluminense de Agricultura*, June 1871, p. 17.

in economic benefits to agriculturalists, but this tack did not address the social value of slaves and political control over rural land. *Fazendeiros* were reluctant to relinquish the status and authority associated with slavery and *agregados*. Additionally, planters in São Paulo preferred to plant coffee trees on hills (terrain that was not conducive to plowing) as this made it easier to oversee slaves during harvest time.

The passage also underscores a deeper and long-standing attitude about the abundance of Brazilian natural resources that would have made paying for expensive materials such as chemical fertilizers or machines appear redundant at best and extravagant at worst. The perceived unending fertility of the nation's tropical landscape underwrote the belief that Brazilian forests were inexhaustible, a characteristic that scholars have identified as the driving force in the destruction of Brazil's Atlantic Forest.[57] Finally, differences between tropical and temperate agriculture were also most likely at play. The pleasing linear aesthetic of plowed fields represented modernity and progress for agricultural modernizers. Yet, while monocrops such as wheat and corn planted in straight rows facilitated mechanization as Argentina and the US Midwest illustrate, the practice was better suited to temperate climates where pests and plant diseases are fewer in number than the tropics where biodiversity amplifies both. As James C. Scot observes, twentieth-century North Atlantic agronomists viewed polycropping (planting different cultivars together in one field) and slash-and-burn cultivation as disorganized and wasteful. Yet these techniques were well suited to combat pests in tropical environments like Brazil. In African and Latin American cultivation, for example, polycropping discouraged the predation of blights and insects and ensured food supplies in the advent of the failure of one crop.[58] Slash-and-burn cultivation was also a successful tactic for combatting pests, at least for the short term, as it moved crops to new locations away from the concentrations of birds, mammals, and especially ants that plagued nineteenth-century *fazendeiros*.[59]

---

[57] See Pádua, p. 73; The expansion of the sugar sector in early nineteenth-century Cuba followed a similar trajectory, Reinaldo Funes Monzote, *From Rainforest to Cane Field in Cuba: an Environmental History since 1492* (Chapel Hill: University of North Carolina Press, 2008), p. 128.

[58] James C. Scott, *Seeing Like a State: How Certain Schemes to Improve the Human Condition Have Failed* (New Haven, CT: Yale University Press, 1998), ch. 8, especially pps. 270–83.

[59] "Losses of standing crops to leaf-cutting ants were sometimes overmatched by the depredations of various mammals – armadillos, cotias, and peccaries – and by seed- and fruit-eating birds – among them maitacas, blackbirds, parakeets, parrots, and oropendola," Dean, p. 193.

The perception of plows as aesthetic instruments gestures toward a deeper rift between modernizers armed with books and diagrams and those they targeted for reform: knowledgeable agriculturalists with many years of practical experience. In the following passage, the planter Jousselandiére complained about the arrogance of immigrant farmers (though his criticism could have applied to Brazilian modernizers as well):

> [Many new immigrants only know agriculture]... through reading books, some of which are good while others are full of errors. They do not have the faintest idea of how to [begin cultivation] in the tropics, and even less about local difficulties. They possess the confidence that sometimes results [in success], but are also ignorant... In the end, their literary education and their intellectual faculties prevent them from believing that they are capable of failure. I have often recommended that new arrivals modify their ideas [but I have received the following response] when I attempted to offer advice, 'I did not come to Brazil to learn, but to instruct.' In the end, many are discredited, and finish in ruin.[60]

In other words, slash-and-burn agriculture employed by Brazilian *fazendeiros* made economic sense given the social and physical conditions in which they operated. Though the burning of forest caused irreparable environmental damage, soil erosion, and drought, all of which were infinitely more expensive in the long run than purchasing and transporting plows and improved machinery, the short-term profits were simply more attractive. Lumbering, rather than burning the forest (though not necessarily less destructive from an environmental perspective), was also often not economically rewarding. In contrast to the forests of North America where tree harvesting was facilitated by the concentration of usable species, Brazil's valuable trees were dispersed over large areas of land that challenged systematic logging. It was expensive and difficult to amass enough raw material once easily exploited forest was depleted or destroyed to make the endeavor profitable, even when transportation networks facilitated the process. The nation's tree species were also slow-growing and resistant to replanting outside of their complex, biodiverse forest habitat.[61] Preserving forests for other economic uses was not attractive in the short run and fraught with uncertainty from an economic perspective in the long run. Brazilian agriculturalists simply took the path of least resistance: the tried and true method of burning the forest into fertile ash. This practice depended on practical knowledge, abundant land, and enslaved or dependent rural laborers – all of which were available in Brazil. The social value of slaves and large numbers of *agregados* certainly also played a significant role in *fazendeiros'* reluctance to embrace new technologies and techniques, but it was not the only consideration. In the

[60] Jousselandiére, p. 48.   [61] Dean, pp. 136–9.

end, reformers' visions of neatly plowed Brazilian fields did not come to fruition in the nineteenth century. Nonetheless, agricultural innovation transformed Brazilian *fazendas* by the 1870s with the mechanization of the coffee sector.

Agricultural Patents

With the diminishing supply of slave labor, the need to improve the quality of exported products, and the high cost of free labor by the 1870s, the demand for machinery increased in the expanding coffee frontier in São Paulo in particular. Despite his criticisms of Brazilian cultivation, Gaston recorded many examples of agricultural innovation by the late 1860s, including a steam machine for washing and hulling coffee beans, a steam-powered sawmill, a cotton gin, and a cotton press on the plantation of José Vergueiro. The new machines replaced a water-powered coffee and sawmill still maintained on the property. Characteristic of many large *fazendas*, Vergueiro's plantation was a veritable village unto itself. It sported a smithy, a carpenter shop, and a brickyard. The on-site production of wagons and agricultural implements supported cultivation, while the brickyard produced tiles, pipes, and brick for construction of houses and farm buildings. Immigrants and slaves together supplied labor for the plantation. These examples illustrate two central points: wealthy *fazendeiros* increasingly began to solve the problem of moving equipment over unimproved roads by meeting a large portion of their construction and technological needs on-site, and *fazendas* themselves became local sites for technological innovation.

Brazil's patent record reinforces the importance of agricultural machinery, both invented domestically and introduced from abroad, after mid-century. Of 1,655 patents granted between 1850 and 1889, 27 percent applied to the agricultural sector. This is similar to the first wave of US agricultural innovation between 1790 and 1846 where 22 percent of patents were for agricultural machinery and implements.[62] It is also clear from Figure 4.2 that the coffee sector drove most of the innovation during this period; coffee patents comprised 46.3 percent (207 out of a total of 447) of all agricultural patents (Fig. 4.2). Patents for machines

---

[62] Patents for textile machinery and railroad equipment were two other important sectors of technology that proliferated in Brazil for the period in question reflecting their importance in transportation and early manufacturing, Leandro Malavota, *A Construção do Sistema a de Patentes no Brasil: um olhar histórico* (Rio de Janeiro: Editora Lumen Juris, 2011), p. 191.

AGRICULTURAL PATENTS 1850-1889 BY APPLICATION

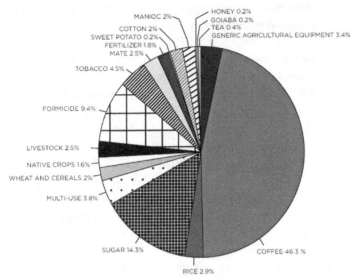

FIGURE 4.2. Agricultural Patents 1850–1889 by application. Figures compiled from the catalog of Privelégios Industriais for the years 1850 to 1889 at the Arquivo Nacional; the database of Brazilian legislation available at the Website of the Senado Federal, www.senado.gov.br/sf/; and the *Relatórios da Secretaria de Estado dos Negocios da Agricultura, Commercio e Obra, 1882–1889*, University of Chicago LAMP Website, http://brazil.crl.edu/bsd/bsd/hartness/agricultura .html. Patent Nos. 1477, 2837, 8899, 9014 are not included in this table. Table design: Alana Baldwin and Christina Frantom.

that processed sugar (64), tobacco (20), mate (11), and cotton (11) followed distantly, correlating both to their lesser importance in the export economy and the availability of foreign inventions. Plagues of leaf-cutting ants in São Paulo also spurred a niche sector for innovation in Brazil; the demand for formicide (ant poison) resulted in 42 patents or 9.4 percent of the total patents granted for agriculture. The Baron of Capenema, the owner of the Orianda Paper Factory from Chapter 2, patented his own formula in 1873.

Importantly, as Luiz Cláudio M. Ribeiro observes, coffee production increased even as the slave population declined owing in large part to labor-saving machines that made processing more uniform and efficient. The coffee boom also produced the wealth needed to improve transportation and finance the purchase of additional mechanical improvements that could cost as much as $30,000 per plantation, as US traveler Herbert Smith claimed in 1879.[63] Slave-operated, indoor steam-powered drying tables (which must have been insufferably hot in Brazil's tropical heat) were one of the improvements Smith described during his stay on a plantation in the Rio de Janeiro province. The steam-room reduced the drying time of coffee beans from sixty days in an outdoor *terreiro* (drying yard) to a few short hours, illustrating the impact of new technology on old methods of production (Fig. 4.3).[64] Increasing competition from coffee plantations in Java, Mexico, and Costa Rica spurred further innovation, and Brazilian inventors, as mentioned previously, began exporting machinery abroad to these regions.[65] By 1868, the Lidgerwood Co. sold coffee machinery through a satellite office in Java.[66] Tropical Brazil was at a disadvantage when competing with wheat producers in the US and Argentina, but the nation emerged as a global leader in coffee and its attendant machinery by the end of the century. When it made economic sense, Brazilian and foreign-born inventors rose to the challenge of meeting Brazilian technological needs.[67]

The success of Brazilian coffee machinery probably also resulted from the nation's competitive advantage in growing the crop. Imported threshers and sugar, corn, and wheat mills appeared in the patent registry, and their availability, at least in Rio, is corroborated in period ads. By contrast, Brazil was the largest supplier of coffee in the world by the end of the century, so it should not be surprising that domestic innovation met the demands of production for this vital sector of the economy. This point is further illustrated by the much smaller number of patents given for inventions related to sugar production, a crop that, while not as important as it had been in the previous century, still represented a sizable portion of the economy. The United States, France, and Great Britain produced sugar-refining machinery and many planters imported this machinery directly.[68]

---

[63] Herbert H. Smith, "Coffee Culture in Brazil," p. 231.   [64] Smith, p. 230.

[65] Luis Cláudio M. Ribeiro, *Ofício Criador: invento e patente de máquina de beneficar café no Brasil (1870–1910)* (Master's thesis, História, Faculdade de Filosofia, Letras e Ciência Humanas, Universidade de São Paulo, 1995), p. 15.

[66] Ema E. R. Camillo, *Guia Histórica da Indústria Nascente em Campinas (1850–1887)* (Campinas, SP: Mercado de Letras, CMU, 1998), p. 50.

[67] Lobo, *História Político-Administrativo*, pp. 77–8; and Ribeiro, p. 39.

[68] Peter Eisenberg, *The Sugar Industry in Pernambuco: Modernization Without Change 1840–1910* (Berkeley: University of California Press, 1974), pp. 49 and 88; Richard Graham, *Britain and the Onset of Modernization in Brazil* (Cambridge: Cambridge University Press, 1968), p. 87.

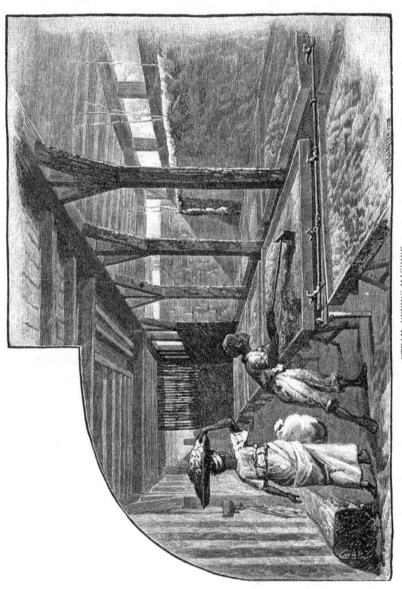

STEAM DRYING-MACHINE.

FIGURE 4.3. "Steam Drying-Machine." *Source: Scribner's Monthly: an Illustrated Magazine for the People,* Volume XIX, November 1879 to April 1880, pp. 228–9. Public domain, author's private collection.

In conclusion, Fig. 4.2 demonstrates that the majority of agricultural patents pertained to the predominant agricultural industries of the southeastern provinces of Rio de Janeiro and São Paulo. Aside from machinery and systems for processing sugar and manioc or preserving meat, relatively few patents were issued for industries specific to Bahia, Pernambuco, or Rio Grande do Sul, where mate, sugar, cotton, tobacco, wheat, and cattle predominated. The preponderance of machinery that benefited the southeastern provinces may reflect a number of realities. As mentioned previously, sugar machinery was less expensive and more easily purchased from abroad with the result that Brazilian inventors may have had less incentive to compete with foreign imports.[69] The patent record may also be biased toward innovators from Rio and São Paulo simply due to their proximity to the capital city. While the patent registry inconsistently indicated the residence of inventors, a significant portion was based in Rio. Inventors in distant provinces were at a further disadvantage; shipping costs to send a model of the invention to Rio (all applicants were required to submit a miniature working version of the invention when applicable), and the registration and possible legal fees for the patent application were additional obstacles. Perhaps inventors in more remote areas did not consider patents necessary under the previously mentioned conditions, or they were unaware of the existence of the registry. Nonetheless, regions outside Rio and São Paulo were also home to technological innovation as evidenced by Recife resident Padre José Azevedo, who won a gold medal at the 1861 national exhibition for his *maáquina de escrever* (writing machine). Designed to record church sermons, the priest never patented the machine nor expressed a desire to develop it commercially. Finally, though only eight patents were registered for machines that processed the native Brazilian cultivars of mate, manioc root, *goiaba*, and *açaí*, many more must have appeared across Brazil, as displays at provincial and national exhibitions and designs published in *O Auxiliador* suggest.

Conclusion

Agricultural technology, especially the plow, represented the pathway to progress for Brazilian modernizers in the nineteenth century. Improved techniques and machinery, they hoped, would provide the key to transforming both Brazilian economic productivity and social realities. The

[69] Eisenberg, p. 49.

plow was much more than an agricultural tool; it was a civilizing force that would replace the relationship of slave and master with self-sufficient, disciplined free labor and scientific farmers. It would preserve the forest, diversify the economy, and promote the production of food crops for domestic consumption. Because the plow would eliminate the need to burn more forest for cultivation, Brazil's rich natural endowment of flora and fauna could be effectively studied in the interest of economic development, thereby making better use of the empire's natural competitive advantage as a tropical nation with vast forest resources and long growing seasons.

Yet, as the sources underscore, the plow met with little success during the period. The expense of fertilizers and the difficulty of purchasing, transporting, and using machinery complicated the picture. Brazil's agricultural regime was lamentable from the perspective that it underutilized valuable forest resources and depended on cycles of destruction and depletion, but it was also extremely profitable, and not much that Sociedade Auxiliadora members proposed was easily or inexpensively adapted. In the end, Rodrigues' agricultural school in Maranhão came to naught. Five years after its inauguration in 1859, the school's French director declared the terrain upon which it was located "unsuitable for cultivation," and the institute subsequently closed its doors.[70]

Agricultural schools established in Juiz de Fora in Minas Gerais, and in Rio de Janeiro failed to attract sufficient students by the 1870s, dashing the hopes of Sociedade Auxiliadora members. Ironically, if agricultural schools did not result in a beneficial revolution of Brazilian agriculture and society, the *fazendeiros* themselves proved to be effective innovators in the end. Descriptions of the demonstration of new machinery and agricultural techniques on local *fazendas* were often published in the *apedidos* section. An example from 1853, for instance, praised the "enlightened *fazendeiro*" Paulo Gomes Ribeiro de Avellar of Vassouras for a demonstration of two machines: a coffee mill and another invention that milled wheat, corn, and rice in addition to processing castor bean oil.[71] Brazilian *fazendeiros* and inventors such as Luiz Goffredo de Escragnolle Taunay, who patented several coffee machines during his many years as a planter, were best poised to combine practical experience and mechanical science. By the end

[70] Teresa Cribelli, *O mais útil de todos os instrumentos: o arado e a valorização da terra no Brasil no século XIX*, in Márcia Motta and María Verónica Secreto, eds., *O Direito às Avessas: por uma história social da propriedade* (Guarapuava, PR: Unicentro, and Niterói: Editora da Universidade Federal Fluminense, 2011), pp. 309–10.
[71] "Industria Agricola," *Publicações a Pedido*, JC, February 22, 1853.

of the imperial period, agricultural technology did indeed improve coffee production, though it ultimately did not engender a transition from slash-and-burn agriculture or transform the underlying social relationships of rural Brazilian society as modernizers wished.

Rodrigues and his contemporaries' vision for rural modernization based on the plow might seem naive, resulting in a blind faith about the possible transformative qualities of technology. But far and above the condescension of reformers towards the unreformed, the actors described here made a sophisticated assessment of the social problems perpetuated by an agricultural and landholding regime inherited from the colonial system. This was not only a desire to "de-Africanize" the nation or to rationalize agriculture, it was also an effort to carefully transform the Brazilian economy and society, reshape attitudes toward the environment and its natural resources, and establish new possibilities for wealth generation through the valorization of land and wage labor. The active engagement that these would-be reformers brought to their work belies assertions of a passive, conservative agricultural elite playing out their days as slavery neared its end. This chapter demonstrates that Brazilians thought deeply and creatively about the possibilities of technological transformation during the years of Brazil's monarchy.

5

Road-Building and Railroads

Challenges to Modernization

"March forward, progress, progress!" they exhort us from all sides. We too desire this, but how do we march forward without roads? ... how do we get by without them when they represent all of the following: low prices, abundance, and commerce in the realm of economics; civilization in the realm of morals; and nationality in the realm of politics?
Correio Mercantil, May 27, 1861[1]

Quem diz Brazil diz estradas. (To speak of Brazil is to speak of roads.)
Jornal do Commercio, July 17, 1860[2]

... I may remark ... that any extended travel in Brazil is styled a voyage, though it be entirely on land.
John McFadden Gaston, Hunting a Home in Brazil, 1867[3]

As the central government in Rio consolidated its power in 1850 after defeating the regional revolts and rebellions that characterized the 1830s and 1840s, bureaucrats and politicians turned their attention to ameliorating the transportation bottleneck that frustrated commerce and interprovincial communication in all regions of the nation. In 1852 alone, exactly two years after the definitive end of the legal slave trade, concessions for some of the most important transportation projects of the period were granted: the Pedro II Railroad linking the port of Mauá in

---

[1] Cited from the writings of Portuguese author Antônio de Oliveira Marreca, "Estrada de Bom Jardim," *Publicações a Pedido, Correio Mercantil*, May 27, 1861.
[2] "Estrada de Mangaritiba," *Publicações a Pedido*, JC, July 17, 1860.
[3] John McFadden Gaston, *Hunting a Home in Brazil: The Agricultural Resources and other Characteristics of the Country. Also the Manners and Customs of the Inhabitants* (Philadelphia: King & Baird Printers, 1867), p. 53.

Guanabara Bay to the mountain city of Petrópolis; the Recife to São Francisco railroad in Pernambuco; the União e Indústria, a macadamized road – the first of its kind in South America – from Minas Gerais to Rio de Janeiro; the Companhia Mucuri, a joint colonization and transportation project in Minas Gerais; and the Companhia Navegação do Amazonas (Navigation Company of Amazonas) destined to facilitate domestic trade on the Amazon river and its tributaries.[4] While railroads and steamships were among the most celebrated modernization projects, less visually impressive (by contemporary standards) all-season wagon roads were also crucial for settlement and economic development.

This chapter is divided into two sections that address aspects of the development of the land-based transportation sector in imperial Brazil. By the 1830s bureaucrats, *fazendeiros*, and merchants recognized the benefits of improved transportation to economy and society, but limited funds, political disunion, and difficult geography impeded the rapid adoption of improvements. Part I explores the welter of differing aims – sometimes conflicting, other times converging – that motivated those who debated how development of land transportation should proceed. A central argument was whether improved ordinary roads or railroads would better meet Brazil's needs. Additionally, railroads emerged as a central component of a Brazilian imagining of modernity.[5] The passion with which anonymous writers argued for railroads in public letters demonstrated that they were not merely economic necessities built to service the coffee sector, but held considerable psychological weight in a nation keenly aware of foreign perceptions of Brazil as backward and uncivilized. This section also examines the challenges to improving overland travel, including the engineering of wagon roads and railroads in Brazil's difficult topography. The technological remedies adopted in Brazil pushed the limits of nineteenth-century road and railroad engineering. Part II investigates the role of railroad workshops in the development and dissemination of local technological knowledge. Scholars have noted that transportation technology was crucial for laying the groundwork of modernization in Brazil, and foreign engineers, capital, and technology played a central role in developing this sector.[6] Yet Brazilian technological

---

[4] Ademar Benévolo, *Introdução à História Ferroviária do Brasil: estudo social, politico e histórico* (Recife: Edições Folha da Manhã, 1953), p. 156.

[5] See Francis Foot Hardman, *Trem-fantasma: a ferrovia Madeira-Mamoré e a modernidade na selva* (São Paulo: Companhia das Letras, 1988, 2005).

[6] Richard Graham, *Britain and the Onset of Modernization in Brazil 1850–1914* (Cambridge: Cambridge University Press, 1968), p. 63.

adaptions were also important for the ongoing construction and maintenance of the transportation network though they remain understudied at present.[7] While it is true that foreign engineers oversaw the construction of Brazil's first railroads, Pedro Marinho observes that by 1880, 75 percent of all railway engineers were Brazilian-born and trained.[8] This contrasted sharply with Mexico where even after nationalization of the railroad system in the early 1900s, US citizens dominated the upper echelons of railway management and only 32 percent of engineers were Mexican nationals.[9] Brazilian railroad workshops also became important sites for local innovation where cadres of skilled laborers and engineers collaborated on, modified, and reconstructed railroad equipment. By the 1880s, thirty years after the completion of the first rail line, Brazilians readily incorporated domestic resources into the construction of rolling stock and produced innovations that better suited local conditions. Railroads did not result in a *revolution* of industry in Brazil along the lines of the United States or Germany, but they sparked an industrial *evolution* that shaped the Brazilian imagining of modernity and resulted in considerable technological expertise.

This chapter focuses on land transportation, but steam navigation was also an important sector that improved interprovincial communication and commerce. As scholars Geraldo Beauclair and Pedro Telles observe, shipyards in Rio de Janeiro, Bahia, and Minas Gerais developed into active centers of technological innovation in the nineteenth century. Emerging out of a well-established colonial shipbuilding tradition, Brazilian and foreign engineers together oversaw the construction of modern vessels suited for the unique seasonal and navigational conditions of Brazil's waterways. During its heyday from 1865 to 1890, the Navy Arsenal in Rio de Janeiro employed 500 workers in specialized workshops equipped to build and appoint ships from top to bottom. Blacksmiths, mechanics, and technicians constructed steam engines and ship hulls; tailors and rope-makers outfitted sailors and ships with clothing and cordage; and carpenters deftly employed hundreds of different Brazilian tree species in ship design. The Arsenal constructed war vessels

---

[7] William L. Summerhill, "Railroads and the Brazilian Economy Before 1914," *Summaries of Dissertations, Journal of Economic History*, Vol. 56, No. 2 (June 1996), pp. 466–7.

[8] Pedro Eduardo Mesquita de Monteiro Marinho, "Engenharia Imperial, O Instituto Politécnico Brasileiro," (Ph.D. dissertation, Universidade Federal Fluminense, Niterói, Rio de Janeiro, 2002), p. 147.

[9] Rodney D. Anderson, *Outcasts in their Own Land: Mexican Industrial Workers, 1906–1911* (DeKalb: Northern Illinois University Press, 1976), p. 236.

that served in the Paraguayan War (1865–70) and exhibited scale models of its ships and steam engines at international exhibitions to favorable review.[10] Along with newly professionalized Brazilian engineers by the 1870s, workshops for the transportation sector played an important role in the creation and dissemination of technological knowledge. The lack of recognition for Brazilian engineering has resulted in part from the fact that European and North Americans were the trailblazers in engineering technology and thusly dominated the railroad and shipbuilding industry in the nineteenth century. But technological accomplishments also suffered from the perception of Brazil and Brazilians as backward. Richard Burton observed as much in his comments on the macadamized road, the União e Indústria, in 1868 when he noted that Harvard Professor Louis Agassiz credited the road's success to French engineers and not Captain Bulhões, the road's Brazilian chief engineer, "Thus foreigners in the Brazil often claim and manage to carry off the honours due to the natives."[11]

Part I Debates and Controversies

The heirs to an extensive coastal trading network established in colonial times, Brazilians increased efforts to improve inland transportation via ordinary roads, canals, and steam navigation after independence from Portugal. One early scheme involved the concession, granted in 1835 by Pedro II's regent Diogo Antônio Feijó, which awarded the exclusive right to a "company or companies" to construct a railroad linking Rio de Janeiro, Minas Gerais, Rio Grande do Sul, and Bahia. Though thoroughly impractical and overly ambitious in terms of cost and the difficult terrain and distance of the proposed route (it would have connected southeastern and northern Brazil), the concession demonstrated that Brazilian officials were well aware of the benefits of transportation improvements. Feijó's

[10] Geraldo de Beauclair Mendes de Oliveira, *A Construção Inacabada: a economia brasileira, 1822–1860* (Rio de Janeiro: Vício de Leitura, 2001), pp. 153–67; Pedro Carlos da Silva Telles, *História da Construçao Naval do Brasil* (Rio de Janeiro: LAMN, FEMAR, 2001), p. 52, as cited in Pedro Marinho, "Engenharia Imperial," p. 139. At the 1876 Exhibition in Philadelphia, Brazil displayed, " . . . a number of very good models of ironclads, casemate and monitor ships, steam launches and corvettes sent from Rio de Janeiro . . . " Richard Kenin, ed., *A Facsimile of Frank Leslie's Illustrated Historical Register of the Centennial Exposition, 1876* (New York: Paddington Press Ltd., 1976), p. 272.

[11] Richard Burton, *Explorations of the Highlands of the Brazil; with a Full Account of the Gold and Diamond Mines, Also, Canoeing Down 1500 Miles of the Great River São Francisco, From Sabará to the Sea*, Vol. I (New York: Greenwood Press, 1869, 1969), note, p. 35.

decree appeared just five years after the construction of the first commercial railroad in the US, the Baltimore and Ohio in 1830, and was contemporary with the first rail-building boom in Great Britain.[12] No part of the concession was ever actualized, though it provides an early example of the desire to impose government sovereignty and promote national unity through overland communication.

While railroads and steamships received most of the attention, transportation improvements also included more traditional conveyances. Road-building technologies such as the macadam process (comprised of layers of packed gravel designed to drain rainwater), improved carriages and freight wagons, and the selective breeding of draft animals fit hand in glove with new steam technologies in bringing products to market and moving people from place to place. Far from rendering animal-dependent technologies obsolete, railroads relied heavily on horses and wagons to move freight to and from stations and passengers between transfer points in the nineteenth-century US.[13] Draft animals were therefore crucial for the commercial growth of nineteenth-century cities, and in Brazil mules and horses increasingly hauled freight through crowded city streets from busy ports to merchant houses. By 1887, 5,471 mules supplied the muscle that pulled passengers along Rio's trolley lines.[14] The need for new animal-drawn conveyances for handling the increasing volume of consumer goods was illustrated in an 1876 Brazilian patent application for a specialized wagon configured to safely transport pottery and mirrors. Sociedade Auxiliadora member José Rego Filho urged the Ministry of Agriculture to hold a competition to further promote the development of improved wagons and carriages, complaining that Rio's "cumbersome and inefficient" freight wagons damaged streets and held up traffic.[15] The Sociedade Auxiliadora also published a treatise on horsebreeding, *Ensaio sobre a regeneração das raças cavalares do Império do Brasil*

[12] *O Brazil na Exposição Internacional dos Caminhos de Ferro em Pariz em 1887* (Rio de Janeiro: Imprensa Nacional, 1887), p. 11.

[13] Ann Norton Greene, *Horses at Work: Harnessing Power in Industrial America* (Cambridge, MA: Harvard University Press, 2008), p. 45.

[14] Rodrigo Augusto da Silva, *Relatorio apresentado á Assembléa Geral na Terceira Sessão da Vigesima Legislaturapelo Ministro e Secretario de Estado dos Negocios da Agricultura, Commercio, e Obras Publicas* (Rio de Janeiro: Imprensa Nacional, 1888), p. 364. http://brazil.crl.edu/bsd/bsd/u1973/.

[15] "Concede privilégio a José Luiz Alves de Mirandella para fabricar, usar, e vender carroças de sua invenção, destinadas ao transporte de trastes," *Privilégios Industriais*, Ministério da Agricultura, Comércio, e Obras Publicas, Caixa 831, Pacote 2, Decreto 6284, August 9, 1876. *Arquivo Nacional*.

(The Improvement of Horse Breeds in the Empire of Brazil) in 1856, underlining efforts to improve on older modes of transportation even as steamships and locomotives appeared.[16]

The desire for new roads and the improvement of existing roads in Brazil was primarily an economic matter – *fazendeiros* and farmers wanted to move their agricultural products, especially export crops, efficiently and cheaply to market – but modern roads were also important material representations of nineteenth-century progress. Many Brazilians desired the status – and what they referred to as the moral impact – that modern roads and railroads conveyed, as will be explored later in this chapter. In the realm of commerce, the difficulties of travel discouraged agricultural producers from risking their harvests during periods of turbulent seasonal weather, and merchants sometimes faced dangerous obstacles in bringing their wares to remote regions. The president of Mato Grosso in 1850 complained that the lack of a bridge over the river Coxipó was literally killing business during the rainy season. "People and mule-trains" drowned while they attempted to cross the swollen river outside the capital city of Cuiabá. The obstacles to building a bridge were twofold: the lack of funding and a competent engineer to design and oversee construction.[17]

Facilitating economic growth through improved transportation was also a primary concern of the imperial government as evidenced in annual provincial reports. The state's dependence on customhouse receipts for the majority of its revenue underscored the need to facilitate the movement of export commodities from the interior to the coast.[18] But if the economic objectives of improved transportation were apparent to provincial presidents, they were even more pressing for rural producers who experienced the lack of improved roads firsthand. Complaints, protests, and occasional praise of road-building efforts filled the *Publicações a Pedido* section of the *Jornal do Commercio* in the 1850s and 1860s. No other figure was vilified or sanctified as much as the civil engineer who was lauded when a new road functioned well, and scorned when neglect, real or exaggerated, left roads impassable. The following example from

---

[16] Frederico Burlamaque, *Ensaio sobre a regeneração das raças cavallares do Imperio do Brasil* (Rio de Janeiro: Tip. Dous de Dezembro, 1856).

[17] João José da Costa Pimentel, *Falla dirigida à Assembléa Legislativa Provincial de Mato Grosso na abertura da sessão ordinaria em 3 de maio de 1850, pelo exm. sr. presidente da provincia* (Cuiabá: Tip. do Echo Cuiabano, 1850), p. 14.

[18] José Murilo de Carvalho, *A construção da ordem: a elite política imperial e Teatro de sombras: a política imperial* (Rio de Janeiro: Civilização Brasileira, 2006), p. 267.

an anonymous critic in Rio de Janeiro province illustrated the frustration of rural residents with engineers and bureaucrats alike. Signed "Voice of the people," the author appealed to the provincial president to speed the completion of a bridge on a wagon road that linked the town of Cacaria to the Dom Pedro II railroad in Belém:

No one can deny the necessity of maintaining the road [between Belém and Cacaria] in good condition, and even less so the need for its upkeep, and if any one dares to challenge such a fact... we will ship them off to the insane asylum of D. Pedro II.

The importance of this road seems to have not reached the notice of your Excellency, because the construction of a bridge over the Santa Anna River, which services the road, is more than two months overdue. This results in great danger to travelers who are obliged to cross on small, decrepit bridges, and at times are even forced to swim to the applause of the... engineers in charge of the bridge's construction. The lack of a bridge also results in the loss of cargo carried away by the river's current.[19]

The author further protested the toll charged on the road, which he complained, only "added another affliction to the afflicted." The letter ended with a threat, warning the provincial president that the only way to prevent "further inflammation of feeling" was to see to the matter quickly, "as the results of such reactions are almost always of the worst kind."[20] Dilapidated roads and lax engineers were an incendiary topic indeed during the imperial period.

Completed roads, on the other hand, were cause for celebration. An *apedido* from May of 1860 applauded the engineers of a new road that serviced the port town of Ubatuba in São Paulo province:

May 17 was a day of true celebration for the citizens of [Ubatuba], who fully appreciate the value and benefits that a good road brings to a community.

Since its founding, Ubatuba... was condemned to communicate with the interior by a tortuous road lined by precipices that belonged more to the edge of an abyss than a path for travelers.[21]

---

[19] "Estrada – Cacaria a Belem," *Publicações a Pedido, JC*, February 12, 1860.

[20] "Estrada – Cacaria a Belem," Provincial president Ignacio Francisco Silveira da Motta reported in the 1860 *relatório* for Rio de Janeiro that the bridge was near completion, Ignacio Francisco Silveira da Motta *Relatorio apresentado à Assembléa Legislativa provincial do Rio de Janeiro na 1.a sessão da 14.a legislatura* (Rio de Janeiro, Tip. de Francisco Rodrigues de Miranda & C., 1860), p. 53.

[21] "Ubatuba," *Publicações a Pedido, JC*, May 21, 1860.

Town inhabitants gathered in the church courtyard to witness the arrival of the first caravan to traverse the new road. A decorated wagon carrying the Brazilian flag and a portrait of Pedro II led a short parade of "seven carts loaded with timber" that had just been carried across the *serra* and was destined for export. Celebrated for his role in the road's construction, engineer and town resident Captain Antônio Francisco de Gouvêa e Castro took center stage. The festivities included fireworks, enthusiastic shouts of "viva," and a table of sweets supplied by Captain Castro who also organized the parade. With true Brazilian flair, the celebration, complete with musicians and revelers in carnival masks, lasted into the night and included a visit to "the house of Captain Castro which was crowded round by spectators." The captain was lauded for his perseverance in completing the road after decades of provincial neglect.[22]

The *apedido* about the Ubatuba road served multiple purposes. It alerted interested parties – particularly merchants in Rio de Janeiro – about the road's availability for use. Additionally, it advertised the community's success at procuring state and national resources while also enacting a civic ritual that highlighted membership in the nation. The announcement about Captain Castro's role in constructing the road also served a transparent political purpose. He was elected an alternate city council member for Ubatuba in the following November elections, news of which was likewise published in the *Jornal do Commercio*.[23] Political successes aside, the rather prosaic contents of the wagons on parade – raw timber – was the most valuable result of the road. The shipment represented the future commercial prosperity of Ubatuba, and demonstrated that roads brought prestige, political recognition, and increased commerce to municipalities and regions.[24]

---

[22] "Ubatuba," *Publicações a Pedido, JC*, May 21, 1860.

[23] "Ubatuba: Resultado das Eleições Municipaes," *Publicações a Pedido, JC*, September 19, 1860.

[24] The *apedido* stated that 2 *contos* were raised from private investors in the town of Ubatuba, with another 20 *contos* provided by the province of São Paulo. The provincial reports for 1860 and 1861 offer no specific information about the construction of the road, but the 1861 report declared that the port at Ubatuba was considered of strategic importance and was therefore to be given priority in funding public works, confirming the political success of the town's efforts to secure provincial monies. *Discurso com que o illustrissimo e excellentissimo senhor conselheiro Antônio José Henriques, presidente da provincia de São Paulo, abrio à Assembléa Legislativa Provincial no anno de 1861* (São Paulo: Tip. Imparcial de Joaquim Roberto de Azevedo Marques, 1861), anexo, p. 5.

Central Authority and the Projection of State Power

In the second half of the eighteenth century, the consolidation of Portuguese colonial territory and the projection of state power into unpopulated regions became a matter of heightened importance for the Portuguese crown. Expeditions were sent into Pará, Mato Grosso, and other unexplored areas toward the aim of establishing Portuguese sovereignty over remote and valuable regions. In the wake of revolts and rebellions after independence in 1822, the need for state control of remote provinces intensified further. Sovereignty was crucial in a nation as topographically varied, geographically extensive, and sparsely populated as Brazil. Historian Janaina Amado observes that Brazil's post-independence territorial delineation preceded settlement; the borders that appeared on nineteenth-century Brazilian maps differed markedly from the actual physical control of territory by the white population.[25] Vulnerable areas included the northern Amazonian region, the western portions of Mato Grosso, and the southern provinces that abutted the Spanish republics of Uruguay, Paraguay, and Argentina. Brazilian officials were particularly concerned about commercial encroachment and military threats from the nation's Spanish-speaking neighbors to the south. In 1853, the provincial president of Rio Grande do Sul attributed the proliferation of illegal trade with Uruguay less to the profitability of contraband than because it was simply too difficult and expensive to bring in merchandise from the capital Porto Alegre on poorlymaintained provincial roads. In the far north enormous swaths of the Amazonian region remained unsurveyed, a matter of increasing importance as other nations cast a covetous eye at the resource-rich region by the 1850s.[26] Internal conflicts with indigenous peoples also posed a threat to settlement and safe transportation as the war with the Botocudos in Minas Gerais illustrated in the first decades of the nineteenth century.[27]

---

[25] Janaina Amado, Warren Dean, and Walter Nugent, "Frontier in Comparative Perspectives: The United States and Brazil," Working Papers No. 188, Latin American Program, The Wilson Center, Washington, DC, 1990, p. 31.

[26] J. Valerie Fifer, *United States Perceptions of Latin America, 1850–1930: a "New West" south of Capricorn?* (Manchester, UK: Manchester University Press, 1991), p. 10; and Katherine Emma Manthorne, *Tropical Renaissance: North American Artists Exploring Latin America, 1839–1879* (Washington: Smithsonian Institution Press, 1989), pp. 51–3.

[27] Hal Langfur, *The Forbidden Lands: Colonial Identity, Frontier Violence, and the Persistance of Brazil's Eastern Indians, 1750–1830* (Stanford: Stanford University Press, 2006), p. 164.

As early as 1835, the president of Rio de Janeiro province noted the effect of political dissension on national unity in his annual report, arguing that improved roads were the answer. By facilitating commercial exchange and *indústria*, roads would engender fellow feeling among Brazil's factions and regions. Roads were essential for knitting together political and national unity (as indeed the road in Ubatuba illustrated), thereby channeling discord into more peaceful and profitable competition in the marketplace, a reflection of Enlightenment thought in which commercial activity sublimated political tensions.[28]

Nineteenth-century improved roads – though they appear little more than packed dirt to contemporary eyes – were also monuments of progress that represented a nation's level of civilization. During the era of feverish turnpike construction in the late eighteenth- and early nineteenth-century US, for example, improved roads invoked the prestige and authority of Roman imperial roads.[29] In Brazil in 1860, M. A. Monteiro da Silva, a young medical student from Minas Gerais, marveled at the newly constructed União e Indústria, an engineered road that linked Petrópolis in Rio de Janeiro province to Juiz de Fora in Minas Gerais:

As soon as the coach's bugle . . . announced that we had left Petrópolis, my spirit was enchanted by the brilliant and exhilarating sight before my eyes, one of the largest public works of the country, and the first of its kind in my province . . . the *União e Indústria* . . . I salute my home province of Minas Gerais for this magnificent accomplishment that will open new pathways for civilization, and for its native son, [M. P. Ferreira Lage] the director of the first [macadamized] wagon road in Brazil . . . [30]

The student compared Lage's perseverance in the face of material and social obstacles to the sixteenth-century accomplishments of the Cardinal Richelieu, hinting at the controversies that surrounded the road's construction.[31]

---

[28] *Falla com que o presidente da provincia de Rio de Janeiro, o conselheiro Joaquim José Rodrigues Torres, abriu a primeira sessão da primeira legislatura da Assembléa Legislativa da mesma provincia, no dia primeiro de fevereiro de 1835* (Nitheroy: Tip. de Amaral & Irmão, 1850 [*sic*]), pp. 34–5. Torres' argument reveals influences from Enlightenment thought: with the notion that violent passions could be directed into peaceful self-interest via competition in the marketplace, see Albert O. Hirschman, *The Passions and the Interests: Political Arguments for Capitalism before Its Triumph* (Princeton: Princeton University Press, 1977, 1997).

[29] Greene, p. 50.

[30] "A Estrada União e Industria," *Publicações a Pedido, JC*, April 10, 1860.

[31] *Ibid.*

Despite the young Monteiro da Silva's excitement upon seeing the road for the first time, the more spectacular locomotive became the emblem of nineteenth-century progress, and for good reason. The railroad flattened distances and conveyed overland travelers and cargo along their way at speeds unimaginable in the previous century. It opened up new territories to resource extraction and settlement and transferred raw materials quickly and efficiently to manufacturing centers and ports, a technology of great utility for a nation of continental size like Brazil. During his visit to the United States in 1876, Pedro II was impressed by the fact that an express trip from New York to San Francisco took just three and a half days on the continental railroad.[32] Only twenty-seven years previously the emperor had personally witnessed the arrival of thousands of California gold-rush travelers in Rio en route from the Eastern US to San Francisco on a six- to eight-month journey around Cape Horn.

The railroads did more than move freight and people; they became crucial for narratives of progress in the United States and Brazil, nations linked by the desire to incorporate enormous stretches of unsettled territory into the national body. In the former, the locomotive was an important symbol in the creed of *Manifest Destiny*. In the 1872 painting, *Westward Ho (American Progress)* described in Chapter 4, artist John Gast portrayed *Manifest Destiny* in the form of white settlers marching across the western plains accompanied by the railroad and telegraph, stagecoach, and covered wagon. Though technology enables the westward march, the hardy pioneers are the central catalysts of US progress. Hovering over them is a luminous "ambassador of liberty" – a female figure in the style of a Greek Muse – floating in the center of the painting. In one arm she holds an uncoiling telegraph wire, in the other a book representing science. A group of Native Americans, bison, and a lone bear flee the approaching pioneers as they head toward a darkened sky, an allegory for their eventual demise in the face of progress. Their flight blandly gestures toward the violent appropriation that characterized white/native encounters on the western plains by the 1860s.[33]

The railway's conquest of wilderness and distance with coal-fire and speed also captured the imagination of Brazilians who gazed upon their "colossal empire... immense with forests," and saw a nation of

---

[32] Teresa Cribelli, "A Modern Monarch: Dom Pedro II's Visit to the United States in 1876," *The Journal of the Historical Society*, Vol. IX, No. 2, June 2009, pp. 244–5.

[33] Richard Grusin, *Nature, Technology, and the Creation of America's National Parks* (Cambridge: Cambridge University Press, 2004), pp. 71–2.

continental scale with enormous – and daunting – organic wealth, but little civilization.[34] A poem celebrating the locomotive's transformative powers appeared in the positivist *Gazeta Acadêmica* in 1876, roughly contemporary with *Westward Ho*. Like Gast's depiction, the locomotive's arrival in the Brazilian forest carried undercurrents of violence:

> In the distance a cry is heard that bursts forth in the palm groves
> A crest of smoke lifts into the air
> A monster appears, accelerating, urgent
> And an astonished Indian, ruddy-hued and naked, asks:

> Who art thou, terrible vision?
> What comes forth, shaking our feet?
> What comes forth, awakening the forest
> With your thundering cry?[35]

The personified locomotive responds, linking the figure of the Wandering Jew (Asheverus) from medieval Christian mythology to the feverish spirit of nineteenth-century progress:

> I am the Asheverus of Progress[36]
> Who circles the world over
> I carry in my feet the *pampeiro*[37]
> And in my bosom, steam-power.

> I am the spark of an idea
> A fever of human ingenuity
> I am from the sovereign genius
> The most vivid luminescence.

> A wise one declared as he contemplated

---

[34] Joaquim Lins de Albuquerque, "A locomotiva no Brazil," *Gazeta Academica*, Anno I, January 22, 1876, p. 13. My thanks to Sarah Moody for assistance with this translation.

[35]
> *Ao longe ouve-se um grito que estruge nos palmares*
> *Um penacho de fumo eleva-se nos ares...*
> *Um monstro se apresenta, vem acelere, apressado,*
> *E o indio rubro nú pergunta admirando:*

> *II*
> *Quem és tú visão terrivel*
> *Que vens sacudindo as patas?*
> *Que vens acordando as matas*
> *Com teu grito estrugidor?*
>   Lins de Albuquerque, p. 13.

[36] In the Christian legend, Asheverus mocked Jesus as he carried the cross to Golgotha. In punishment, Asheverus was condemned to wander the earth, never able to stop or rest. The *Judeu Errante* (Wandering Jew) was a well-known figure in nineteenth-century Brazilian culture.

[37] The *pampeiro* is a powerful wind that blows across the Pampas (a region of fertile grasslands) of Argentina, Uruguay, and Southern Brazil.

My urgent passing:
I leave from the hands of the past
Into the arms of destiny.[38]

The railroad arises from the past, rushing into the future, a common trope in representations of nineteenth-century progress. But key elements link the locomotive explicitly to the Brazilian wilderness, harnessing both powerful natural forces (the *pampeiro*) and mechanical power (steam) into a machine of "vivid luminescence." The railroad renders the unorganized and organic Brazilian forest into efficient, rational, and *mechanical* order.[39] Importantly, and in contrast to Gast, no human figure, other than the startled native and the "wise one," appears. This is a significant omission; at the time undeveloped forest was inhabited by indigenous groups, or more likely in locations closer to established settlements, by free poor populations comprised of mixed-race *caboclos* (Indian and European) and *mulattos* (African and European), *matutos* (backwood dwellers), or *posseiros* (squatters). In this Brazilian imagining of progress, the *locomotive* is the hardy pioneer, the central actor, and the land is a catalyst for its power. Less-desirable populations that would have been considered unsuitable for colonization of the frontier by elites back in Rio do not appear at all.

After the startling arrival of the locomotive in the virgin forest, the tone of the poem softens, transitioning into a celebration carried out by the indigenous flora and fauna rather than a scene of their triumphal extermination. His role as herald complete, the native Brazilian conveniently disappears while nonhuman forest denizens join together to welcome the locomotive. In contrast to the doomed wildlife of Gast's painting, the

---

[38]

Sou o Asheverus do progresso
Que circula o mundo inteiro
Trago nos pés o pampeiro,
Trago no seio o vapor.

Eu sou o chispa de idéia
Ferida no craneo humano,
Sou do genio soberano
O mais vivido lusir.
Diz o sabio a contemplar-me
No meu correr apressado:
Sahio das mãos do passado,
Corre aos brações do porvir.
Lins de Albuquerque, p. 13.

[39] Lygia Segala and Paulo Garchet, "Prescriptive Observation and Illustration of Brazil: Victor Frond's Photographic Project (1857–61)," *Portuguese Studies*, Vol. 23, No. 1 (2007), p. 63, fn. 27.

jaguars, tropical birds, and trees joyfully receive the civilizing smokestack in their midst:

> The mountains salute me as I pass
> On the margins laughter quiets
> Hymns of complaint and love
> Seeing me in nature's bosom,
> Everything expands to receive me
> The bird, the startled beast
> The nest, the crater, the flower
>
> In the vertigo of speed
> The genies of the forest dance in my honor
> The cedars, the waterfalls
> The snake, the ocelot, the jaguar
> In my brilliant story
> I join light and work
> In this plume of smoke
> that I set aloft.[40]

In this florid example, speed and light are the transformative catalysts that (after the locomotive's startling entry in the forest) serenely set Brazilian modernization in motion, creating an ethereal tone for the arrival of the "machine in the garden" quite in opposition to the doom and disruption ascribed to the locomotive by North American writers like Henry Thoreau.[41] The locomotive coupled the light of science to the material work of transforming the landscape, turning it from an idyllic

[40]
> *As motanhas[sic], quando eu passo,*
> *Me saúdào na passagem,*
> *O riso cala na margem*
> *Hymnos de queixa e do amor*
> *Tudo se expande me vendo*
> *No seio da natureza:*
> *A ave, á fera sorpresa,*
> *O ninho, a cratera, a flor*
> *Na Vertigem da carreira*
> *Dansão-me os genios das matas;*
> *Os cedros, as cataratas,*
> *A cobra, a onça, o jaguar.*
> *Na minha historia brillhante*
> *Luz e trabalho resumo;*
> *N'este penacho de fumo*
> *Que arremeço para o ar*
>   Lins de Albuquerque, p. 13.

[41] Leo Marx, *The Machine in the Garden: Technology and the Pastoral Ideal in America* (Oxford: Oxford University Press, 1964, 2000), pp. 15–16.

(but uncivilized) scene to one of order and progress. Unlike Gast's terra-formed Western vistas where the old landscape is utterly reshaped, the Brazilian forest is receptive and nurturing of technological progress in a metamorphosis that is as emotional as it is physical. In practice Brazil's forests and mountain ranges proved to be much less compliant.

The Difficulties of Travel in Imperial Brazil

Imagine if you will ... a narrow wooden bridge on a tortuous road of five kilo-meters, upon which you traverse a sea of clayish mud 3 to 4 hands deep laid over a roadbed full of potholes; add in a parade of ten to 12 wagons, each bearing weight in upward of 100 arrobas (3300 pounds), some of which are immersed up to their axles ... figure in the mule trains struggling in this muddy sea, with the shouts and curses of the drivers against the government and the engineer dominating the scene, and you will finally have a remote idea of the *Morro do Bicho* (Paraná, 1874).[42]

As this example illustrates, steep *serras*, landslides, and muddy roadbeds churned by seasonal rain routinely vexed those who attempted to travel by wagon or horseback across the Brazilian provinces. As in many parts of Latin America, pack mules proved the most effective method for con-veying goods and people from the coast into the interior and back in most parts of Brazil, though they were far from an efficient mode of transportation.[43] Visiting foreigners were routinely astonished by the physical obstacles to overland travel in the tropical nation. In 1864, our confederate observer of Brazilian agriculture from Chapter 4, John Gas-ton, poignantly described a train of savvy mules laden with provisions as they negotiated a series of muddy slopes in São Paulo province:

The [mules] ... would glide down [the hillsides] as boys descend a steep clay bank ... making a continuous impression like the trail of a small narrow slide upon the side of the hill, from top to bottom. The two pack-mules were kept ahead, and upon reaching the top of one of the hills, away they would go one after the other, and as soon as they were out of the way, then down went the

[42] *Relatorio com que o excellentissimo senhor doutor Frederico José Cardoso de Araujo Abranches abriu a 1.a sessão da 11.a legislatura da Assembléa Legislativa Provincial no dia 15 de fevereiro de 1874* (Curityba: Tip. da Viuva Lopes, 1874), p. 33.

[43] Herbert S. Klein, "The Supply of Mules to Central Brazil: The Sorocaba market, 1825–1880," *Agricultural History*, 64, no. 4 (Fall, 1990), p. 1; Maria Lúcia Lamounier, *Ferrovias e mercado de trabalho no Brasil do século XIX* (São Paulo: Editora da Univer-sidade de São Paulo, 2011), pp. 87–9; and Robert H. Mattoon, Jr., "Railroads, Coffee, and the Growth of Big Business in São Paulo, Brazil," *The Hispanic American Historical Review*, 57:2, May 1977, pp. 275–6.

[rest]... as if upon skates, in quick succession [descending]... almost with the velocity of a locomotive-engine.[44]

But locomotives they were not. Mule trains, the "scourge of the *fazendeiro*," as one frustrated *apedido* writer put it in 1860, were expensive, slow, and dependent on favorable weather. Many *fazendeiros* maintained their own sizable troops, but supporting veritable armies of mules for the larger plantations necessitated the fabrication or purchase of hundreds of packsaddles and halters, the employment of experienced muleteers, the dedication of valuable agricultural land for fodder and grain, and capital for the purchase of fresh mules.

The physical limitations of mule carriage also dictated the type of products that planters were able to send overland. José Tomás Nabuco de Araújo, president of São Paulo in 1851, attributed the rise of coffee production to its superior transportability over sugar, the latter a cumbersome and delicate product that spoiled easily upon exposure to the elements as was wont to happen in mule packsaddles.[45] Transporting bottled spirits, honey, prepared foodstuffs, or bulky items including furniture and agricultural machinery by mule was especially difficult and expensive, if not impossible, and was one of the most important factors limiting economic growth in interior regions.[46] Unsurprisingly, damage and loss of cargo were continual complaints among farmers, planters, and merchants. Introducing new methods for safe, efficient, and quick transport was the highest priority for frustrated *fazendeiros* and necessary for economic growth.

Human obstacles also impeded road building; four reasons for the difficulty of road improvements put forth in the 1855 report for São Paulo included the absence of a properly "scientific" and centralized state

---

[44] Gaston, p. 315.

[45] "The transition from cultivation of sugar to that of coffee and tea is... currently [being] undertaken by our *fazendeiros*... the transition... to this type of cultivation is not only advantageous and easier than that of sugar, but it is less subject to the problems inherent to the horrible condition of our network of roads and the impossibility of traveling... " *Discurso com que o illustrissimo e excellentissimo senhor dr. José Thomaz Nabuco d'Araujo, presidente da provincia de São Paulo, abrio a Assembléa Legislativa Provincial no dia 1.o de maio de 1852* (São Paulo: Tip.do Governo arrendada por Antonio Louzada Antunes, 1852), p. 36; and Mattoon, p. 275.

[46] William Summerhill, *Order Against Progress: Government, Foreign Investment, and Railroads in Brazil, 1854–1913* (Stanford: Stanford University Press, 2003), pp. 18–33, and Stephen Haber, *How Latin America Fell Behind: Essays on the Economic Histories of Brazil and Mexico, 1800–1914* (Stanford: Stanford University Press, 1997), pp. 96–7.

authority in charge of overseeing provincial projects, a lack of geographical surveys, a general disorganization in the administration and inspection of public works, and finally the "unjustifiable obstinacy" and "bad will" of *fazendeiros* who refused to grant right of way across their land. Short-sighted planters, the report's author accused, promoted their own interests at the expense of the greater community with their "fervor in requesting new roadways [to service their *fazendas*] without attending first to the necessity of improving main arteries and communal roads."[47] Indeed, in 1884 a *fazendeira* angry about the construction of a road across her land in São Paulo published a series of incendiary *apedidos* in the *Jornal do Commercio* and sent out "her adminstrator and sixty slaves" to block a startled road crew, effectively stopping construction.[48] Complaints about uncooperative planters also appeared in reports for Rio de Janeiro.

The twenty-first-century image engendered by the term "road" suggests a more developed image of overland transportation than is warranted for much of nineteenth-century Brazil. *Picada* referred to the most primitive of overland trails, often simply a pathway hacked through the forest, and many were footpaths first used by indigenous peoples. An *estrada* or *estrada normal* was usually passable by animal-drawn vehicles, though this did not necessarily mean it had been surveyed or engineered. Some of these were older colonial routes built by slaves in the eighteenth century and paved with stones such as the *Estrada Real* (Royal Road) that linked the gold fields in Minas Gerais to the port of Paraty. Road-building techniques varied widely, from little more than beating out a path by hoof or human foot that followed the contours of the local landscape, to surveys and the sophisticated steam machinery used in the construction of the União e Indústria. *Estrada de rodagem* (wagon road) referred specifically to roads usable by animal-drawn wagons. Construction usually included macadamizing the road surface, erecting wood or iron bridges,

---

[47] *Discurso com que o illustrissimo e excellentissimo senhor dr. José Antonio Saraiva, presidente da provincia de S. Paulo, abrio a Assembléa Legislativa Provincial no dia 15 de fevereiro de 1855* (São Paulo: Tip. 2 de Dezembro de Antonio Louzada Antunes, 1855), p. 24.

[48] "Documentos sobre o recurso interposto por Dona Francisca Amalia de Oliveira Camargo, contra o ato de presidente do Estado de S. Paulo resolvendo as questões sussetadas sobre a abertura de uma estrada de Rodagem entre Capivary e a estação de Kilombo, de estrada de ferro Itaúna," manuscript, Arquivo Nacional, IT4 Maço4, GIFI 43177, Código de Fundo: OI, Seção de guarda: SDE, pp. 14 and 27.

flattening grades, and configuring embankments and drainage to prevent rainwater from cutting ruts into the road surface. Slave and immigrant labor were both employed in road-building, sometimes simultaneously, in what was some of the most difficult and dangerous work of the imperial period.

Road-building technology in the nineteenth century centered on improving the efficiency of animal-drawn wagons and coaches. One horse or mule could carry about 200 pounds upon its back while a team of two to four horses could draw ten times that amount in a wagon. In terms of the cost-benefit ratio, the superiority of freight wagons over pack animals was obvious. But the amount of energy that a draft animal expended pulling a wagon, and therefore, the speed and distance across which it could move cargo, was directly related to the quality of the surface over which it traveled. The ideal road for draft animals supplied a surface rigid enough to grant easy passage to wagon wheels and flexible enough to provide traction to hooves. Building uniform roadbeds with gentle grades suitable for draft animals in all types of terrain including swamps, hills, and forests and adaptable to the vagaries of seasonal conditions (wet, soggy soil during rain and dusty, hard-baked ruts in dry periods) challenged engineers, frustrated travelers, and proved exceedingly expensive to build and maintain in the nineteenth century.[49]

In Brazil, mountainous tracks – particularly over the Great Escarpment that extended inland from the Atlantic coast all the way from Salvador past São Paulo – exacerbated the use of wagons, requiring significant engineering and expense to build gentler grades on the steepest slopes. In addition to the challenges of hilly territory, provincial reports, *apedidos*, and travelers' accounts give the impression that nineteenth-century Brazil had no shortage of mud. In 1853, a US traveler in Rio de Janeiro was scandalized by the ostentation of a carriage with "four-in-hand" sent to convey him to a party. The passenger was later grateful for the extra horsepower when the carriage became mired in mud two feet thick outside the city.[50]

On the other hand, cutting-edge finishing techniques such as the macadam process employed to combat mud and ruts posed a challenge to slaves and the poor who went unshod, making the use of the layers of small stones crucial for draining rainwater off the road surface

---

[49] Greene, pp. 45–6.
[50] C. S. Stewart, *Brazil and La Plata: the Personal Record of a Cruise* (New York, G. P. Putnam & Co., 1856), p. 234.

problematic for the majority of the population.[51] Indeed what solved one problem, often merely created others. In mid-nineteenth-century France, for example, Napoleon III's insistence on the construction of showy macadam roads in Baron Haussman's 1860s renovation of Paris resulted in daily inconveniences for those who traversed the city on foot. Designed for hooves and carriage wheels, macadam roads were dusty in summer and muddy in winter, making foot traffic uncomfortable and difficult.[52]

As the previous examples illustrate, solutions to Brazil's transportation woes were very much on the mind of the public in the 1850s and 1860s. *O Agricultor Brazileiro*, an agricultural journal sponsored by the same US merchant, Nathaniel Sands, from Chapter 2, published a scheme for the gradual improvement of Brazilian roads in 1854.[53] Arguing that railroads were beyond the financial means of Brazil at the time (though it was conceded that they were the best transportation option), the article called for the government to organize gangs of military laborers to build and maintain ordinary roads in rural areas. Once constructed, the roads were to be serviced by privately owned carriage companies modeled after stagecoach lines in the US. Road workers were to simultaneously construct and police the roads in addition to providing a seed population for the settlement of sparsely populated regions. The proposal illustrated obstacles to overland travel beyond poor road conditions: brigandage, the lack of services for travelers, and the need for a settled workforce for road upkeep.[54] In Mato Grosso, for example, the distance between settlements meant that travelers had no place to purchase fodder for their animals aside from a "few kernels of corn" at the occasional humble settlement. Muleteers were forced to pack enough supplies for "weeks, if not months," adding to the number of pack animals and expense required

---

[51] Viviane Alves de Morais, *Carros, viandantes, cargas e as comunicações durante o Império: estudo sobre as estradas interprovinciais entre 1832 e 1860*, unpublished conference paper, *Anais do XIX Encontro Regional de História: Poder, Violência e Exclusão*, ANPUH/SP – USP, São Paulo, September, 2008, n.p.

[52] Marshall Berman, *All That is Solid Melts into Air: the Experience of Modernity* (New York: Simon & Schuster, 1982), p. 158.

[53] Nathaniel Sands owned an import business for agricultural machinery in Rio. He was also associated with one of Brazil's first mechanized textile mills, Santo Aleixo, located in Rio de Janeiro province. The journal is mentioned in the 1857 edition of the travel narrative by American missionaries D. P. Kidder and J. S. Fletcher, *Brazil and the Brazilians: Portrayed in Historical and Descriptive Sketches* (Philadelphia: Childs and Peterson, 1857), pp. 252–3.

[54] "Systema de Transportes," *O Agricultor Brazileiro*, Vol. I, No. 3, January 1854, pp. 3–5.

to carry cargo, all of which was paid by the consumer at the end of the line. São Paulo coffee *fazendeiros* were often at the mercy of landowners who charged exorbitant rates for grazing and fodder en route to the port of Santos.[55]

Later in the same year, another article in O *Agricultor* suggested that plank roads were a viable solution to the perennial problem of muddy Brazilian roads. The article conceded that wooden planks were certainly less efficient and glamorous than steam locomotion, but "necessities demand remedy in the now," and gradual improvements, however small, were better than the status quo.[56] As the name suggests, plank roads consisted of elevated wooden planks laid above the roadbed. They were sturdy enough to support the weight of animal-drawn wagons and durable enough to function in all seasons. Celebrated as an all-weather, cost-effective alternative to the macadam method, plank roads experienced a construction boom by mid-century in the US; between 1846 and 1853, 3,500 miles of plank roads were completed in New York state alone. The wooden planks deteriorated quickly, however, and the system fell out of use by the 1860s as rail lines proliferated.[57]

Perhaps inspired by the initial success of plank roads in North America, the Viscount of Barbacena and the Baron of Novo Friburgo began construction of a plank road in Rio de Janeiro province in 1854. The road crossed a portion of the *serra* between Cantagallo and Novo Friburgo and employed gentle inclines, they reported, that were more easily constructed and ascended than the macadam system. The road extended at least fourteen miles and accomplished the dual goal of providing a smooth road surface and leveling steep inclines.[58] Despite the enthusiasm of the 1855 report, however, no further mention of the road appeared in subsequent years, suggesting that it was ultimately not a viable construction technique. Moist tropical conditions that rotted wood and the ants

---

[55] *Relatório do presidente da província do Mato Grosso, o capitão de fragata Augusto Leverger, na abertura da sessão ordinaria da Assembléa Legislativa Provincial em 10 de maio de 1851* (Cuiabá: Tip. do Echo Cuiabano, 1852), p. 34; and Mattoon, p. 276.

[56] "Vias de Communicação," O *Agricultor Brasileiro*, Vol. I, September 1854, pp. 1–2.

[57] John Majewski, Christopher Baer, and Daniel B. Klein, "Responding to Relative Decline: The Plank Road Boom of Antebellum New York," *The Journal of Economic History*, 53:1, (March 1993), pp. 106–7; E. L. Powers, "History of Road Building: First Law to Improve United States Highways passed in 1639" *New York Times*, January 2, 1910, p. AU5.

[58] *Relatório apresentado ao Exm. Vice-Presidente da Província do Rio de Janeiro o Snr. Doutor Joé [sic] Ricardo de Sà Rego pelo Presidente o Conselheiro Luiz Antônio Barboza por occasião de passar-lhe a administração da mesma provincia* (Nictheroy: Tip. de Quirino & Irmão, 1855), pp. 64–5; and E. L. Powers, "History of Road Building," p. AU5.

and termites that plagued agriculture would have almost certainly been a problem for plank roads as well. The example nonetheless demonstrates that Brazilians looked far and wide for solutions to their transportation bottleneck and experimented with new technologies beyond railroads.

The questions posed by the *Agricultor Brasileiro* about the efficacy of ordinary roads versus railroads foreshadowed the debates that swirled around the construction of the União e Indústria. The initial outlay of capital for railroad construction was high, especially in Brazil which was distant from European capital markets, raw materials were inaccessible or not of industrial grade, and even coal had to be imported from England.[59] But ordinary roads engineered through challenging territory were also expensive to construct and maintain, calling into question, in the minds of many Brazilians, whether railroads were a better investment in the long run. The dilemma came to a head in a series of critical *apedidos* published in response to the completion of Brazil's first "monumental road," the União e Indústria in 1861.

Roads and Rails: Debates and Controversies

The nineteenth-century belief that the rigid schedule and fixed tracks of the railroad imposed order on uncivilized landscapes and people obscured the fact that technological innovation was and is deeply embedded in social relationships rather than the other way round.[60] Nineteenth-century Brazil was no exception. Beyond complaints about the poor conditions of roads, impassioned debates about which type of transportation was best suited for the tropical nation appeared in newspapers and journals. The macadamized road that stirred the emotions of the young *mineiro* Monteiro da Silva was both a monument to Brazilian progress and the center of an acrimonious exchange between five anonymous writers and a Hungarian refugee and lawyer Kornis Totvarad, then residing in Rio, that unfolded in the *Publicações a Pedido* sections of the *Correio Mercantil* and the *Jornal do Commercio*. Even before the vastly ambitious project for the macadamized road had entered the thoughts of Mariano Procúpio Lage, the road's director and a *fazendeiro* from Minas Gerais, there were murmurings of discontent and doubt as to its usefulness. Some saw such "monumental roads" as an effective solution to a major problem; others saw them as squandering resources better

---

[59] Colin M. Lewis, "Public Policy and Private Initiative: Railway Building in São Paulo 1860–1889," (London: Institute of Latin American Studies, University of London, 1991), research paper, p. 4.

[60] Berman, p. 159, note.

invested in railroads that were a long-term and ultimately more cost-effective mode of transportation. The debates were bitter, the language mean-spirited. Arguments and counterarguments reflected the crisis in the national mind concerning progress: should this be moderate improvements to the status quo, or more aggressive with an eye to transforming the land, creating new ways of life for thousands of people, funneling immigrants into remote regions, and raising the national image. Interestingly, in the debates over the União e Indústria, European observers and Brazilians differed on whether railroads or ordinary roads were better suited for the young nation. Daunted by the nation's size and "backward" population, the Hungarian Totvarad argued that Brazil was too undeveloped for the railroad.

Mariano Lage received a concession for the União e Indústria in 1852. Three years later, French engineers J. R. Vigouroux and Th. Flajolot surveyed the road's proposed route and submitted a report to the imperial government. The engineers appreciated the railroad, that "marvelous instrument of modern civilization," but they advised the government that a macadamized wagon road was indeed the best option for the region. Their recommendation was primarily based on economic reasons. Asserting that the agricultural and industrial capacity of the region was insufficient to support a railroad capable of turning a profit, they argued that Brazil's sparse population, unlike the US where rail-lines connected already populated and productive regions, could not support railway freight charges.[61] The report contrasted with the 1834 observations of the Marquis of Abrantes (a member of the conservative party and later the president of the Sociedade Auxiliadora), that transportation networks were crucial for opening up interior lands to immigration. Abrantes noted that in the US new immigrants, traveled cheaply and quickly via steamship, canal, carriage, and railway from port cities to interior regions. He recognized the utility of a comparable infrastructure for feeding immigrant streams into unpopulated regions of Brazil where new arrivals often required expensive provisions, pack mules, and guides to reach settlements.[62] And once settlers arrived, they sometimes lived

---

[61] "Mémoire sur la comparaison d'une route ordinaire et d'un chem de fer entre Parahyba et Barbacena, et sur les limites qu'il convient d'adopter dans la trace d'une route pour les déclivités et les rayons des courbes," Diversos Códices 1612 a 1984, Códice 807, Volume 16, 1794–1883, Arquivo Nacional.

[62] Milguel Calmon du Pin e Almeida, *Ensaio sobre o fabrico do assucar offerecido a Sociedade D'Agricultura, Commercio, e Industria da Provincia da Bahia* (Bahia: Tip. do Diario, 1834), pp. 13–15.

unhappily in isolation at the end of poorly maintained roads, as a small group of Confederate émigrés in Pará lamented in the 1870s.[63] One central question remained, which came first: roads or the populations that used them?

Construction on the União e Indústria began in 1856, and ultimately linked the burgeoning coffee-growing region of southwestern Minas Gerais to Rio via the Pedro II railway in Petrópolis. Upon its completion in 1861, the União e Indústria was the first engineered road of its kind in South America. It included 91 miles (144 km) of macadamized surface complete with state-of-the-art bridges, gentle grades, comfortable station houses, stables, and modern stagecoaches. The road also employed the latest in construction machinery. In 1868, Richard Burton observed:

I saw, without surprise, in the virgin forest, French road-rollers, civilized appliances which had not reached London by May, 1865, when the hoofs [*sic*] of blood-horses, and the costliest wheels from Long Acre, still did the dirty work.[64]

In conjunction with the road, Lage founded an agricultural school and a German immigrant colony in Juiz de Fora, underscoring the importance of roads to colonization projects.[65] The road, settlement, and school demonstrated three central modernizing schemes of the imperial government: the improvement of internal transportation, European immigration, and the dissemination of modern agricultural practices through scientific education.[66]

The opening of the final leg of the União e Indústria in 1861 inspired admiration and enthusiasm from the public. The road reduced what

[63] Herbert H. Smith, *Brazil, the Amazons and the Coast* (New York: Charles Scribner's Sons, 1879), pp. 143–4.

[64] Burton, p. 35.

[65] By 1858 around 1,000 souls had settled in Juiz de Fora where many of the men found employment as carpenters, sawyers, and blacksmiths in the workshops of the *União e Indústria*. Wilson de L. Bastos, *Mariano Procópio Ferreira Lage: Sua vida, sua obra, descendência, genealogia* (Juiz de Fora: Paraibuna, 1994), pp. 68–9.

[66] The agricultural school was first proposed in 1864, and inaugurated in 1869. The organizers hoped that the school would improve agriculture in the region, but despite the support of Pedro II himself, the project ultimately met with little success. The school's failure was attributed to a general lack of interest and "the small intellectual advancement of [Brazilians], as well as the 'congenital defect' of the national character, always inclined to assurances of governmental protection, and distrustful of private initiative," *Relatorio Apresentado á Assembléa dos Accionistas da Companhia União e Industria em 16 de Fev. De 1875 pela Directoria da Mesma* (Rio de Janeiro: Tip. G. Leuzinger & Filhos, 1875), p. 12.

had been a four-day journey on horseback to a nine-hour drive in a comfortable coach serviced by well-maintained rest stations.[67] Pedro II personally inspected the new road in June of 1861, traveling in a special coach to the inauguration festivities in Juiz de Fora. A series of articles published in the *Jornal do Commercio* illustrated the psychological impact of the road:

> We witnessed a mule-train loaded with coffee off in the distance as it crossed the old road on the *fazenda* of d. Lina. This sight offered up for our contemplation... the contrast between routine and progress... [on one side] the donkeys bent under the weight of their pack saddles as they climbed the steep slopes (the same animals that served the contemporaries of Pedro Alves Cabral [the discoverer of Brazil in 1500]) contrasted to the gentle slopes [of the new road], rising so slowly as to be imperceptible, and quickly traversed by the modern coach, perfected and improved in conformity with the civilized world![68]

Despite such glowing responses, the road was also criticized as a wasteful vanity project. An anonymous author who appears to have been a Brazilian with intimate knowledge of the road's construction published an *apedido* attacking the road's high cost, the fact that it did not meet the deadlines stipulated in the contract, and the construction techniques of its chief engineer Captain José Maria Oliveira Bulhões. Signing with the moniker "A.," he argued that macadamized roads were indeed a necessity when constructed frugally, but the high cost of the União e Indústria rendered it a poor return on investment. A. claimed that the road cost nearly 500 contos per *légua*, or approximately 83 contos (£ 8,875) per kilometer, in his view an exorbitant cost in a country with so many pressing material needs.[69] A.'s figure, probably exaggerated to make his point, contrasted with the 1861 report for the Ministry of Agriculture, which listed the cost per *légua* at 359:135$566 milréis or nearly 60 contos (£ 6374) per kilometer including "obras de arte" (bridges and buildings), still an extravagant figure for the day. Despite A.'s argument that a railroad could have been erected in its stead for a similar or only slightly higher cost, railroads were in reality far more expensive. The first 48 kilometers of the Dom Pedro II line cost £625,991 (£13,041 per

---

[67] Peter L. Blasenheim, "Railroads in Nineteenth-Century Minas Gerais," *Journal of Latin American Studies*, Vol. 26, No. 2 (May, 1994), p. 352.

[68] *Viagem Imperial de Petrópolis a Juiz de Fóra por occasião de colleção de artigos publicados no "Jornal do Commercio" do Rio de Janeiro em 1861 e no "Diario Mercantil" de Juiz de Fóra em 1918* (Juiz de Fóra: Tip. Sul, 1919), p. 12.

[69] "Melhoramentos Materiaes," *Publicações a Pedido, Correio Mercantil*, May 4, 1861.

kilometer), while the São Paulo Railway came in at 214:598$920 *milréis*, approximately 215 contos or £24,432 per kilometer.[70]

What rankled the anonymous author, and other voices chimed in to support him, was exactly what so impressed the young medical student: the road's expensive bridges, smooth surfaces, and gentle grades that resulted in its extravagant cost. In a country like Brazil, where "backwardness and routine" were the rule, A. argued, the government needed to invest in improvements that offered the biggest value to society, and railroads were simply a stronger stimulus to *indústria*. In addition to their economic value, A. declared that the moral improvementof the Brazilian people depended on the introduction of speed. "[S]low transportation has a negative influence on the moral and material interests of a people," he asserted, while "velocity" resulted in the opposite.[71] Speed changed the fabric of society by injecting energy into lethargic populations and by imposing a mechanical rhythm on the land and its inhabitants. A.'s rhetoric mirrored the British narrative that telegraphs, railways, and steamships were crucial for civilizing backward populations in colonial India where, imperial modernizers asserted, locomotives did not merely transport passengers, they edified them.[72] Railroad tracks, telegraph lines, and rigid time schedules imposed symmetry and order on the chaotic Indian landscape and brought the colony into sync with historical (European) time.[73] Train cars also provided newly configured public spaces that, it was asserted, would eradicate Indian social distinctions through the intermingling of different castes.[74] Colonial administrators further declared the railway a stimulant to productivity and innovation by introducing India's artisans and manufacturers to a wider range of goods produced in distant villages.[75] As Ritika Prasad observes, railways were more than mere technology; they transformed space and unified time, they opened up continents and brought Enlightenment rationality

---

[70] Figure for the São Paulo Railway from Mattoon, p. 280; figure from the Dom Pedro II railway from Graham, p. 58. Converted at 9.39 *mil-réis* per pound sterling in 1861 for the Dom Pedro II and 8.8 *mil-réis* per pound sterling in 1863 for the São Paulo Ltd. For conversion values, see Nathaniel H. Leff, *Underdevelopment and Development in Brazil, Vol. I: Economic Structure and Change, 1822–1947* (New York: George Allen & Unwin, 1982), p. 246.

[71] "Melhoramentos Materiaes," May 4, 1861.

[72] Michael Adas, *Machines as the Measure of Men: Science, Technology, and Ideologies of Western Dominance* (Ithaca: Cornell University Press, 1989), pp. 225–6.

[73] Francis Foot Hardman, *Trem-fantasma: a ferrovia Madeira-Mamoré e a modernidade na selva* (São Paulo: Companhia das Letras, 1988, 2005), p. 239.

[74] Adas, pp. 225–6.   [75] *Ibid.*

to backward populations in both material and psychological terms; in sum they accelerated and harmonized the march of progress.[76]

In a similar vein, A. averred that the railway would impose a mechanical rhythm on the landscape and the human body in Brazil, resulting in the creation of a work ethic and a new valuation of time that would disseminate *indústria* in backward regions. The anonymous author's assertion was not mere hyperbole; one of the earliest train travelers in Great Britain remarked that the speed of the locomotive created new perspectives for the passengers within in a most curious and stimulating way, a sentiment also related in Indian literature.[77] Brazilians eager to overcome the perceived insufficiencies of their nation's non-European population were inspired by the possibility for elevating the masses through technological transformation, as A. demonstrates. From the eighteenth-century French philosopher, the Marquis of Condorcet, to Auguste Comte's nineteenth-century positivism, technology as a catalyst for social improvement found a ready audience in Brazil.

The French engineers of the União e Indústra were not the only foreigners to suggest that Brazil was not yet ready for the railroad. Carlos Kornis de Totvarad, the opinionated Hungarian lawyer who appears to have represented Lage in the *publicações apedido*, asserted that steam locomotion was not the answer to Brazil's transportation woes. Ordinary roads were of greater utility to Brazil's economic development, he claimed. Railroads lost in their "limited access to a particular territory" what they might gain in velocity, an argument also put forth by the French engineers. Totvarad asserted that "... the accelerated transport of passengers and coffee at eight or ten leagues per hour [a bracing 24 to 30 mph] is not a pressing necessity" in Brazil.[78] Money spent on a larger, well-maintained ordinary road system that was passable in all seasons of the year would benefit a greater portion of the populace than the "illusory progress" of an "object of momentary fashion" implying that Brazilians merely wanted to put a modern veneer on their "backward nation."[79] Unsurprisingly, his argument revealed a tone of racial superiority as he further claimed that Brazilians, unlike their North American counterparts, were "indolent" by nature and therefore not ready for the "sublime speed" of the locomotive. For Totvarad, there were no transcendent

---

[76] Ritika Prasad, "'Time-Sense': Railways and Temporality in Colonial India," *Modern Asian Studies* 47, no. 4 (Jul 2013), pp. 1253–4, 1258 and 1268.

[77] Hardman, p. 35.

[78] "Melhoramentos Materiaes," *Publicações a Pedido, JC*, May 15, 1861.   [79] *Ibid.*

technological possibilities in bringing the railroad to primitive Brazil. In his view, improved roads were sufficient to meet the nation's current state of progress, which the lawyer described in rather uncharitable terms:

[Brazilians are] a people in its infancy who are satisfied...to cover their nudity with simple cotton shifts, and to satisfy their hunger with scanty amounts of corn meal...or the root of whatever plant meets the need...and as the centuries pass they remain content [to travel via] horses and mules, traveling not on improved roads, but on small trails etched by [the feet] of travelers and the so-called muleteers.[80]

Needless to say, such provocative charges were not well received by Totvarad's Brazilian audience. An ally of A., the anonymous *O Amador das curiosidades raras* (the Admirer of Curiosities), responded with especial venom, sarcastically challenging the charges of Brazilian indolence.[81] Yet notwithstanding the Hungarian's obvious racial bias and his affront to Brazilian sensibilities, he offers the modern reader insight that says as much about his Brazilian interlocutors as it illuminates his outsider's perspective. Both he and his opponents advocated for the same result: the transition from a "backward," non-European population to a Europeanized landscape and people. At stake was more than commerce. Totvarad's criticism condemned the "miserable" appearance of the nation's interior settlements, communities that often appeared very poor indeed to arriving immigrants. This was a version of Brazil that would-be modernizers were hoping to overcome. Totvarad also expressed awe for the vastness of Brazilian geography – in his mind incomparable to the United States because it was larger and possessed a more challenging landscape – a response that still strikes many Europeans as they encounter the immense territories of American nations. He saw railway technology as *insufficient* to meet the needs of modernizing Brazil, a nation of continental scale:

These so-called cities and settlements in the nation's vast interior are located at such great distances from each other, in addition to the distance in time in which they were originally founded, that today they present themselves so miserably, and on such a small scale, whether in relation to their population or their products, that only an extravagant dreamer could propose the railroad as a reasonable project for linking together the most remote points of the country. The sublime

---

[80] "Melhoramentos Materiaes," *Publicações a Pedido, JC*, May 13, 1861.
[81] "Melhoramentos Materiaes: resumo dos valentes argumentos do Sr. Kornis em Favor da Estrada União e Industria e Sua Administração," *Publicações a Pedido, Correio Mercantil*, May 16, 1861.

speed of the locomotive is proposed as a remedy, without any consideration for the demand this would place on the nations' resources, now and for future generations... [82]

In other words, the Hungarian imagined the locomotive would sputter out in the great distances of the Brazilian nation.

In contrast, A. and his *apedido* allies saw the railroad as the only technology consequential enough to conquer both material distance and social backwardness in Brazil. They wanted change, and quickly. Whereas Europeans associated with the União e Indústria were more conservative about the ability of the railroad to increase economic development and settlement in Brazil, A. saw the railroad as the most important catalyst for modernizing the nation, and they were not wrong. In economic terms, railroads spurred Brazilian growth in the latter part of the nineteenth century and into the twentieth, even if an attendant "civilizing of the population" remained elusive in the eyes of many Brazilian elites.[83]

Despite Totvarad's reservations about Brazilian railways, the arrival of the first railroads in the 1850s and 1860s greatly alleviated the transportation bottleneck. But in contrast to the image of a joyful forest celebrating the arrival of the railroad, reality proved to be quite the opposite. In Brazil, engineers faced some of the most difficult railroad-building terrain of the nineteenth century. The São Paulo Company Limited, a line that began in the port of Santos and extended to Jundiahy in the interior of the province, rose from sea level to an impressive 2,625 feet in just seven miles as it tackled the Great Escarpment.[84] Gaston described the obstacles that engineers faced in constructing the line:

[W]e passed the termination of the iron rail twelve miles from the city of São Paulo, and learned from a man engaged on the road that there would be an interruption of some months, from a landslide at the Serra de Santo having stopped the transportation of iron. This serra is likely to be a very serious obstacle to the success of the road, as even when in working order the inclined plane, with four stationary engines to draw up the cars, is an inconvenient arrangement, and not by any means free from danger.[85]

[82] "Melhoramentos Materiaes," *Publicações a Pedido*, JC, May 15, 1861.
[83] Summerhill, pp. 4–5.   [84] Lewis, p. 4.
[85] Gaston, p. 207. An additional description of the railroad was printed in *Brazil and the Brazilians*, "The great difficulty for this road was the almost perpendicular wall of the Serra do Cubitão, which was only overcome by a series of inclined planes, up which the cars are drawn by stationary engines. This road, under Mr. Fox, an eminent English engineer, has been a great success in every point of view," Fletcher and Kidder, p. 365.

Despite the technological difficulties encountered in construction, the railroad later became one of the most commercially successful lines in Brazil.

The Dom Pedro II railroad in Rio de Janeiro province faced similar challenges. The company exhausted its capital three years into construction as its engineers attempted to conquer the formidable *Serra do Mar*. The Brazilian government subsequently guaranteed the railway's loans, and took over the line.[86] An article printed in the US in 1890 acknowledged the difficulties that railroad engineers faced in Brazil:

> We have been apt to regard Brazil as far behind Argentina in the energy in which she has pushed her commercial development. The fact is that the Brazilians have accomplished far more in the way of railroad building than they have had credit for. The vast difference in the topographical features of Brazil and Argentina accounts largely for the far greater mileage of railroads completed in the Argentine Republic... But Brazil had to begin her railroads under the most expensive difficulties. Her roads from the sea level to the elevated table have cost $150,000 a mile. Five hundred miles of Argentine lines could be laid down in less time and more cheaply than fifty miles of these early Brazilian roads.[87]

Crossing the Great Escarpment called for expensive mechanical remedies such as the four stationary engines described by Gaston that hoisted train cars up the *serra* when grades were too steep for locomotives. In addition, costly, slow, and dangerous tunnel excavation and complicated trestles and bridges were required to ascend the escarpment in Rio de Janeiro. At its completion, the Dom Pedro II line included fifteen tunnels ranging from 300 to 7,300 feet of which 5,700 feet, or nearly a mile, were shored up by interior masonry.[88] Louis Agassiz described a portion of the Dom Pedro II Railway as it crossed the *serra* in 1864:

> The last three miles of our journey was over what is called the "temporary road," the use of which will be discontinued as soon as the great tunnel is completed. I must say, that to the inexperienced this road looks exceedingly perilous, especially that part of it which is carried over a wooden bridge 65 feet high, with a very strong curvature and a gradient of 4 per cent (211 feet per mile). As you feel the engine laboring up the steep ascent, and, looking out, find yourself on the edge of a precipitous bank, and almost face to face with the hindmost car, while the train bends around the curve, it is difficult to resist the sense of insecurity. It is certainly to the credit of the management of the line that no accident has occurred under circumstances where the least carelessness would be fatal.

---

[86] Blasenheim, p. 357.

[87] "Railroad Building in Brazil," *New York Evangelist*, December 4, 1890, 61.49. p. 9.

[88] Elizabeth Cabot Cary Agassiz and Louis Agassiz, *A Journey in Brazil* (Boston: Ticknor and Fields), 1868, p. 528.

To this, Agassiz appended the following:

Some weeks after [my travel on the Dom Pedro II] I chanced to ask a beautiful young Brazilian woman, recently married, whether she had ever been over this temporary road for the sake of seeing the picturesque scenery. "No," she answered with perfect seriousness, "I am young and very happy, and I do not wish to die yet." It was an amusing comment on the Brazilian estimate of the dangers attending the journey.[89]

These impressive engineering feats were achieved at great expense – both human and financial – and often with significant delays. Mosquitos, thick vegetation, and disease also thwarted railroad construction; the most notorious example of this was the Madeira Mamoré line that was begun in 1872 in Amazonas (now the state of Rondônia) and completed thirty years later. Built in the challenging conditions of the Amazon forest, the railroad was constructed to bring landlocked Bolivian rubber through Brazil to market. The railway's engineers encountered the same difficulties that thwarted the French attempt to construct the Panama Canal in the 1880s, especially the periodic outbreak of mosquito-borne disease. Subsequently the line was referred to as the "railroad of death" due to the high mortality of its workers. Many laborers shipped to the region to work on the railway returned before even disembarking upon discovering the horrendous conditions.[90]

It was not until advancements in engineering technology, and many years of experience working with Brazilian conditions, that railroad construction more easily met geographical challenges by the end of the imperial period. At Brazil's first Railroad Exhibition in 1887, the Minister of Agriculture, Commerce, and Public Works commented, "Brazil has conquered formidable natural obstacles, subjugating them through mechanical works of art that deserve recognition among the . . . victories of science and industry."[91] Beyond the minister's nineteenth-century hyperbole about the power of engineering to conquer nature, Brazil was home to

---

[89] Agassiz, p. 56.

[90] José Marcello Salles Giffoni, "Trilhos Arrancados: história da Estrada de Ferro Bahia e Minas (1878–1966)," (Ph.D. dissertation, Universidade Federal de Minas Gerais, 2006), pp. 62–3; and Lamounier, pp. 126–35. For a full treatment of the difficulties of building the Madeira Mamoré railroad, see Manoel Rodrigues Ferreira, *A Ferrovia do Diabo* (São Paulo: Melhoramentos, 1959, 2005).

[91] Rodrigo Augusto da Silva, *Discurso Proferido por Occasião da Abertura da Primeira Exposição dos Caminhos de Ferro do Brazil*, in *O Brazil na Exposição Internacional dos Caminhos de Ferro em Pariz em 1887* (Rio de Janeiro: Imprensa Nacional, 1887), pp. vi–vii.

some of the most difficult terrain confronted by the railroad engineer. But if physical limitations and the lack of capital sometimes thwarted technological ambitions, locomotives nonetheless began to profitably speed and spark across the Brazilian landscape, inspiring commentary in the public sphere.

Part II Railroad Workshops and Local Technological Dissemination

Brazil's dependence on imported railroad materials, technology, and engineering personnel inhibited the large-scale industrialization that resulted from railroad construction in the United States and Germany. Great Britain provided the capital, engineers, machinery, rolling stock, tracks, and coal for Brazil's first railroads. US manufacturers later competed with European producers as US-produced Bessemer steel tracks and machinery, especially Philadelphia's Baldwin locomotive, were less expensive and often better suited to Brazilian needs.[92] Colin Lewis attributes the absence of railroad-based industrialization in Brazil to deposits of low-grade iron ore unsuitable for heavy construction, the difficult accessibility of high-grade coal, and isolated and outmoded foundries such as the São João de Ipanema located in rural São Paulo province.[93] Innovations in foreign steel production and the international decline in the price of railroad materials after the 1870s further prejudiced domestic production.[94] William Summerhill agrees that Brazilian railroads failed to spark industrialization, but counters that unlike the United States, where railroad construction tapped into existing manufactories that never fully depended on the railroad sector, Brazil had no widespread and preexisting industrial capacity from which to supply its railroads. Though Summerhill overlooks the importance of shipyards in producing the first steam

[92] Bernardo Avelino Gavião Peixoto, *Relatorio apresentado á Assembléa Legislativa Provincial do Rio de Janeiro na abertura da segunda sessão da vigesima quarta legislatura em 8 de agosto de 1883* (Rio de Janeiro: Tip. Montenegro, 1883), p. 22.

[93] A large coal deposit was discovered in Rio Grande do Sul at the beginning of the nineteenth century, but was unavailable for wide-scale exploitation until 1883 when the *Companhia das minas de carvão de pedra do Arroio dos Ratos* was founded. The coal was transported from the mine via rail thirty kilometers to the river Jacuhí, where it arrived in Porto Alegre via steamer. A sample of coal from *Arroio dos Ratos* won a bronze medal at the International Exhibition in Antwerp in 1885. Before the construction of the railway, coal from the mine was transported overland by ox cart, an inefficient mode of conveyance that greatly hampered its industrial application. *O Brazil no Exposição Internacional de caminhos de ferro*, pp. 64–5.

[94] Lewis, p. 6.

engines and industrial machinery in Brazil – the Baron of Mauá's Ponte d'Areia shipyard assembled Brazil's first locomotive – workshops with the capacity to produce machinery and parts for railroads were limited to large urban centers with shipbuilding facilities until later in the century.[95]

Railroads did not spur industrialization in nineteenth-century Brazil, but railroad *oficínas* (workshops) nonetheless became important local sites for on-the-job mechanical training and technological dissemination. Workshops produced passenger and freight cars, wheels, and in the case of the Cantagallo line in Rio de Janeiro, agricultural equipment for local *fazendeiros*.[96] The *oficínas* also provided meeting places for machinists, engineers, and inventors. As illustrated in Chapter 3, the facilities of the Pedro II Railway, located in Engenho do Dentro on the outskirts of Rio de Janeiro, also served as an exhibition space for inventions by local entrepreneurs.[97]

Brazilians may not have manufactured locomotives, but they assembled (imported locomotives were shipped in pieces and put together on-site), repaired, and modified them for local conditions in railroad workshops. By the 1870s, Brazilian engineers also evaluated foreign equipment and made decisions about which locomotive systems were better suited for domestic needs. The Pedro II railroad workshop repaired and rebuilt locomotives from the ground up, in many cases incorporating significant modifications. The line employed wheels, wagon components, and iron appliances fabricated in the Ipanema foundry. By 1881 the Pedro II workshops had produced 1,343 wagons and passenger cars.[98] At the 1887 International Exhibition of Railroads in Paris, one line from provincial Rio de Janeiro featured a photograph of a first-class passenger car constructed entirely from Brazilian materials. Other railroads developed specialized pumps, an apparatus for applying oil to wheel axles, and a system for joining together railways of different gauges.[99] In 1876 Engineer Joaquim Galdino Pimental designed an improved

[95] Beauclair, *A Construção Inacabada*, p. 41 and pp. 153–67.

[96] Ernesto Eugenio da Graça Bastos, *Relatório do Engenheiro Fiscal da Estrada de Ferro de Cantagallo, anexo ao Relatório apresentado á Assembléa Legislativa Provincial do Rio de Janeiro na primeira sessão da decima nona legislatura no dia 29 de setembro de 1872 pelo presidente, conselheiro Josino do Nascimento Silva* (Rio de Janeiro: Tip. Perseverança, 1872), pp. 7–8.

[97] "Gaz de Turfa," *Gazetilha, JC*, January 19, 1880.

[98] *Archivos da Exposição da Industria Nacional: actas, parecers e decisões do jury geral da exposição da industria nacional realizada no Rio de Janeiro em 1881*, (Rio de Janeiro: Tip. Nacional, 1882) p. CXXXIV.

[99] *O Brazil no Exposição Internacional dos Caminhos de Ferro*, pp. 42, 48, and 70.

"distribution apparatus" for locomotives, demonstrating that Brazilians readily modified imported technology for their local needs. Based on a European design, the Engineering Commission of the French Government declared the device an improvement over the original.[100]

Of special note was the use of native woods in the construction of rolling stock, furniture, train stations, and railroad ties. A majority of the 22 Brazilian railways listed in the 1887 catalog enumerated the varieties of wood employed in railroad construction. The Dom Pedro II line, for instance, listed 45 different tree species used in its rolling stock: first-class cars employed distinguished tropical hardwoods such as mahogany, while less valuable woods served in second- and third-class cars. The Macaé e Campos, also in Rio de Janeiro, listed a total of 72 species of trees used in its equipment, including two varieties of mahogany and one of exotic black oak. Coal and iron may have been scarce, but Brazilians readily adopted domestic lumber in all aspects of railway construction, a fact that was underscored by engineer André Rebouças' *General Index of Brazilian Wood* described in Chapter 3.[101]

Provincial reports from the 1870s reveal a flurry of activity in the *oficínas* of the Cantagallo Railroad. In 1872, the workshop forged its own material for an extension of the line and manufactured replacement parts for repairs. As mentioned previously, the Cantagallo *oficínas* took private commissions for agricultural machinery from local *fazendeiros*, a fact that the fiscal engineer was quick to assert did not prejudice the needs of the railroad, and indeed, generated more than 4 *contos* (£426) in additional revenue in 1872.[102] Likewise, two British engineers in Pernambuco oversaw repairs to sugar *engenhos* on plantations in the 1850s, suggesting that railroads facilitated the dissemination of agricultural technology into the interior, again contrasting with the United States where machine shops produced parts for the railroad, not the other way around as in Brazil.[103]

Built through some of the steepest mountain grades in Brazil, the Cantagallo railroad used the English Fell system, which was specially designed for mountainous territory. Due to the difficult terrain, wear and tear

---

[100] Sebastião José Pereira, *Relatorio apresentado à Assembléa Legislativa Provincial de S. Paulo em 2 de fevereiro de 1876* (São Paulo: Tip. do Diario, 1876), p. 9.

[101] André Rebouças, *Ensaio de indice geral das madeiras do Brazil*, 3 vols. (Rio de Janeiro: Tip. Nacional, 1877).

[102] Bastos, *Relatório do Engenheiro Fiscal da Estrada de Ferro de Cantagallo...*, pp. 7–8.

[103] Mansfield, Charles, *Paraguay, Brazil, and the Plate: Letters Written in 1852–1853* (Cambridge: Macmillan & Co., 1856), p. 44.

on machinery required constant upkeep. The 1875 report, for example, included sixteen pages of detailed descriptions of repairs completed in the line's workshops.[104] The demands of maintenance – and the ability of workers to repair everything from broken axles, to springs, fuel valves, and gauges, in addition to forging wheels and replacement parts and building cars from the ground up – required expertise and technical skill from railroad machinists. At the same time, repairs were sometimes rendered more time-consuming and difficult due to the lack of up-to-date machinery that required much of the work to be measured and completed by hand.

In 1875, the Cantagallo line employed 227 rail yard workers including five machinists, three lathe workers, eleven metal workers and their apprentices, twenty-three carpenters, six fitters, one telegraph repairman and apprentice, and nine smiths, among others. While it is impossible from the report to determine how many of those employed in the workshops were Brazilian-born or trained (the chief engineer was French), it is reasonable to assume that Brazilians comprised a portion of the workforce. This meant that they acquired a hands-on understanding of the mechanics not only of locomotives, but of the construction of freight cars, and all of the myriad working parts of the railway that supported a line's safe operation. The Cantagallo workshops also suggest that engineers and machinists in Brazil had to be resourceful in reconditioning and maintaining their equipment. Unlike Mexico and Cuba where US engineers dominated railroad construction and maintenance and the proximity to manufacturers ensured faster shipping times and lower costs for materials, Brazil's distance from production centers necessitated self-sufficiency.[105]

Another example of local technical expertise was evidenced in a competition held by the Ministry of Agriculture in 1884 for the invention of a safety device for street trolleys that prevented passengers from slipping and falling beneath trolley wheels. Of nine surviving entries (and ten inventors) seven applicants were Brazilian, one was from the US, and two were French. One Brazilian entrant was a land surveyor from Campinas who first envisioned the design for his "Expulsor

---

[104] Bernardo Augusto Nascentes de Azambuja, *Relatorio apresentado á Assembléa Legislativa Provincial do Rio de Janeiro na segunda sessão da vigesima legislatura no dia 8 de setembro de 1875* (Rio de Janeiro: Tip. do Apostolo, 1875), pp. 12–28.

[105] Anderson, *Outcasts in their Own Land*, pp. 89 and 236; Louis A. Pérez, Jr., *On Becoming Cuban: Identity, Nationality, and Culture* (Chapel Hill: University of North Carolina Press, 1999, 2008), pp. 19–21.

Mascarenhas" in 1876 when he was a student at Rio's Polytechnic School. Two others were "married merchants" residing in Rio, and another was a civil engineer. The occupations of the remaining Brazilians were not listed, though several held patents for their devices from the Ministry of Agriculture, which suggested they were experienced engineers or machinists (Fig. 5.1).[106]

While a later Ministry of Agriculture report declared that experiments with the submitted designs had not produced "satisfactory results," and that some of the applicants "hadn't a minimal understanding of mechanics," the alacrity with which local inventors responded to the call for the safety device indicated an active community of professional and lay inventors in Brazil.[107]

British engineers and capital built the first railroads in Brazil in the 1850s and 1860s, but Brazilians dominated railroad engineering by the 1870s.[108] A course on the construction of "ordinary roads, railroads, bridges and viaducts" was added to the engineering curriculum at the Polytechnic School in Rio de Janeiro in 1874, and by 1880 a full 75 percent of all railway engineers were Brazilian-born.[109] At the 1887 International Exhibition of Railroads in Paris, the majority of Chief Engineers for railways across the nation had Portuguese names. Unlike the United States, where up until the 1870s engineers and machinists learned their profession on-site, Brazilian engineers were formally trained and thoroughly professionalized by the 1880s.[110] By the end of the century Brazilians still imported railway machinery and material, but on the ground, the nation's railways were thoroughly Brazilianized.

Conclusion

Improving transportation during the Second Empire was one topic most elite Brazilians agreed upon, even as they remained divided on how

---

[106] *Diversos Códices* OI, GIFI, 6D-52, *Arquivo Nacional.*

[107] Rodrigo Augusto da Silva, *Relatorio apresentado à Assembléa Geral na Terceira Sessão da Vigesima Legislatura...*, 1888, p. 366.

[108] Colonel Charles Garnett made his career in the US South where he constructed railroads in the mountainous regions of Tennessee and Alabama, *American Railroad Journal and Iron Manufacturer and Mining Gazette*, Second Quarter Series, Vol. V, No. 1, January 6, 1849, p. 28.

[109] Pedro Eduardo Mesquita de Monteiro Marinho, "Engenharia Imperial, O Instituto Politécnico Brasileiro" (Ph.D. dissertation, Universidade Federal Fluminense, Niterói, Rio de Janeiro, 2002), p. 147, and fn.381, p. 147.

[110] *Ibid.*, p. 147 and fn. 381, p. 147.

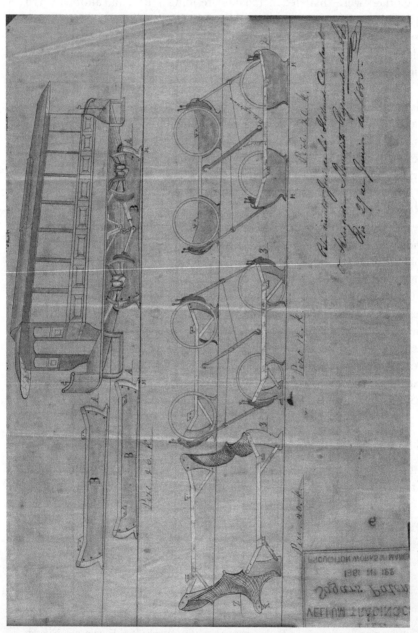

FIGURE 5.1. The "Preservador Calvacanti," complete with metal wheel covers and a safety net at both ends of the trolley, was designed by José de Sá Hollanda Cavalcanti to prevent fallen passengers from being crushed beneath trolley wheels. *Source: Diversos Códices* OI, GIFI, 6D-52. Courtesy of Arquivo Nacional, Brazil.

best to proceed. The difficulties of travel in the new nation put a stranglehold on economic development, discouraged immigration, and caused anxiety about Brazil's backward appearance. A scarcity of capital was also a serious obstacle, and how best to apply limited funds for improvements resulted in bitter public debates. In the end the railroad did indeed triumph, resulting in impressive development of engineering skills on the part of foreign and Brazilian engineers alike. Railroad construction did not spur domestic industrialization on the scale of the United States or Germany, but it did stimulate the economy and the dissemination of mechanical knowledge within Brazil. Yet if Brazilian railroads were without doubt an economic success, they did not necessarily engender progress and civilization in the social sphere, as the next chapter demonstrates.

6

Trolleys, Railroads, and Factories, or Civilization and Barbarism

It was Christiano who opened the conversation with the remark that train travel was very tiring, to which Rubião replied that it was, indeed, and added that for one accustomed to donkey-back it was especially so, and wholly without charm. It was undeniable, though, that it marked progress.

Machado de Assis[1]

The 1870s were a pivotal decade in the modernization of nineteenth-century Brazil. Among the significant developments of the period was the passage of the Law of Free Birth in 1871, an important, albeit inconsistently enforced and ambiguously effective step toward the full abolition of slavery in 1888.[2] In the political sphere, the increasing popularity of republicanism, positivism, and racial ideologies such as those espoused by British philosopher Herbert Spencer added new debates and participants to the established contours of conservative Brazilian politics.[3] Actors from outside the traditional agricultural elite and state bureaucracy began to assert their influence in military, social, cultural, and political venues,

---

[1] Machado de Assis, *Philosopher or Dog?*, Clotide Wilson, trans. (New York: The Noonday Press, 1954, 1992), pp. 27–8.

[2] The Law of Free Birth emancipated slaves upon majority at age twenty-one, or at the age of eight with indemnification from state funds. In reality, the law did little to impact the lived status of slaves, many of whom were bought and sold, despite the free status they would achieve upon majority, Robert Conrad, *The Destruction of Brazilian Slavery, 1850–1888* (Berkeley: University of California Press, 1972), ch. 7.

[3] Angela Alonso provides a recent interpretation of this important decade and the "Generation of 1870" that infused the political and social spheres with new ideas such as positivism, see especially ch. 2, *Idéias em Movimento: a geração 1870 na crise do Brasil-Império* (São Paulo: Paz e Terra, 2002). See also Richard Graham's chapter on the appeal of British biologist and philosopher Herbert Spencer's ideas on progress and race in Brazil, Richard Graham, *Britain and the Onset of Modernization in Brazil: 1850–1914* (Cambridge: Cambridge University Press, 1968), ch. 9.

culminating in the relatively uncontested coup of the emperor Pedro II in 1889. As Chapter 5 demonstrated, foreign and Brazilian-made inventions increasingly appeared in urban and rural settings. Railroads and streetcars rambled across the countryside and through city streets; factories and mechanized production increased; and new and marvelous machines appeared in homes, on plantations, and in cities and towns, as period newspaper advertisements demonstrate. But if sewing machines, grain mills, steam-powered factories, streetcars, ice machines, and household call systems transformed material circumstances, they also impacted Brazilian social norms, redefining, or at least calling into question, the ways in which individuals interacted. This chapter will examine the social anxieties that surrounded modernization in two areas in particular: railroads and factories.

An advertisement for a *campainhas eléctricas* (electric bell) call system published in 1875 provides one advertiser's imagining of how a new technology could both mesh with and improve upon the existing social hierarchy in Rio (Fig. 6.1). The advertisement features a slightly startled-looking black servant who appears to have been roused from dozing. He is dressed in formal livery in a domestic setting seated beneath a row of bells labeled for the different stations of the household staff, (doorman, butler, cook, etc.). The servant and the neatly arranged, geometrical wires of the call board occupy the central pane of the illustration, serving as a visual and metaphorical barrier between the lady of the house sitting quietly in her parlor and a top-hatted gentleman calling at the door. The central message is that the new technology improves upon existing social hierarchies within the household, and in this case, reinforces the gendered division of space. In nineteenth-century Brazil the house was the domain of respectable middle- and upper-class women who required protection from the potentially corrupting and reputation-damaging influences of the street.[4] The emphatically capitalistic phrase placed above the figures, "Time is Money!! O Tempo É Dinheiro," asserts that the call system will introduce the efficiency of the factory into the home by improving communication between servants and mistress. The additional terms, "Frugality! Promptness! Elegance! Neatness!" and "Call! Speak! Order!" reinforce the authority of the lady of the house, appeal to the aesthetic expectations of middle- and upper-class domestic space, and invoke mechanized

---

4 The street was inhabited by unfamiliar men, women of questionable virtue, and slaves and servants who served as intermediaries between the corrupting street and the safety of the house. Sandra Lauderdale Graham's classic study explores this gendered division of house and street in Rio, *House and Street: the Domestic World of Servants and Masters in Nineteenth-Century Rio de Janeiro* (Cambridge: Cambridge University Press, 1988).

FIGURE 6.1. "As Campainhas Eléctricas" – an electric bell system marketed for the Brazilian household. *Source*: "Anúncios," *Jornal do Commercio*, September 18, 1875. Courtesy of the Acervo da Fundação Biblioteca Nacional, Brazil.

efficiency. Traditional social roles and the emergence of a new, capitalist arrangement of social space are brought together in the household. The call system modernizes and improves upon domestic management, reinforcing nineteenth-century conceptions of gender and the proper relationship between servants (or slaves) and those they served.[5] Finally, the illustration asserts, the new technology is beneficial for all levels of society.

While it is unknown to what extent the electric call system was adopted in Rio households, the illustration demonstrates an awareness of the potential for technology to impact social organization. If the modernizers of Chapter 4 hoped to transform rural Brazilian society through agricultural technology, manufacturing was seen as a way to reinforce and improve upon existing social hierarchies, and demonstrate the viability of wage labor through factory-sponsored education. In contrast, when technologies were experienced as disruptive, as sometimes occurred with railways and streetcars, the public forcefully expressed their umbrage in the *Publicações a Pedido* section.

Modernization and its Discontents

If the railways desired by Brazilian modernizers did successfully facilitate the efficient and rapid movement of agricultural commodities from the interior to port cities, conquer Brazil's difficult geography, and elevate the human spirit by the 1870s, they also created unforeseen problems in the social sphere as Rubião's remarks to Christiano at the beginning of this chapter reveal. The new – often cramped – public spaces on rural train cars and city trolleys raised questions about the proper deportment between railway workers and passengers and caused anxiety about intermingling between members of different social castes and women and men, making the railroad discomfiting to those accustomed to the more congenial travel by "donkey-back."[6] An example from the *Revista Illustrada* in 1888, for example, lampoons the effect of abolition on trolley ridership: a white, well-dressed male passenger is nearly crowded out by two portly Afro-Brazilian women, presumably ex-slaves. More ominous still, the next panel shows the formerly enslaved chaotically scrambling onto a moving street car (Fig. 6.2). Railroads and tramways were also among the

[5] "Annuncios," *JC*, September 18, 1875.
[6] Rosa Maria Barboza de Araújo discusses the democratization of public space on board street trolleys in the late nineteenth- and early twentieth-century Rio, *A Vocação do Prazer: A cidade e família no Rio de Janeiro republicano* (Rio de Janeiro: Rocco, 1993), p. 295.

Nos bonds.

FIGURE 6.2. "A festa da Gloria e alguns efeitos da lei de 13 de Maio" (The celebration of the neighborhood of Gloria, and some of the effects of the law of the 13th of May (abolishing slavery). The *Revista Illustrada* reveals anxieties about sharing public space on board trolleys after the abolition of slavery. The top-hatted gentleman in the center is squeezed between two portly Afro-Brazilian women; on the right, the formerly enslaved crowd onto a moving trolley. *Source: Revista Illustrada,* Anno 13, n. 510, 1888, p. 8. Courtesy of the Acervo da Fundação Biblioteca Nacional, Brazil.

first modern Brazilian companies to employ wage earners who worked directly with the public.[7] As wage earners, railroad operators existed outside the slave hierarchy, yet their status as service workers suffered from pejorative perceptions of manual labor. As a result, the integration of railway workers into a slave society with a hierarchical racial caste system was fraught with tension as revealed by numerous *apedido* accusations of rudeness and insubordination. Conductors, train engineers, and *cocheiros* (trolley drivers) enforced rules that maintained safety and kept trains running on time, actions that passengers sometimes interpreted as impertinence and disrespect. On Rio's congested streets near the port, long the center of the city's commercial and cultural life, trolley lines also pitted wagoners, pedestrians, and merchants against streetcar operators and passengers over right of way and the use of public space, resulting in heated debates about the definition of progress. Complaints about the trolley and railway illustrated that Rio was undergoing social and technological changes that did not always proceed in the peaceful manner that modernizers envisioned.

Concern over how to integrate wage labor into existing social structures also appeared in debates about the labor force in factories. Uncertainty about free workers in a society where manual labor was defined by slavery came to the fore, especially as calls for abolition mounted in the early 1870s. Reformers sought models that would prepare workers for the order and rhythm of the factory regime while maintaining the paternalistic relationships of Brazilian society. Factory schools were celebrated as an effective model for transitioning to wage labor in Brazil, a central motive of which was to create a docile workforce and contain owner/worker relationships within a traditional Brazilian social structure.

The Social Price of Progress

Mr Editor:

I humbly request that you print this notice of the following incident that occurred on the Dom Pedro II railroad. As is well known, the insolence of certain employees of this railroad is becoming proverbial in this country, and a stop to the practice is sorely needed. Yesterday, a passenger arriving on the six o'clock train from Belém was grossly insulted by one of these employees... [When] he politely inquired about a missing bag, the... employee's response was, "Get out,

---

[7] Maria Lúcia Lamounier, *Ferrovias e mercado de trabalho no Brasil do século XIX* (São Paulo: Editora da Universidade de São Paulo, 2012), p. 41.

and get out now!" spoken with all the inappropriate arrogance of a subaltern employee who should know his place . . .

   One who was there,

                              – Jornal do Commercio, November 19, 1860[8]

Excitement over the arrival of Rio de Janeiro's first railways in the 1850s and the first animal-drawn *bondes* (trolleys) in the court city in 1859 quickly turned to complaints about poor administration, high fares, irregular schedules, and especially rude employees. No other category of free worker, with the exception of the road engineer, received as much negative attention in public letters as did conductors and *cocheiros* (trolley operators). Indeed, it was quite the opposite with ship captains and crews, a group that was frequently praised for successful voyages as demonstrated by an *apedido* published by a group of twenty-four satisfied steamship passengers in 1875.[9] Part of the frustration with conductors stemmed from their role as both service providers and rule enforcers who directed passengers, operated mechanical equipment, collected tickets, and made change, all while hewing to a schedule. Furthermore, any one passenger's encounter with a trolley conductor was fleeting, measured in short periods of time, amid the hustle and flurry of a growing city on the move. The anonymity and speed of interactions on the trolley necessitated by tight schedules and crowded conditions meant that conductors had little time for personal interactions with passengers. The ever-astute Machado de Assis observed the effect of the *bonde* on public life in Rio: "As one *bonde* climbs to the top of the hill, another descends; there is no time on the way for a pinch of snuff; at the most, all two fellows can do is give a tip of the hat."[10] Under these circumstances, conductors were often, one might assume, impatient with passengers, especially during peak hours. Frustration with trolley conductors gained greater urgency by the 1880s as Rio residents from the middle-class neighborhoods of Botafogo to the less affluent communities in Vila Isabel and the North Zone increasingly depended on *bondes* for their daily movements around the city. Dissatisfaction with trolley service in the 1860s and 1870s took a more ominous turn with Rio's first politically significant popular protest:

---

[8] "Estrada de Ferro de D. Pedro II," *Publicações a Pedido, JC*, November 18, 1860.

[9] "Vapor 'Pará'," *Publicações a Pedido, JC*, May 7, 1875.

[10] Joaquim Maria Machado de Assis, "Bonde de Santa Teresa," *Obra Completa: Vol. III*, Afrânio Coutinho, (Rio de Janeiro: Aguilar, 1962), p. 363, as cited in Antonio Luciano de A. Tosta, "Exchanging Glances: The Streetcar, Modernity, and the Metropolis in Brazilian Literature," *Chasqui*, 32:2 (November, 2003), p. 37.

the Vintem Riot of January 1880. The riot was instigated by an unpopular tax on trolley fares that resulted in street protests against streetcar companies, their operators, the police, and the emperor himself, signaling a new era of popular participation in political culture in the capital city.[11] Those involved with the protests were comprised of literate middling to low-level bureaucrats and clerks, while a series of violent riots that broke out at the beginning of the protests appears to have been led by lower class "persons of little importance," or so the Rio authorities described them. The latter group was most likely not comprised of regular trolley riders as fare was beyond the reach of Rio's poorest classes.[12] While the causes of the Vintem Riot appear to have been different from the complaints voiced in public letters, both examples demonstrate that trolleys and trains emerged as a flashpoint for the underlying tensions caused by modernization.[13] Reaction to the new technology was diverse, even contradictory as the public adapted to and came to depend on the streetcar for transportation around the city.

Uncivilized Spaces

Crowded *bonde* cars brought Rio's residents together, often uncomfortably so. Men and women found themselves face-to-face and elbow-to-elbow in the small quarters on board. An illustration from the *Revista Ilustrada* in 1869 shows a well-to-do father and his daughter (Fig. 6.3) turn away from a Rio trolley car, alarmed at the crowded conditions. Gender or racial mixing do not appear to be the issue in this case (the passengers are respectfully dressed and from the same circle of society), but cramming into the car nonetheless threatens to unmake social standing by turning passengers into a processed commodity. While the freed slaves in the previous example threaten the social order with their uncivilized behavior on board, in the case of the human "sardines," technological modernization itself poses a menace by depersonalizing

[11] Sandra Lauderdale Graham, "The Vintem Riot and Political Culture: Rio de Janeiro, 1880," *The Hispanic American Historical Review*, 60:3, 1980, pp. 431–7; and Paulo Cruz Terra, "Cidadania e trabalhadores: Cocheiros e carroceiros no Rio de Janeiro (1870–1906), (Ph.D. dissertation, Universidade Federal Fluminense, 2012), pp. 86–7. See also Déborah Raison, "Ventos da Modernidade: os bondes e a cidade do Rio de Janeiro – 1850/1880" (Master's thesis, Universidade Federal do Rio de Janeiro, 2000).

[12] Graham, pp. 440–1.

[13] Araújo, pp. 295–300; Teresa Meade, *"Civilizing Rio" Reform and Resistance in a Brazilian City, 1889–1930* (University Park: Pennsylvania State University Press, 1997), pp. 58–60, and 104–9; Terra, ch. 1.

BONDS PARA BOTAFOGO.
— Não é carro, é uma caixa de sardinhas. Eu não sou sardinha nem camarão.
— Então vamos embora, papae !

FIGURE 6.3. "This isn't a car, it's a can of sardines! I'm neither a sardine nor a shrimp!" "Let's leave then, Papa." *Source: Semana Illustrada*, n. 457, September 12, 1869, p. 3652. Courtesy of the Acervo da Fundação Biblioteca Nacional, Brazil.

passengers. An additional illustration depicts a trolley conductor who is sarcastically maligned for his philanthropy as he lets passengers board the car in excess of the limit, presumably to collect more fares.[14] Greed, and by extension, the commodification of people result in the unpleasantly crowded conditions.

Another example from the *Semana Illustrada* (Fig. 6.4) depicts the intrusion of the public into the private sphere in an illustration that also caricatures gender, class, and age. An elderly woman of modest means (she purchases a second-class passage) is offended when the railway clerk inquires where she is going, obviously a necessary query in order to sell her the correct ticket. The assumption here is that men do not make personal inquiries of unknown women. But the joke is ultimately on the woman who is depicted as a country bumpkin, ignorant of the requirements of railway travel and behind the times in an old-fashioned costume. She stands out from the elegantly attired gentleman and lady in the background who are presumably dressed for first class. In this example, travel by railway does not threaten to decompose social hierarchy, but instead emphasizes it.

Gender norms were also at stake. The presence of women in crowded *bonde* cars led to anxiety about their exposure to unfamiliar men. Whether or not they were rightly accused of doing so, conductors came under fire for flirting with and making suggestive gestures toward women. In a sarcastic play on the Portuguese words for "made of iron" (*férrea*) and "beast" or "savage," (*féra*), one anonymous *apedido* writer complained about inappropriate comments made to a young woman on the Riachuelo line. The author described the Carioca and Riachuelo trolley lines as "uma – férrea e a outra *féra*" (one line is made of iron, and the other is savage). The Carioca line, being constructed of iron, represented progress, while to the anonymous author the *Riachuelo* line, with its rude employee, represented savagery, quite the opposite. Furthermore, the author asserted that the Carioca line employed workers noted for their *mansidão* (docility or subservience – a quality valued in slaves) toward passengers, while the Riachuelo employed "insubordinate and uneducated" workers who "offended the modesty of families" with "indecent phrases and gestures."[15] The exact threat to the modesty of families is

---

[14] "Reverso e Anverso de um Bonde," *Semana Illustrada*, n. 424, January 24, 1869, p. 3388.

[15] The adjective form of *mansidão*, *manso*, was the term for an acculterated and docile African slave. "Itinerario de uma viagem nos bondes da empreza Carioca e Riachulo," *Publicações a Pedido, JC*, January 10, 1875.

— Uma passagem da 2ª classe.
— Para onde ?
— Que se importa o senhor para onde eu vou !

FIGURE 6.4. "One second class ticket." "Where to?" "Sir, what business is it of yours where I am going!" *Source*: *Semana Illustrada*, n. 685, July 20, 1873, p. 5260. Courtesy of the Acervo da Fundação Biblioteca Nacional, Brazil.

unclear, but it might have involved the conductor directly addressing a young woman rather than an accompanying male from her family, or it could have been a more provocative comment or gesture. Either way, the perceived rudeness of railway workers was interpreted as a direct threat to paternal authority. A challenge to an uncle, father, or grandfather's control over his extended collection of dependents, especially young women, was a serious charge in a society constructed around paternalistic authority in both the public and private spheres, as the letter of another angry father indicates. Even more egregious in the eyes of the writer were the conductors of passing trolleys who made suggestive gestures towards the families on his street as the latter watched from their windows or enjoyed themselves in their gardens. The invasion of the private space of the home by public trolley workers was one step too far, the "Indignant Head of a Family" fumed.[16]

Another example from 1874 (Fig. 6.5) depicts a family, *sans* father, gathered at the window of a wealthy house to watch the trolley passing by in the stylish neighborhood of Botafogo. Technology is a spectacle that draws the family's attention away from the domestic sphere, where it should be focused, to the outside world. Written in the voice of the exasperated father, the caption describes a scene of domestic disorder instigated by the trolley:

... since the arrival of the *bonde* on the streets of the city, my house has been completely turned upside down!... The result is that the windows are always occupied, and the kitchen always empty.[17]

The wife has abandoned her proper role as a mother overseeing household matters to marvel at the passing streetcar along with her children.[18] The joke of the illustration is that the father is apparently ignorant of the fact that the spectacle that has captivated his spouse is not the "animals," nor the streetcar, but a passenger – the conductor? – waving from the rear of the trolley. The wife stands at the window dressed for an evening out, complete with earrings and a flirtatious handkerchief in a manner evocative of a prostitute soliciting clients. The man with whom she flirts brazenly waves to her while her children look on. Improprieties abound as the trolley rolls down the street, disrupting households and inciting improper female conduct. If the previous example of the electric bell seamlessly integrated technology into the home in a way that reinforced gendered space and social order, this depiction intimated that the

---

[16] "Bondes da Tijuca," *Publicações a Pedido*, *JC*, May 25, 1870.

[17] *Semana Illustrada*, N. 695, Anno XIV, April 5, 1874, p. 5557.

[18] Similar concerns regarding women's presence on trains and trolleys arose in the nineteenth-century United States, Amy Richter, *Home on the Rails: Women, the Railroad, and the Rise of Public Domesticity* (Chapel Hill: University of North Carolina Press, 2005), ch. 2.

EFFEITOS DOS *BONDS*

Desde que temos *bonds* nas ruas da cidade, a minha casa está totalmente transtornada! O Antonico quer ouvir os apitos, a Anninha e a Clara gostam dos carros novos, e minha mulher, não sei que diabo lhe deu, parece gostar dos... dos animaes! Emfim as janellas estão sempre cheias e a cozinha sempre vazia.

FIGURE 6.5. "The *Bonde's* Effect," "Since the arrival of *bondes* on the streets of the city, my house has been completely turned upside down! Little Antonio wants to hear the whistles, young Ann likes the new cars, and my wife, who knows what devil has got her, she seems bewitched by the . . . the animals! The result is that the windows are always occupied, and the kitchen is always empty." *Source: Semana Ilustrada*, N. 695, Anno XIV, April 5, 1874. Courtesy of the Acervo da Fundação Biblioteca Nacional, Brazil.

trolley could lead to illicit profits (the wife resembles a prostitute) that quite literally turned the home "upside down."

In the midst of this social disruption, conductors had a difficult job. Amy Richter describes the multiple duties performed by conductors in the United States:

[They were responsible for] checking the supplies and cleanliness of the cars, collecting and turning in fares, counting tickets and passengers, seating passengers, answering travelers' questions, handling disorderly passengers, enforcing company rules, regulating the car's temperature and ventilation, calling out station stops, helping passengers alight at the right stations, and assisting them with parcels.[19]

Conductors balanced their duties between serving the public with respectful goodwill and enforcing the regulations required of a large, complex, schedule-driven technological operation. They were at once charged with making passengers comfortable, in a role similar to a subordinate servant or slave, and they were the representatives of an impersonal business that sometimes had to sacrifice one passenger's wishes or comfort for the safe and efficient operation of the line.[20] Yet despite their highly visible and very public role, they owed their allegiance – and their obedience – to their employers: railroad companies with managers hidden from the public eye. Likewise, the rigid schedule that facilitated the safe functioning of the railroad imposed anonymity onto its passengers and its workers. Engineers and conductors were under pressure to hew to schedules not only in the interest of profit, but because it was an absolute necessity for safely coordinating the movement of trains that often traveled in both directions on single tracks.[21]

Complaints about rude employees were in part an expression of frustration with this impersonal structure of the trolley or railway company, where higher-ups were removed from direct public interaction and conductors represented the human face of the trolley.[22] Additionally, trolleys were subsidized by public funds, and passengers felt entitled to good

---

[19] Richter, p. 123.

[20] In the United States, gentlemanly behavior was expected of conductors and porters, especially regarding female passengers, Richter, ch. 5.

[21] Telegraph messages, strict schedules, and the establishment of time zones were essential for synchronizing train movement and avoiding collisions. Stephen Salsbury, "The Emergence of an Early Large-Scale Technical System: The American Railroad Network," in Renate Mayntz, Thomas P. Hughes, eds., *The Development of Large Technical Systems* (Boulder, CO: Westview Press, 1988), pp. 40–5.

[22] Terra, p. 93.

service.[23] At the same time, railway workers exercised a certain amount of freedom on their daily rounds in the city or the countryside, and the fact that interactions took place away from the watchful eyes of managers probably empowered them to talk back or refuse service to what they saw as demanding passengers.

If illustrated weeklies called attention to the disruptive forces of the trolley in a humorous way, the *apedido* section contained very sincere grievances about the perceived impertinence of railway workers. As a result, angry letters about the behavior of these transportation workers appeared regularly in the pages of the *Jornal do Commercio* from the 1860s to the 1880s. The majority complained of rude and insubordinate behavior. A "Dr. J. Ferreira de Campos," for example, complained when the engineer of the Leopoldina railway line, perhaps in an effort to make up lost time, left the station of Volta-Grande before his luggage could be loaded and despite the efforts of the local station manager to signal the train to halt. The matter resulted in much consternation for the passenger as he was delayed in traveling to "other parts" where, he pointedly emphasized, he had been summoned by "powerful interests." Despite the eventual and satisfactory return of his luggage, "minus a pair of sandals," the Doctor was deeply affronted, and called upon the railroad administration to "make the proper amends" against the "inattentive and insubordinate" behavior of the engineer in question. In another letter, an aggrieved passenger complained:

In Brazil, there are certain public employees who have completely forgotten the duties implied by the title they hold. Rather than undertake the zealous service of those to whom their service is due, such employees, on the contrary, treat the public with an utter lack of civility and with extreme and reprehensible rudeness.

While waiting for the luggage to be transferred (as is the custom) at Cachoeiras station on the Cantagallo line during a trip from the court city to the village of Nova Friburgo, the present company experienced just such an act of incivility. We were the impassive witnesses of a display of inept and uncouth behavior on the part of the man in charge of operations at the station. The employee in question conducted himself with a manner of reprehensible arrogance, unleashing a flurry of offensive language, and utterly forgetting his place regarding his obligations to the public.

The offensive impression of this individual stands in stark contrast to the kind and civilized treatment of another station manager on the same line. We had

---

[23] Paulo Cruz Terra, "Conflitos cotidianos e motins: os usários de bondes no Rio de Janeiro no final do século XIX e início do XX," *História Social*, n. 22 e 23, primeiro e segundo semestres de 2012, p. 252.

the good fortune to experience this man's gentlemanly service at the Friburgo station, where we witnessed him provide considerate and civilized treatment [to passengers], and even to a poor slave... [24]

The author demanded the employee be fired in the interest of maintaining social order for "... those who value the interests of companies such as the Cantagallo railroad, which are of great importance to national prosperity and which have such a profound effect on public harmony." Like the angry fathers in the previous examples, the *apedido* writer described the interaction as a showdown between the forces of civilization and barbarism, which if left unchecked warned of ominous disruptions to the public order. Indeed, in 1889 another author accused the stokers of the locomotive steam engines, whom he described as "uneducated and unscrupulous... workers recruited from the dregs of society," of starting fires by deliberately throwing sparks from the steam furnace onto wooden fences along the Leopoldina line. Though the fires were more likely a result of the sometimes dangerous inefficiency of the locomotive engine rather than human malice, the author's harsh words underscored both his sense of violation and his feeling of superiority over the workers. [25] Even more ominous, the burning of private property, the writer intimated, invoked a specter of the city in flames at the hands of a riotous and uncontrollable underclass employed by the railroad.

On the other hand, there is evidence that conductors did indeed abuse their authority over passengers. In 1880, one *cocheiro* was accused of arbitrarily refusing service to passengers when he barred a mother and her two children from boarding his trolley because he did not want "a carful of children." [26] Another trolley rider complained that conductors cheated passengers out of the change owed to them. Because conductors did not immediately make change upon payment for a ticket on board open-air cars, more than one passenger forgot to collect the money they were due before exiting the trolley. [27]

The previous examples suggest that ethnic, class, and racial prejudices played a role in perceptions of "uncivilized" railroad workers. The fact that less-esteemed jobs reflected poorly on the individuals who performed them also contributed to disparaging views of wage workers, especially

[24] "Estrada de Ferro de Cantagallo," *Publicações a Pedido, JC,* September 5, 1875.

[25] Not infrequently, railroad furnaces spewed wayward ashes and sparks that resulted in fires. Rail lines were prohibited from city centers in the US for this very reason. Ann Norton Greene, *Horses at Work: Harnessing Power in Industrial America* (Cambridge, MA: Harvard University Press, 2008), p. 81.

[26] *O Corsário,* October 9, 1880, p. 4.   [27] *O Corsário,* October 2, 1880, p. 1.

because manual and service work was still associated with slavery. The emergence of wage labor in the North Atlantic also often resulted in social anxiety. In the northern part of the United States in the early 1800s, for example, wage labor was considered less respectable than the self-sufficient labor of economically independent farmers and fisherman. Erie Canal workers, the itinerant workforce necessary to move ships and barges on the canal, were especially disparaged. Wage laborers were considered dependents of their employers and were therefore not truly free to participate in politics, a suspect social position in the young republic. Fears about the development of a permanent underclass of laboring poor following the example of industrial England contributed to this pejorative image even with the realization that wage workers were a necessity for large-scale transportation projects like the Erie Canal.[28] In Brazil, many trolley workers, like the engineers who built the nation's first railroads, were foreigners and therefore not necessarily sensitive to social rank, unspoken protocol, and local custom. Of 384 conductors and drivers arrested between the years 1890 and 1906, 56 percent were immigrants, the majority of whom were Portuguese.[29] Negative stereotypes about Portuguese immigrants as "cunning... and marginally dishonest..." would have amplified perceptions of conductors as rude and "not knowing their place," and would have contributed to the already disparaging view of wage workers."[30]

Trilhos e Carroças (Tracks vs. Wagons)

Another vivid example of the disrupting presence of the *bonde* came to the forefront in 1875, when a conflict erupted between merchants and wagon drivers on one side, and *bonde* conductors and owners on the other. The narrow streets of the old commercial center of Rio de Janeiro, a congested area located near the port, proved too small for the simultaneous passage of trolley cars, freight wagons, and pedestrians. The

---

[28] Carol Sheriff, *The Artificial River: The Erie Canal and the Paradox of Progress, 1817–1862* (New York: Hill and Wang, 1996), p. 38.

[29] Terra, *Cidadania e trabalhadores*, pp. 102–3. Terra observes that Portuguese immigrants also worked as wagoners in Rio between the years 1837 and 1870. Among wagoners for whom there is data on nationality, 78 percent were Portuguese, unpubl. paper, "História social do transporte do Rio de Janeiro – final do século XIX e início do XX," *Núcleo Interdisciplinar de Estudos e Pesquisas sobre Marx e o Marxismo*, Universidade Federal Fluminense, 2011, p. 12.

[30] Meade, p. 93.

trolley lines established there came to dominate the narrow streets, much to the consternation of local merchants who were often prevented from unloading their goods. An image from *O Mosquito* in 1874 illustrates the tight fit on narrow streets (Fig. 6.6). To the left, a well-dressed gentlemen crouches against a wall, while on the right a *quitandeira* (street vendor, probably a slave) spills her basket of produce as they both scurry to get out of the way of a passing trolley car. The *bonde* is undiscriminating in its threat to all levels of Brazilian society.

The conflict among *carroceiros* (teamsters), merchants, and *bonde* owners erupted over the former's practice of parking their *carroças* (freight wagons) directly on trolley tracks on the narrow streets of the old city during the loading and unloading of cargo. This meant that conductors had to wait for the wagoners to finish their work before the trolley could pass, causing a disruption in schedules and aggravation all around. The law came down in favor of the trolley owners when the *câmara muncipal* (town council) of Rio passed an edict in March of 1875 making it illegal to park *carroças* on the tracks for the loading and unloading of cargo for more than six minutes, an impossibility for most deliveries.[31] The enforcement of the edict provoked an angry polemic in the *Publicações a Pedido* section when an unnamed *carroceiro* was fined and his wagon impounded after parking the vehicle on the tracks on São Pedro Street. Luiz Fortunato Filho, a lawyer hired on behalf of the merchants affected by the trolley lines, described the conflict:

The gathered crowd protested the violence of the urban guard against the *carroças*, even as they [the guard] remained indifferent to the four or five *bondes* that are constantly parked on *Primeiro de Março* street, prohibiting the businesses established there from freely transporting their goods.

The indignation of the crowd confirmed the following sad truth – there will be serious conflicts regarding the question of – *trilhos e carroças* (tracks and wagons).

On one side we find the *bonde* companies inciting the situation with the swift and powerful wheels of their cars, assisted by the police with a display of force and terror!

On the other side we find the people [*o povo*] and businessmen, flying the flag of liberty, law, and justice![32]

In a rhetorical flourish intended to inflame passions, Fortunato turned the narrative of progress on its head. The "swift and powerful" trolley wheels

31 "Trilhos e carroças," *Publicações a Pedido*, JC, September 12, 1875.
32 "Trilhos e carroças," *Publicações a Pedido*, JC, September 14, 1875.

O peior é que nas ruas, lá para que digamos, naõ há muito espaço para se andar a pé.

FIGURE 6.6. "The worst part is that in the streets . . . there isn't much space to go about on foot," (Detail). *Source*: *O Mosquito*, March 28, 1874, pp. 5–6. Courtesy of the Acervo da Fundação Biblioteca Nacional, Brazil.

Muito mais desagradavel ainda, é, ficar partido
do meio, mas, já que queremos ser Americanos,
soyons le jusqu'au bout.

FIGURE 6.7. "Bonds e mais Bonds, Trilhos e mas Trilhos (More and more tracks and trolleys)," "Even more disagreeable is to be split in two... let's go all the way [in becoming Americans]," (Detail). *Source: O Mosquito*, March 28, 1874, pp. 5–6. Courtesy of the Acervo da Fundação Biblioteca Nacional, Brazil.

not only menaced city dwellers, but threatened to destroy the commerce on which the city's *true* progress depended. *O Mosquito* echoed this theme with an illustration of a trolley car cutting a well-dressed gentleman in half; the *cocheiro* maliciously leers at the top-hatted victim caught beneath the trolley wheels (Fig. 6.7). The reference to "wanting to be Americans" in the caption is a criticism of the relocated US businessman Charles B. Greenough, the owner of several streetcar companies who was then under fire for his intention to build more lines that would add to the congestion. Another panel in the cartoon decried, "Eight *bonde* lines! Good heavens, not even in New York!"[33] The image portrayed the center of Rio de Janeiro divided and dominated by trolley lines. Another illustration depicted the sarcastic proposition that pedestrian walkways be built above the rooftops as an extreme solution for Rio's congested streets (Fig. 6.8).

The lawyer's attack on the trolley owners began with an *apedido* printed two days before the incident on São Pedro street. Arguing against the "barbaric" influence of the trolley system, the lawyer defended the merchants as the true promoters of civilization as it was they who bought and sold the raw material that would transform Rio from an "old-fashioned" city to a modern conurbation "composed of gigantic and solid buildings." How was this transformation to take place, he argued, if "heavy materials such as stone and wood" could not be delivered to the "*fábricas*" and businesses that manufactured and sold them? How were the *bonde* lines, which merely saved passengers a "few steps," more important than the merchants who provided the materials for the reconstruction of the city and presumably, the real work of civilizing Brazil? And as if this were not enough evidence, he further lauded the good works that merchants did for the less privileged, underscoring their position as philanthropists who financed diverse causes such as an asylum for invalids, public education, weapons for the army, funds for freeing slaves, and care for the sick during epidemics of yellow fever. These men were vital members of the community, and the true promoters of progress in the city.[34]

The *bonde–carroça* controversy inspired a rush of commentary in the *Publicações a Pedido* in support of both sides. If the arguments of Fortunato and his opponents touched on matters of civilization and progress, who had the legal right to use public space, and the particulars of the law governing the rights of merchants' interests against those of the owners of trolley lines and their passengers, other writers revealed concern about class and economic status. The *apedido* of a group of "citizens" who supported the "free circulation" of the trains, argued in favor of the *bonde* lines over the *carroças* because the former aided the poor and promoted public health:

---

[33] "Bonds e mais Bonds, Trilhos e mas Trilhos," *O Mosquito*, March 28, 1874, pp. 5–6.
[34] "Trilhos e carroças," *JC*, September 12, 1875.

Esperamos que brevemente haverá um projecto de se fazerem ruas por cima dos telhados para as pessoas que gostam de andar socegadamente a pé.

FIGURE 6.8. "We hope that soon there will be a project to build roads over the rooftops for those who like to stroll peacefully on foot," (Detail). *Source: O Mosquito*, March 28, 1874, pp. 5–6. Courtesy of the Acervo da Fundação Biblioteca Nacional, Brazil.

These eminently popular vehicles provide a great progress for the less fortunate classes. For a small sum, the worker is transported from the inexpensive neighborhood where he lives into the heart of the city. He can [therefore] do four times the work without tiring; social relations are encouraged through frequent encounters; [while] transportation to the outskirts of the city and the opportunity to breath oxygenated air facilitates the improvement of hygiene; in sum, [*bonde* travel] encourages healthful activity in all its aspects.[35]

Another contributor seconded this argument, adding that the frequent social contact on the *bonde* benefited the rich and poor alike through an "elevated moral influence" upon the passengers that encouraged the "joining together of forces" in camaraderie.[36]

Another writer signing as *um fluminense* (a resident of the province of Rio de Janeiro) came down against the *carroceiros*, complaining that *bonde* riders should not be required to wait for the drivers to unload their "rustic and monstrous" wagons, especially as the "cargo," being inanimate, had more patience than passengers. The *apedido* was answered by "another *fluminense*" who asserted that *bonde* passengers, on the contrary, were idlers who had no right to discomfit pedestrians or to get in the way of commerce:

[Why should] merchants and those who travel by foot be forced to wait while a half dozen idlers who are too lazy to take a half dozen steps are carried about on the *bondes*... Since when has idleness taken precedence over activity?[37]

Like the complaints about rude conductors, the *carroceiro* controversy gave voice to deeper conflicts and anxieties about the changing city. Because of their daily engagement with the public, trolley companies remained a flashpoint for tensions about modernization into the early twentieth century, as frustration with city transportation resulted in riots and protests in later decades.

An image (Fig. 6.9) from the *Semana Illustrada* in 1869 provides a closing visual metaphor for the displacement felt by those who opposed the proliferation of trolley lines on Rio streets. In the left illustration, pedestrians and a carriage peacefully amble along a cobblestone street. To the right the same street has been completely torn apart while one lonely soul observes the rubble left from the installation of gas lines and streetcar tracks from the shelter of a doorway. These improvements, as the wry Machado de Assis observed, may have been undeniable markers of

---

[35] "Viação ferrea urbana," *Publicações a Pedido, JC*, September 28, 1875.
[36] "Viação ferrea urbana," *Publicações a Pedido, JC*, September 20, 1875.
[37] "Viação ferrea urbana," *Publicações a Pedido, JC*, September 28, 1875.

Vista de uma rua do Rio de Janeiro, calçada a paralellipipedos,

ANTES

DEPOIS

do gaz, do esgoto e dos bonds.

FIGURE 6.9. "View of a street with cobblestones and sidewalk in Rio de Janeiro, BEFORE and AFTER the installation of gas illumination, the sewer, and the *bonde*." *Source: Semana Illustrada*, n. 471, December 19, 1869, p. 3765. Courtesy of the Acervo da Fundação Biblioteca Nacional, Brazil.

progress, but they also represented a chaotic process that was disruptive to the physical and social environment.

Moral Machinery: Factory Schools and the Transition to Wage Labor

In contrast to the disruptions caused by the streetcar on Rio's streets and complaints about railway workers, many opponents of slavery saw factory work in combination with owner-sponsored factory schools as a measured pathway for developing a free labor system that demonstrated, or so its proponents hoped, that wage labor could in fact function well in a slave society. At the forefront of discussions about free labor at the beginning of the 1870s was a renewed debate about gradual abolition that resulted in the passage of the Law of Free Birth in 1871. The new law, considered the first step toward full abolition, stipulated that all children born to slave mothers be freed either through government indemnification at eight years old by way of a special abolition fund, or at the age of twenty-one. Here the shoemaker's complaint about the low social value of manual labor in Chapter 2 points to an important consideration for modernizers: how to valorize wage labor in opposition to slavery and how to prepare Brazil's poor population for the rigidly scheduled factory day in a manner that maintained existing social hierarchies. Brazil was not the only nation to grapple with the social ruptures associated with the replacement of preindustrial work regimes by wage labor. The shift from agrarian and guild labor to the factory system in England, the center of the Industrial Revolution, was, as is well known, a fraught process. Workers often had to be persuaded (and not infrequently) directly coerced into abandoning agriculture, home production, and work in guilds in order to labor in England's early factories.[38] Absenteeism was a central challenge as "[workers] resented... the discipline; the factory bell...; [and] the time-keeping which over-rode ill-health, domestic arrangements, or the choice of more varied occupations."[39] In England, both the carrot and the stick were used to entice workers to the factory floor, and physical punishment was a technique employed especially against child laborers.[40] The Brazilian situation differed, of course, from Industrial Revolution-era

---

[38] Jeff Horn, *The Path Not Taken: French Industrialization in the Age of Revolution, 1750–1830* (Cambridge, MA: MIT Press, 2006), pp. 91–125.

[39] E. P. Thompson, *The Making of the English Working Class* (New York: Vintage Books, 1963), p. 305.

[40] Sidney Pollard, "Factory Discipline in the Industrial Revolution," *The Economic History Review*, New Series, 16:2 (1963), pp. 254–6.

Britain in significant ways. Slavery and a racial caste system that included free and freed blacks influenced elites' views not only of manual labor but of the aptitude of free Brazilian-born workers to labor for wages. The perception that Africans and their descendants only worked well under coercion inspired heated debates about potential sources of docile immigrant labor primarily for the agricultural sector.[41] Beliefs about the deficiencies of free Brazilian agricultural workers also influenced discussions of factory labor. Though not always explicitly stated, concern for social order and assurance that immigrants and Brazilians alike could be made into obedient and reliable workers were two motivations for the establishment of schools for workers and their children at Brazilian factories by the 1870s. Many opponents of slavery saw owner-sponsored factory schools as a measured pathway for developing a free labor system. As mentioned previously, a renewed and fevered debate about gradual abolition resulted in the passage of the Law of Free Birth in 1871, spurring concerns about the transition to wage labor in this decade.[42]

It was in the year leading up to the passage of the Law of Free Birth that an anonymous *apedido* in the *Jornal do Commercio* celebrated the Imperial Fábrica de Tabaco de São João de Niterói (São João de Niterói Imperial Factory of Tobacco, located across Guanabara Bay from Rio) as a showcase for preparing the poor to work in factories. The factory featured the latest in processing equipment, including three steam-powered tobacco processors, gas illumination, and heated water for hygienic purposes. These technological advances cast the factory in a progressive light, but it was the social innovation of the factory school for the 110 poor and orphaned boys employed there (out of a total of 200 workers) that received the highest praise. Above and beyond earning a regular wage, medical care, and job training, the boys received a free primary education. The poorest of the lot were additionally allocated shoes, clothing, and meals at the factory's expense, and the earnings of orphans were reportedly deposited into a savings account held on their behalf.[43]

---

[41] Jeffrey Lesser, *Negotiating National Identity: Immigrants, Minorities, and the Struggle for Ethnicity in Brazil* (Durham, NC: Duke University Press, 1999), pp. 14–15; and George Reid Andrews, *Blacks and Whites in São Paulo: 1888–1998* (Madison: University of Wisconsin Press, 1991), pp. 47–9.

[42] Conrad, ch. 6, and pp. 90–3 in particular.

[43] "Imperial fabrica de cigarros de Nitherohy," *Publicações a Pedido*, JC, May 12, 1870. Luciana de Araújo Pinheiro observes that the problem of "uncivilized orphans" in Rio de Janeiro became increasingly important in Rio de Janeiro as the date of emancipation of children born after the Law of Free Womb neared. By the end of the 1870s and 1880s, concern for how to "civilize" orphans was evident in the government's intervention in

The *apedido* celebrated the factory's combination of charity with enlightened "self-interest"; it brought mechanized production to Brazil, but without the brutal exploitation of the infamous British factory system, or the runaway "progress" exemplified by the malicious conductor in Figure 6.7.

Also lauding the factory, the 1870 *apedido* of antislavery advocate, republican, and outspoken critic of the agricultural elite, Augusto Emilio Zaluar (a Portuguese immigrant), exemplified the goal of wage labor proponents to elevate the social value of paid work while also ensuring stability in social relations:

In a moment when the public spirit is occupied almost exclusively with a practical method for replacing the servile element and of ennobling wage labor even in its most rudimentary manifestation, we believe it an opportune occasion to describe some of our industrial establishments, and to make the triumph of individual initiative evident [to the public at large]... [44]

Other *apedido* authors celebrated the paternal responsibility of the factory owners to their young workers. C. Azevedo Coimbra referred to the boys as the "adopted sons" of the proprietors. This was not merely cast as a beneficial financial relationship between child worker and factory owner, but an opportunity for the former to fully join the "Brazilian family":

If the future happiness of a nation depends on the family, if its prosperity depends principally on the education given to its sons, then its greatness and its future elevation also depend on the education that its youth receive from their infancy [to adulthood]. A nation is no more than the union of families [into one] great family. [45]

The Imperial Fábrica de Tabaco combined charity and profit safely embedded within a traditional social relationship even as it incorporated wages, mechanized production, and free education. Zaluar's celebration

---

the care of such minors, placing them in foster care or as apprentices to local businessmen at the state's expense. Pinheiro suspects that many of the children taken as wards of the court were probably not orphans in the true sense, but the children of slave mothers abandoned by owners reluctant to provide for their care, as well as children abandoned by their own parents due to poverty or other dire circumstances. "A civilização do Brasil através da infância: propostas e ações voltadas à criança pobre nos anos finais do Império (1879–1889)," (Master's thesis, Universidade Federal Fluminense, 2003).

[44] "Imperial fabrica de cigarros de S. João de Nitherohy," *Publicações a Pedido, JC,* May 20, 1870.

[45] "Imperial fabrica de cigarros de S. João de Nitherohy," *Publicações a Pedido, JC,* September 23, 1870.

of the school is evocative of the educational programs provided for workers at the Lowell textile mills in Massachusetts in the 1840s. Mill owners enticed young Yankee farm girls away from their families to temporarily labor in the mills for wages before marriage by creating a safe, paternalistic environment that included supervised boardinghouses, education, and church. Male overseers were charged with the moral guidance of their female crews, church attendance was mandatory, and evening classes and lectures were offered after hours. These extracurricular programs were a response to the US perception of the British factory girl as overworked, malnourished, and sexually vulnerable, but they also reassured fathers that daughters would be protected while away from home.[46] The example of the orphans employed at the tobacco factory reflected different circumstances in Brazil, namely the effort to demonstrate that the poor, orphaned, and mixed-race could be moralized through wage labor. Factory school proponents pointed to the Imperial Fábrica de Tabaco as a viable example of enlightened industrial development that ensured social stability between different classes.

Articles in *O Auxiliador* and exhibition catalogs extolled factory schools – and the owners who supported them – for the moral benefits they provided workers, foremost of which was the inculcation of a work ethic. The factory moralized its workers through a regimented schedule signaled, in a now iconic metaphor, at beginning and end by the factory whistle. As with the locomotive, the steady rhythm of factory machines worked on the human body, imposing order and discipline from the outside in aspiration of an internal transformation of the spirit toward progress of the self and ultimately the nation. Education was an important component of this system as the "light" of instruction prepared workers to effectively direct the "raw force" of machinery.[47] Narrative flourishes aside, basic literacy skills were also a necessity for the safe operation of complicated machinery in addition to counting and organizing finished products, and many other tasks on the factory floor, revealing a more strategic aim of factory-sponsored education. Owners also wanted a reliable and docile pool of workers, a deeper motive for imposing a schedule on factory hands' free hours.[48]

---

[46] Harriet Robinson, *Loom and Spindle or Life Among the Early Mill Girls*, rev. ed., (Kailua, HI: Press Pacifica, 1976), pp. 37–8.

[47] "Industria Nacional," *Publicações a Pedido*, *JC*, September 1, 1870.

[48] Michael Sanderson, "Education and the Factory in Industrial Lancashire, 1780–1840," *The Economic History Review*, New Series, 20:2 (August 1967), p. 273.

Factory schools were not limited to Rio de Janeiro. The government-run iron foundry of São João de Ipanema in São Paulo province offered a school of *primeiras letras* for minors and night classes for hirelings that included elementary mathematics, and the basics of mechanical and industrial design.[49] Engineer Antônio Augusto Fernandes Pinheiro, a member of Rio's Associação Industrial (Industrial Association of Rio de Janeiro), celebrated the Santo Aleixo textile mill in rural Rio de Janeiro province for the beneficial influence it asserted over its workers by providing a "literary, artistic, and moral" education and for ensuring new generations of skilled and reliable workers:

. . . [the factory] maintains a regular school for the workers and their children. They live under prudent and moralizing guidance, receiving the most edifying example of honorable work from the estimable manager and his family.

[M]any working families are well established at *Santo Aleixo*, their children are raised with good work habits and receive the light of education; the daughters bring as a dowry the worthy principles of honesty and frugality to their marriages, in addition to good work habits and skills to the factory.

In this manner generations of well-mannered and habile workers remain linked to the factory.[50]

Fifty-three percent of the 130 workers at the Fábrica do Cedro textile mill in Minas Gerais attended factory-sponsored night classes in *primeiras letras* and "general science."[51] A wool factory in Rio Grande do Sul provided instruction on Sunday to the twenty-six Brazilian boys under its employ.[52] The Caçú textile mill in Uberabu, also in Minas Gerais, provided a night school for the "primary instruction" of its workers, as well as to local children unaffiliated with the factory. Pointedly, the article emphasized the fact that " . . . the most secure order reigns [at the mill]. Not one disaster or disturbance of public order or work has occurred

---

[49] "Fabrica de Ferro," "Industria manfactureira," *O Auxiliador*, June 1882, p. 136.

[50] *Archivos da Exposição da Industria Nacional: actas, pareceres e decisões do jury geral da Exposição da Industria Nacional realizada no Rio de Janeiro em 1881* (Rio de Janeiro: Tip. Nacional, 1882), pp. LXXXVIII–LXXXIX. The Santo Aleixo factory, reportedly the first profitable and long-running textile mill in Rio de Janeiro province, was founded by an American immigrant though it later came under Brazilian ownership. A nearby river that flowed year round powered the looms. North American missionaries James C. Fletcher and Daniel P. Kidder reported that the factory employed European immigrant workers from the colony at Petrópolis in the 1850s; it is unknown if this was still the case by the 1880s. Fletcher and Kidder, *Brazil and the Brazilians*, 1857 ed., pp. 275–6.

[51] "Fabrica do Cedro," *Archivos Da Exposição da Industria Nacional*, 1881, p. XCIII.

[52] "Fabrica de tecidos de lã de Rheingantz & C.," *O Auxiliador*, June 1882, p. 145.

since its establishment," providing further evidence for a socially safe and financially viable transition to wage labor in contrast to the violent social clashes between labor and capital that occurred in industrializing Europe.[53]

Other examples celebrated the explicitly paternalistic responsibilities of owners toward their hirelings. An article in the *Auxiliador* in 1885, for example, praised the owner of the Tatuhy textile factory in São Paulo province for his benevolence:

The poor population of the area [near Tatuhy] finds in Sr. Pinto Guedes a protector and benefactor... [Guedes] provides for the future of those he employs by ameliorating their harsh existence and making them useful to society... the city of Tatuhy owes much to him.[54]

Saturnino Braga, a mill owner in the city of Campos in Rio de Janeiro province, was "repaid for his capital investment by the honest work of several hundred [previously] idle hands, especially women and children... condemned by age and sex to be a burden on their families."[55] Descriptions of the moralizing effect of honest work and factory-sponsored education echoed the long-standing (though not necessarily enforced) responsibility of slave owners to make good Christians out of their slaves and to provide them with moral direction. A laudatory description in the *Jornal do Commercio* of a *fazendeiro* from Vassouras who employed steam machinery on his plantation and treated the local poor with gentle paternalistic concern demonstrates a similar sentiment and language:

... I witnessed the delicate manners of the esteemed *senhor* as he received visitors from all levels of society on his *fazenda*. Some were from his own class, but many more were poor. He took a great interest in them, as if the business of the most wretched [among them]... were his own.[56]

To be sure, the opportunities given to workers through the factory school and the payment of wages distinguished the mill owner from the slave-owning *fazendeiro*. Nonetheless, despite the promotion of a work

---

[53] The factory employed 56 individuals: Sixteen women over twelve years of age, eight girls under eleven, six boys between the ages of seven and ten, twenty men between the ages of twelve and twenty-five, and five slaves. Twenty students attended the factory school, comprised of workers and local children, "Fabrica de tecidos em Uberaba," *O Auxiliador*, January 1885, pp. 6–7. Article reprinted from the *JC*.

[54] "Fabrica de Tecidos do Tatuhy," *O Auxiliador*, January 1885, pp. 4–5.

[55] "Industrial Campista," *O Auxiliador*, May 1885, p. 114.

[56] "Vassouras," *Publicações a Pedido, JC*, May 19, 1861.

ethic, or proclamations of progress, the wage labor relationship described here was still embedded in a larger social construction of paternalistic responsibility rooted in Brazil's slave society. Mill owners were responsible for guiding their hirelings, much as the *fazendeiro* owed fatherly protection to his slaves and dependents. In these examples mill owners were commended as much for their benevolence and reform of the poor as they were for the sophisticated technology they employed or their business acumen. Factory school proponents went so far as to invoke this paternalistic relationship as a shield to worker and owner alike from the excesses of "self-interested" manufacturing capitalism:

Far from imitating other manufacturers, who, with a few honorable exceptions, only pursue their own interests, Souza Novaes & Co. [the owners of the Imperial Fábrica de Tabaco] envision the principles of humanity and patriotism... with the noble... intention of protecting... more than one hundred youths.... [57]

Though these sentiments were most likely genuine, an underlying motive was also to prove to a wider audience that factories were beneficial to Brazilian society and economy through their potential to moralize and bring progress to the poor.

At the same time, there is little information on the pedagogy employed at factory schools, who taught the classes, whether tuition and the cost of books were deducted from wages or provided at the factory's expense, or what the workers themselves thought of the experience. Nor do we know to what extent factories or factory schools were successful in educating or improving the material and social conditions of workers. Certainly, for some the experience of working in a factory was as exploitative as regimes in other industrializing societies, whatever benefit the factory school might have provided. For others the rare opportunity to gain at least a basic education, particularly in locations outside cities where access to public schools was extremely limited, would have certainly been attractive. Factory wages and schools probably were an attractive opportunity for the free poor population.

Additional institutions that provided instruction in artisanal and industrial skills also began to appear by the 1840s and 1850s in Brazilian cities. The prestigious Academia de Belas Artes, originally founded in 1820, added courses on the *artífices* (mechanical arts) to its more traditional fine arts curriculum in 1855.[58] In 1858 the Liceu de Artes e Ofícios

---

[57] "Imperial Fabrica de cigarros de S. João de Nitherohy," *Publicaões a Pedido, JC*, September 23, 1870.

[58] Luiz Antônio Cunha, *O ensino de ofícios artesanais e manufatureiros no Brasil escravocrata* (São Paulo: UNESP, and Brasília: FLACSO, 2005), pp. 127 and 129.

(School of Manual Arts and Trades) was established under the auspices of the Sociedade Propagadora de Belas-Artes (Society for the Promotion of Fine Arts) in Rio with the aim of providing free classes in basic literacy and manual arts, " ... not only for associates and their children, but to any individual, free or freed who has no compromising situation that will stand in the way of admission." This last point referenced slaves, who, along with women, were prohibited from enrolling. Despite the exclusion of women and girls, the vision of the Liceu as a "school for the people" was underscored by the donation of gas lighting by the Baron of Mauá that facilitated the offering of evening courses " ... with the exception of those [subjects] that are incompatible with artificial light," rendering the school innovative and progressive for its day on two counts: it provided free instruction in basic literacy and the manual arts for "Brazilian nationals and foreigners alike" and it employed cutting-edge technology that expanded the hours in which the courses could be taught, making the curriculum available to day workers.[59] In its first thirty years (with a break between 1864 and 1867 when it was closed due to lack of funding) 33,881 Brazilian-born and foreign students passed through the doors of the Liceu, signaling that there indeed was a demand for education in basic literacy and the manual arts in Brazil.[60]

Beyond free classes, the Liceu published a journal with prints of works by Brazilian artists and artisans, compiled a library on fine and manual arts, and provided free public lectures on the manual arts.[61] Through these activities, Liceu founders hoped to elevate the social standing of skilled labor and manual arts in Brazil. In contrast to the paternalism of the factory schools, Liceu organizers aspired to a more egalitarian setting that celebrated brotherhood, not fatherly guidance, at least on paper:

> Here, the poor do not humble themselves before the rich
> Both are equal in this school of citizens,
> Here, the glory of work is valued
> Everyone is a brother in the classrooms of the Liceu.[62]

Indeed, the Liceu's original founder, architect of the Casa Imperial, and professor of architecture at the Escola Central, Francisco Joaquim

---

[59] Alvaro Paes de Barros, *O Liceu de Artes e Ofícios e seu Fundador* (Rio de Janeiro: n/p, 1956), p. 15.

[60] Cunha, p. 127.   [61] Cunha, p. 15.

[62]   Aqui o pobre ao rico não se humilha
            São iguais nesta escola os cidadãos.
            Aqui só vale a glória do trabalho.
            Nas aulas do Liceu há só irmãos,
                                    Barros, p. 24.

Bethencourt da Silva, was a follower of Socialism who wished to see, "labor valued equally to capital" in Brazil.[63] The Liceu in Rio was maintained through member fees and donations in combination with state funding, a model followed in the opening of unaffiliated Liceus de Artes e Ofícios in Salvador, Recife, São Paulo, Maceió, and Ouro Preto between 1872 and 1886.[64]

Despite the progressive curriculum of the Rio Liceu (the institute opened its doors to women in 1881) the manual arts remained less socially prestigious than the professions taught at the Academia de Belas Artes or the schools of law and medicine. Furthermore, the Liceu prepared workers for artisanal crafts and not necessarily the skilled industrial labor necessary for large-scale manufacturing or heavy industry. The Mechanics School of the Navy Arsenal in Rio, founded in 1860, was one of the only options for industrial training in the capital city at that early date. It was later joined by a school of telegraphy in 1881, illustrating the growing need for qualified workers as railroads expanded.[65]

In addition to *liceus*, ten provinces established workshops or "educational houses" for training poor or orphaned children in manual arts between 1840 and 1865. In comparison to the egalitarian tone invoked in descriptions of the Liceu in Rio, these enterprises were explicitly charitable institutions intended to moralize the impoverished and orphaned children under their care. Founded in 1840, A Casa dos Educandos Artífices do Pará (House for Students of the Manual Arts of Pará) prepared students for employment as gunsmiths, carpenters, shoemakers, tinsmiths, blacksmiths, cabinet makers, and sawyers in the local Navy and Army Arsenals, and on the docks. Discipline was modeled on the military, and the workshops were viewed less as sites of public education and more as state-sponsored charity similar in tone, if not necessarily form, to England's Industrial Revolution-era workhouses and poorhouses.[66]

In the same mold as the Liceu, the Sociedade Auxiliadora also opened a night school for instruction in basic literacy and industrial arts for adults in 1871 and an industrial school that emphasized instruction in manual arts for adolescents in Rio de Janeiro. The curriculum of the night school resembled that of the Liceu (against which it competed for students), with courses ranging from Portuguese grammar and composition to geography, architecture, mechanics, industrial design, and mechanical drafting, among others. Data on enrollees demonstrate that it was mostly

---

[63] Barros, p. 203.   [64] Cunha, p. 122.
[65] Cunha, p. 121.   [66] Cunha, pp. 113–14.

artisans who attended the night school, and between 1871 and 1891, 3,859 (male) students received instruction within its walls. Likewise the industrial school, which admitted students at fourteen years of age, provided a five-year course on basic literacy, math, and industrial skills to 1,078 youths between 1873 and 1891.[67] Like the Liceu, the Sociedade Auxiliadora invoked a more lofty discourse of progress than the paternalism evidenced in the factory school descriptions while retaining the same sense of moralizing the enrollees, "when men are guided by intelligence they are more advantageously able to resist the ruin brought about by vice and passion, and they claim their sacred rights and how to the fulfillment of the obligations that society places upon them."[68]

Invoking the language of progress was also a tactic used to defend and promote industrial and manual arts in other venues as well, as evidenced by the Sociedade dos Artistas Mecânicos e Liberais in Recife, Pernambuco, in the 1860s. Comprised of mixed-race artisans and mechanics, society members attempted to elevate their status and protect their lost corporate privileges after a series of liberal reforms were enacted in the 1860s. Whereas the Rio merchants described earlier in the chapter claimed the language of progress in their struggle against the trolley companies, members of the sociedade invoked the same in order to elevate their trades and jockey for a better economic and social position vis-à-vis the more prestigious professional vocations.[69]

In conclusion, these examples illustrate that Brazilians sought different pathways for a gradual and controlled transition to and valorization of free labor in the 1870s and 1880s. Whereas the Rio Liceu promoted notions of equality through work and citizenship, the factory schools and the night school of the Sociedade Auxiliadora saw basic literacy and training in the manual arts as a way to moralize the poor and prepare them for the discipline of industrial production. Even the Associação Industrial de Rio de Janeiro, a firmly pro-manufacturing organization at a time that agricultural interests still held considerable sway over Brazilian politics and economy, counseled caution in the transition from an economy based on agriculture and slavery to factory production and wage labor:

Only a gradual transformation will ensure our secure arrival at an [industrial future]. Modest undertakings at the beginning will, little by little, become bolder. Like nature, industry does not take large leaps.

[67] Cunha, p. 139 and pp. 142–3.   [68] Cunha, p. 137.

[69] Marcelo MacCord, *Artifiícies da Cidadania: mutualism, educação, e trabalho no Recife oitocentista* (Campinas, SP: Editora Unicamp, 2012), p. 206.

We know that these sentiments are not appealing to those impatient . . . for under-takings compatible only with a much more advanced state of industry. But . . . we are sincere promoters of industry, and [we believe] that only gradual and prudent improvement can ensure a future without dangerous outcomes. . . . [70]

What "dangerous outcomes" does the previous passage allude to? As economist Karl Polanyi has shown, a significant component of the wrenching shift to industrial capitalism in England described as the "Great Transformation" was the dis-embedding of people from the tra-ditional social networks that governed economic relationships.[71] During the reign of Pedro II, rare was the Brazilian voice that advocated for a radical transformation of society.[72] Antislavery proponents may have wanted to see an end to slavery and its replacement with wage labor, but they wanted to do so within the secure framework of patron to underling, of father to son, and of employer to worker. In the case of the factory schools, the harsher aspects of mechanized production and the transition from slavery to wage labor were to be guided by the filial relationship of owner and worker in the hope of ensuring the desired "*aperfeiçoamento progressivo*" (progressive improvement). Factory schools provided a con-trolled method to make free laborers into productive members of the nation.

The promotion of factory schools as one model for transitioning to free labor points to three conclusions. The first was the assumption shared by Brazilian elites from all sides of the political spectrum that those on the lower rungs of Brazilian society needed the guidance of those above, be it as kindly *fazendeiros* or benevolent factory owners. Transforming Brazilian orphans into honest workers was a new invocation of an old theme, one that ensured the safe introduction of industrial production and the creation of a reliable and docile free workforce. Second, even as supporters of benevolent companies such as the Imperial Fábrica de Tabaco praised the benefits of educating and moralizing the poor, it ensconced the same firmly into a social structure with factory "father" at the top and skilled worker "son or daughter" at the bottom. This offered

---

[70] *Archivos da Exposição da Industria Nacional*, p. CLVIII.
[71] Karl Polanyi, *The Great Transformation: The Political and Economic Origins of our Time* (Boston: Beacon Press, 1944, 1957, 2001), chs. 5 and 6.
[72] André Rebouças' *Agricultura Nacional* provides an exception in his proposal for the distribution of land to the Brazilian-born poor. André Rebouças, *Agricultura nacional: estudos econômicos: propaganda abolicionista e democrática, setembro de 1874 a setembro de 1883*, 2nd ed. facsimile (Recife: Fundação Joaquim Nabuco, Editora Massangana, 1988, 1883).

a step up out of ignorance and poverty, but provided no alleviation or exit from the oppressive paternalistic hierarchy. Third, the call to "en-noble" wage labor "even in its most rudimentary forms," echoed the shoemaker from Chapter 2 and his frustration with the low regard for manual trades. The acrimonious descriptions of railway workers in *apedidos* suggest that part of the problem was the continued pejorative view of manual labor and service work, and the anxiety caused by this new class of laborers outside of the paternalistic hierarchy. It is important to remember that negative views of wage-labor were not limited to Brazil. In the early nineteenth century, US citizens were also suspicious of those who worked for wages, as disdain for boat operators on the Erie Canal illustrated in the 1820s and 1830s. Like Brazil, nineteenth-century views of wage labor in the United States were invariably set against a backdrop of slavery, as the implications of working for money necessitated new legislation and new definitions of labor and citizen as the nation developed.[73]

73 Sheriff, pp. 38–40; Amy Dru Stanley, *From Bondage to Contract: Wage Labor, Marriage, and the Market in the Age of Slave Emancipation* (Cambridge: Cambridge University Press, 1998), pp. 60–2.

Conclusion

The original idea for this project emerged from a paper I wrote as a graduate student titled "Modernizing Monarchy: Dom Pedro II's visit to the United States in 1876," in which I used newspaper accounts of the emperor's coast-to-coast travels to reconstruct his three-month tour of US cultural, industrial, and education sites. A self-congratulatory mood prevailed in US newspapers whether printed in Cheyenne, San Francisco, or New Orleans. Progress was the word of the day, and the Centennial Exhibition in Philadelphia was its physical manifestation. The presence of the Brazilian emperor, a member of royalty and a descendant of the Hapsburgs no less, validated the recent industrial successes of the young republic; US audiences were happy to have such an esteemed witness for their recent technological accomplishments, especially the state-of-the-art transcontinental railroad, completed in 1869. As I examined these sources, I began to consider how progress specifically, and modernization more generally, were understood in Brazil. Pedro II's knowledge about the latest industrial, cultural, and social advances of the United States suggested that Brazilians were well informed of the economic and technological transformations developing in the North Atlantic. This train of thought ultimately lead to my examination of O *Auxiliador da Indústria Nacional* and the paid letters and articles of the *Jornal do Commercio* explored in previous chapters. The term *progresso* appeared in these of course, but *aperfeiçoar* seemed less vague and shed more light on Brazilian conceptions of modernization, as Chapter 2 demonstrated.

A striking difference between the US and Brazilian sources I examined was the self-confident, sometimes brash tone of the former and the contrasting bombast and caution of the latter. The press of both nations embraced the mantra of progress, but the United States seemed more certain of itself, an unstoppable machine steam-rolling a wild continent into a modern nation. Brazilian progress was less confident, more cautious, ever mindful of its deficiencies, and aiming not for a radical transformation but a controlled *aperfeiçoamento* (improvement). In Chapter 2, this notion of *aperfeiçoar* provides shades of meaning and context to the discussions of modernization not only in Brazil, but within the industrializing Atlantic broadly writ. At the beginning of the nineteenth century, words such as industry, improvement, and progress did not yet possess their contemporary meanings. The Industrial Revolution was only then becoming a practical reality, and no concise phrase or concept described it in its entirety. These "terms in gestation" congealed over time, moving back and forth across the Atlantic, acquiring new meanings as the people who used them bore witness to the evolving technologies, economies, and social practices before them. By contrasting the evolution of these terms across cultures and nations it is my hope that a more precise understanding of their "impact on consciousness," is gained, and by extension, a greater understanding of the manner in which nineteenth-century modernization proceeded in diverse settings.[1]

In contrast to the technologically backward period nineteenth-century Brazil is often considered to be, this project, as demonstrated through the letters of the *Jornal do Commercio*, reveals a lively public discussion of modernization. This was a society grappling with the most important transformations of the day: how to best bring about the abolition of slavery and the transition to a wage labor economy; how to efficiently adopt and develop new technologies for local conditions; how to employ technological innovations like the railway for economic and social improvement; how to structure the factory system both economically and socially; how to best apply limited capital for the development of large infrastructure projects such as roads and railroads; and how to identify undiscovered species for new commodities. Chapter 3 outlines the last of these questions in the exploration of the economic thought of the Sociedade Auxiliadora and the Ministry of Agriculture (after 1860) in which Brazil's tropical forests and cultivated fields emerged as potent forces for economic development. The economic nationalism of the society drew from diverse Enlightenment thinkers first introduced into

---

[1] Here I again invoke Leo Marx's call for "a careful study of [the] shift in language" for the concepts behind the following terms: manufacture, industry, machine, and engine. *The Machine in the Garden: Technology and the Pastoral Ideal in America* (New York: Oxford University Press, 1964, 2000), endnote, p. 166.

Brazil during the colonial period. The most important of these included the Smithian concept of industry, especially the relationship between agriculture and manufacturing, the pro-agriculture economic thought of the French Physiocrats, and Carl Linneaus' lesser-known economic nationalism. Brazilian interpretations of these ideas appeared throughout the nineteenth century in the writings of society members, gesturing toward a more sophisticated designation of nineteenth-century Brazil as an "agricultural nation" than scholars have previously acknowledged.

Chapters 4 and 5 converge thematically in that they illustrated the difficulties Brazilians faced in adopting technology in the agricultural and transportation sectors while also showing where they were the most successful in establishing domestic production and innovation. The latest agricultural inventions – designed and developed in temperate climates – were not always easily transferred to Brazilian conditions, as Chapter 4 demonstrated. On one hand, this resulted in frustration and caution about experimenting with imported technology. In combination with other factors, including the social status conveyed by slaveholding, slash-and-burn cultivation and slave labor simply made good economic sense where machines were costly, difficult to move, and often unreliable. On the other hand, the challenges to importing technology in addition to the distance from centers of technological production in the North Atlantic spurred local innovation that met local needs. A central argument of Chapter 5 is that looking for bigger trends in industrialization (the large-scale industrial production that accompanied railroad expansion in England, the US, and Germany, for example) results in the overlooking of smaller spaces of technological adaption and innovation. These spaces, such as railroad workshops and the self-contained smithies and workshops on coffee plantations, I argue, matter too, though their impact may not have been as spectacular or as great in economic terms compared to North Atlantic centers of industry.

Finally, Chapter 6 connects to an overarching theme in the arts, history, and literature of the nineteenth and twentieth centuries: the complications and displacements caused by processes of modernization. The social tensions that erupted around rude railway employees and the physical displacement of pedestrians and freight wagons on Rio streets pointed to deeper social fissures as Brazil's slave society transitioned to wage labor. The transformation of the material shape of the city did indeed result in new rhythms imposed onto human bodies and social relationships, but whereas our modernizers from Chapter 5 saw the precise and measured movement of the railway as a civilizing force, in reality many individuals felt threatened and oppressed by the same, as depictions of the trolley lines that criss-crossed Rio's narrow streets attest. Furthermore, the negative reaction to the enforcement of trolley and railroad rules and regulations by conductors (or the liberties taken by the same) reveals, in part, resistance to their authority, especially because they were perceived as subordinate in the social hierarchy. Reactions to trolleys also revealed anxieties about gender and race as city populations came together in train stations and onboard crowded cars. If trolleys and railways sometimes unleashed uncivilized behavior on the part of conductors and passengers alike, in contrast, great care was taken to describe factory schools, *liceus*, and low-cost night schools as a way to carefully ensure the training of docile and educated factory workers. In both cases, reasserting or maintaining social order remained a central concern, bringing the project of a gradual aperfeiçoamento described in Chapter 2 full circle.

In closing, I consider this project a launching point for further research on themes of modernization in nineteenth-century Brazil. Of particular interest is a deeper understanding of the notion of geography as economic destiny that seemed to direct modernization in both Brazil and the US. The mythology of Manifest Destiny and the mass movement toward an ever-expanding frontier in the US West depended on a particular vision of and relationship to the natural world. A study of attitudes toward the environment in Brazil and its potential for economic development beyond slash-and-burn plantation agriculture would provide an interesting counterpoint and build upon the environmental histories of Warren Dean and José Pádua.[2] The designation of Brazil as an "agricultural nation," by many nineteenth-century Brazilians, as mentioned before, is only partially explained by the influence of its landholding planter elite. This work suggests that a more complicated political economy and emerging sense of national destiny underlied this phrase.

Other little-explored lines of inquiry include the patent applications of the National Archives. Reports from the Sociedade Auxiliadora and the Council of State (Pedro II's advisory council) on patent requests provide a rich, unexplored window into Brazilian technological thought. Additionally, research into the reactions of Brazil's slaves and the illiterate poor to steam machines, railroads, and other innovations would fill a lacuna of

---

[2] Warren Dean, *With Broadax and Firebrand: The Destruction of the Brazilian Atlantic Forest* (Berkeley: University of California Press, 1995); José Augusto Pádua, *Um Sopro de Destruição: pensamento político e crítica ambiental no Brasil escravista, 1786–1888*, 2nd ed. (Rio de Janeiro: Jorge Zahar Editor, 2002).

the present work. The *Publicações a Pedido* might have provided access to a wider public reaction, but they do not include the majority of Brazil's population. The central challenge, of course, is finding such actors in the sources; court documents, letters from soldiers or sailors, and photographs would shed light on this topic. Finally, further investigation of regional reactions to modernization would go far in confirming or contrasting the observations of the public in Rio de Janeiro. Salvador and Pernambuco were also sites of large-scale engineering projects and manufacturing. The Maranhão was home to several printing presses by the 1830s, and Rio Grande do Sul established numerous colonization projects and many of Brazil's earliest factories. The capital city of Mato Grosso, Cuibá, possessed a naval installation for the repair and reconstruction of steamships; its technological connections to the outer world lay through the Spanish republics of the River Plate and not Rio de Janeiro. Investigations into these outlying provinces would provide further insight into regional understandings of modernization and complete a more holistic picture of technological transformation during the nineteenth century.

While this work is directed towards historians of Brazil and Latin America, it also seeks to engage a wider readership by presenting the local context of what was part of a larger, increasingly global transformation. I envision future conversations with US historians that move beyond the consideration of that nation as a normative model for modernization, immigration, and the settlement of new territories. In all of these areas Brazil (and the rest of Latin America) offers a compelling comparison and different, locally nuanced outcomes. Furthermore, as the United States moves into the twenty-first century, its former economic hegemony can no longer be taken for granted. It might serve us well to consider other conversations about and processes of economic, industrial, and technological transformation. Modernization – and all its interconnected, moving parts – is a complicated, often nebulous process that is shaped by economic, political, cultural, environmental, and social factors. It is my earnest desire that this project will contribute to further dialogue and understanding between the "two giants" of the Western hemisphere, the United States and Brazil – and the world beyond.

Brazil's economic and technological potential continues to develop. Recent government investment in scientific education and research, the expansion of the federal university system, and the growth of a Brazilian middle class with greater purchasing power all evidence a "Brazil on the rise." This is a continuation of the processes of modernization that began in the nineteenth century. Since then, developments in Brazil have unfolded within a greater context of economic, social, and technological transformation that originally emanated from the North Atlantic. This does not mean that Brazilian modernity is a shabby reflection of foreign visions of progress. On the contrary, this project has evidenced a long-standing Brazilian-inflected vision of modernization that, while influenced by imported ideas and policies, was never adopted wholesale or without reflection.

Final Thoughts

Secretary of State Colin Powell named Brazil an "agricultural super-power" during his visit to the tropical nation in 2004.[3] In the intervening decade, Brazil has solidified its position as a major agricultural producer and one of the United States' biggest competitors. In addition to dominating world markets in the export of traditional crops such as coffee and sugar, Brazil now surpasses the United States in orange juice production, and is second globally in the exportation of beef and ethanol.[4] As of 2014 the tropical nation became the global leader in soybean exports though overall production was slightly smaller than the US total.[5] Brazil's abundant land and climate (up to three soybean crops can be grown per year in comparison to one harvest in temperate climates) are two of the most important factors in the nation's competitive advantage in agricultural production, just as the nineteenth-century modernizers of the Sociedade Auxiliadora envisioned. Brazil's present-day agricultural boom is also the result of innovations in tillage techniques adapted for acidic tropical soils, genetically engineered cultivars, machinery, and new chemical fertilizer and pesticide regimes researched and developed by Brazilian researchers in domestic institutions.

Another important component of Brazil's present-day rise in global stature has less to do with direct economic development than it does with the transformation of its nineteenth-century image from a nation rich in natural resources, but racially degenerate and home to dangerous tropical flora and fauna, as Chapter 3 demonstrated, to a country with biodiverse

---

[3] Larry Rohter, *Brazil on the Rise: The Story of a Country Transformed* (New York: Palgrave MacMillan, 2010), p. 151.

[4] Marcos Fava Neves and Vinícius Gustavo Trombin, *The Orange Juice Business: A Brazilian Perspective* (The Netherlands: Wageningen Academic Publishers, 2011), p. 22.

[5] Daryl E. Ray and Harwood D. Center, "Brazil Seeks to become Largest Ag Exporter," Agfax, July 10, 2015, http://agfax.com/2015/07/10/brazil-seeks-become-worlds-largest-ag-exporter.

ecosystems essential to the health and well-being of planetary life systems. In other words, Brazil has not only overcome internal challenges such as the lack of investment capital and transportation networks, but has benefited from a newly positive international image of its tropical environment. This last observation points to a less tangible but nonetheless significant obstacle for developing countries: nations on the periphery have faced more than material and logistical challenges – they have also battled negative perceptions of themselves and their products in the developed world. It was not enough to build roads and disseminate credit, as André Rebouças recognized in the nineteenth century; Brazilians had to build a modern "brand" that would appeal to consumers both within and beyond their borders. Visions of the Amazon as a source of life and health have contributed to a more positive image of the tropical nation today.

Industrial Forests – Phytomedicines, Agriculture, and Modern Economic Nationalism

Aché, a Brazilian pharmaceutical company that researches, develops, and distributes synthetic medicines and more recently, phytomedicines and phytotherapies (medications developed exclusively from plant extracts), launched a new product called Achéflan in 2005. Derived from the native Brazilian plant *erva-baleeira*, Achéflan was inspired by a folk remedy popular among fishermen off the coast of São Paulo for treating sprains and inflammation caused by tendonitis and other ailments. The company's Website touted the new medicine as:

... the first medical product totally researched and developed in Brazil ... made with Brazilian raw materials, researched by Brazilian scientists, in Brazilian universities, and developed and launched by the largest Brazilian pharmaceutical laboratory.[6]

While Aché's claim is not entirely true – as Chapter 3 demonstrated, medical experimenters developed treatments from Brazilian species dating back to the colonial period – the medication nonetheless represents a significant accomplishment that combines popular knowledge, scientific research, and capital to transform a local resource into a new product for national and international markets.[7] In other words, Achéflan is

---

[6] Aché Website, www.ache.com.br/ingles/phytomedicines.shtml.
[7] Nineteenth-century national and international exhibition catalogs and the research of experimenters like Theodoro Peckholt demonstrate nineteenth-century attempts to use

the embodiment of what nineteenth-century experimenters like André Rebouças and Frederico Burlamaque desired for Brazil: the commercialization of Brazilian species by Brazilian entrepreneurs in support of the nation's economy. The emphasis on economic and scientific self-sufficiency on the Aché Website echoes the nineteenth-century Brazilian vision of achieving independence from foreign economic influence through the commercial development of domestic resources.

Brazilian scientists are realizing the visions of nineteenth-century modernizers in agricultural production as well. Embrapa (Brazilian Agricultural Research Corporation) a state-run private/public collaboration created under the auspices of the Ministry of Agriculture in 1973 for the purpose of "...conserving natural resources..., the environment, and diminishing external dependence on technologies, basic products and genetic materials," has been instrumental in engineering Brazil's present-day agricultural revolution.[8] New technologies – chemical, mechanical, and genetic – have made the cultivation of temperate crops such as the aforementioned soybeans possible in the acidic tropical soils of the Brazilian interior. Other innovations include "no-till" farming that has proven an efficient method for retaining nutrients in tropical soils while also preventing erosion:

> ... "no-till" agriculture, [is a process] in which the soil is not ploughed nor the crop harvested at ground level. Rather, it is cut high on the stalk and the remains of the plant are left to rot into a mat of organic material. Next year's crop is then planted directly into the mat, retaining more nutrients in the soil. In 1990 Brazilian farmers used no-till farming for 2.6 percent of their grains; today [2010] it is over 50 percent.[9]

Though no-till cultivation comprises a very different technology from the state-of-the-art plows so admired by nineteenth-century modernizers, the underlying vision of creating Brazilian solutions for Brazilian conditions is similar. Sociedade Auxiliadora member José Pereira Rego Filho asserted in 1870 that rather than merely importing European agricultural implements of uncertain utility, Brazilians needed to adapt the

---

folk remedies and indigenous plants in creating new medicines and marketable products from botanical resources. Nadja Paraense dos Santos, Angelo C. Pinto, and Ricardo Bicca de Alencastro, "Theodoro Peckholt: Naturalista e Farmacêutico do Brasil Imperial," *Química Nova*, 21:5 (1998), p. 669; and "Passando da Doutrina à prática: Ezequiel Corrêa dos Santos e a Farmácia Nacional," *Química Nova*, 30:4 (2007), p. 1042.

[8] Embrapa Website, www.embrapa.br/english/embrapa/about-us.

[9] "Brazilian Agriculture: the miracle of the cerrado," *The Economist*, August 26, 2010, www.economist.com/node/16886442.

possibilities presented by foreign technology to the particulars of their agricultural needs.[10] This vision is evocative of the role that Embrapa and other research centers, such as the Centro Pluridisciplinar de Pesquisas Químicas, Biológicas e Agrícolas (Interdisciplinary Center of Chemical, Biological, and Agricultural Research) at the State University of Campinas and the Instituto Butantan (Butantan Institute), both in São Paulo state, and the Fundação Oswaldo Cruz (Oswaldo Cruz Foundation) in Rio are playing in Brazil's agricultural and pharmaceutical research and development.[11] These centers are presently researching the commercial uses of Brazilian species and developing cultivation techniques and technology specifically suited for tropical agriculture. This last point is significant in that agricultural research in nations with temperate climates concentrate on crops such as wheat, corn, and soy. Manioc (cassava), for example, a staple across tropical Africa, Latin America, and Asia, receives little attention from institutions in the US and Europe.[12] Brazilian research is therefore filling a significant lacuna in the development and modernization of tropical agriculture that includes an impressive toolkit of machinery, cultivation techniques, and bioengineering. Today Brazil is poised to transfer this specialized technology to other tropical regions.[13]

By highlighting these Brazilian accomplishments, I do not argue that there is a direct connection between the nineteenth-century writings of the Socidade Auxiliadora and the development strategies of Empraba. Rather, the point is to highlight Brazilian efforts to achieve economic self-sufficiency through agricultural improvement and the discovery of the commercial uses of natural resources in both periods, suggesting that harnessing the productivity of the nation's tropical environment remains a driving force behind visions of economic development. Nonetheless, Embrapa's focus on developing technology ranging from machinery to genetically engineered crops evidences a mission similar in spirit and

[10] José Pereira Rego Filho, "Escola agricola da Companhia União e Industria," *O Auxiliador*, September 1870, p. 475.

[11] For a listing of more than fifty government-supported agricultural research centers in Brazil, see Nienke M. Beintema, Antonio Flavio Dias Avila, and Philip G. Pardey, "Agricultural R&D in Brazil: Policy, Investments, and Institutional Profile," International Food Policy Research Institute, Empresa Brasileira de Pesquisa Agropecuaria, and Regional Fund for Agricultural Technology, Washington, DC, 2001, pp. 97–105.

[12] Larry Rohter, "Scientists are Making Brazil's Savannah Bloom," *New York Times*, October 2, 2007, www.nytimes.com/2007/10/02/science/02tropic.html?pagewanted=all&_r=0.

[13] *Ibid.*

vision to that of the Imperial Instituto Fluminense de Agricultura founded in 1860.[14] Through its regional research centers, Embrapa has fulfilled many of the objectives of the Imperial Instituto: the acclimatization of introduced species, the development of agricultural technologies specifically designed for Brazilian crops and environmental conditions, and research on products derived from native species such as *copaíba* oil extracted from the Amazonian *Copaifera multijuga*, which is used in medicines and cosmetics. Embrapa's research ranges from biopolymers produced by spiders (also envisioned as a source for textile fibers by nineteenth-century modernizers) to biofuel extracted from sugar cane and Amazonian nuts.[15] Brazil's successful transformation of the Cerrado – an inland tropical savannah in the northeastern and central interior long considered an economically unproductive wasteland – into one of the most vibrant and agriculturally productive regions in the nation, and indeed the globe, is truly a technological and scientific revolution on the scale of the nineteenth-century transformation of midwestern US grasslands into farmland that was so admired by Brazilian modernizers.[16] Together these examples represent a long-standing Brazilian conception of economic development enmeshed in the nation's tropical biome.

At the same time, these recent successes have resulted in new challenges and controversial outcomes: the ongoing habitat destruction and environmental degradation of the sensitive ecology of the Cerrado, land grabs and speculation, and the continuation and heightening of economic disparity with the introduction of export-oriented agro-business to remote regions.[17] It remains to be seen whether the agricultural boom

---

[14] Embrapa Website, www.embrapa.br/english/embrapa/about-us.

[15] Rohter, "Scientists...."

[16] Sod-busting plows were a key innovation in the agricultural revolution on the midwestern plains in the nineteenth-century US. The successful breaking up of thickly rooted prairie sod led to further mechanical innovations that amplified human and animal labor and fully exploited the region's flat geography to reach new economies of scale in the production of wheat and corn. William Cronan, *Nature's Metropolis: Chicago and the Great West* (New York: W. W. Norton and Co., 1991), pp. 98–102; for a description of John Deere's adaption of plows for prairie soils see Neil Dahlstrom and Jeremy Dahlstrom, *The John Deere Story: A Biography of Plowmakers John and Charles Deere* (Dekalk, IL: Northern Illinois University Press, 2005), pp. 11–17.

[17] See Carlos A. Klink and Ricardo B. Machado, "Conservation of the Brazilian Cerrado," *Conservation Biology* 19:3, June 2005, pp. 707–13; Emma Marris, "The forgotten ecosystem," News Feature, *Nature*, October 13, 2005, pp. 944–5; Maria Luisa Mendonça, "Brazil: Sugar cane plantations devastate vital Cerrado region," *Pacific Ecologist*, Summer 2009, pp. 25–7; Richard C. Morais, "Deadwood Brazil," *Forbes Magazine* July 25, 2005, www.forbes.com/free_forbes/2005/0725/080.html; Thomas D.

will address historic social and economic inequalities while also avoiding ecological degradation.

From Dangerous to Healthful: Changing Perceptions of Tropical Forests

Mate's purported healthful properties were not enough to sell it to North Atlantic consumers in the nineteenth century, but today exotic-sounding and exotic-looking Amazonian fruits such as *açaí* and *guaraná* are lauded on blogs and television shows in the US and Europe as superfoods replete with health-sustaining antioxidants.[18] Indigenous and popular knowledge are recast as more traditional, wiser, and "better for you" in the advertisements of Aveda (US), The Body Shop (founded in the UK), and the Brazilian company Natura, all corporations that manufacture beauty products from indigenous and "exotic" plants sourced from around the globe. The Amazon – and the tropics in general – once seen as a source of degeneracy and disease that threatened European bodies, is now advertised as a pristine font of all that is natural, healthy, and pure.[19] The old trope of the New World tropics as a dangerous and corrupting space has been turned on its head; today the Amazon *heals*. Ironically, Europe's industrially contaminated environment is declared dangerous and unnatural in Brazilian marketing strategies:

"If you pick a rose from the Amazon and a rose from the middle of France, the Brazilian one will be a lot less polluted," said Eduardo Rauen, commercial director of Amazonia Natural... "Amazonia is more natural and that is our selling point."[20]

Rodgers, *The Deepest Wounds: A Labor and Environmental History of Sugar in Northeast Brazil* (Chapel Hill: University of North Carolina Press, 2010), p. 210; and Donald Sawyer, "Climate change, biofuels and eco-social impacts in the Brazilian Amazon and Cerrado," *Philosophical Transactions of the Royal Society* 363 (2008), pp. 1747–52.

[18] Seth Kugel, "Açaí, a Global Super Fruit, is Dinner in the Amazon," *New York Times*, www.nytimes.com/2010/02/24/dining/24acai.html?pagewanted=all&_r=0; Lindsey Duncan, "So What's so Good about Açaí? A Whole lot." Dr. Oz Show Website, www.doctoroz.com/blog/lindsey-duncan-nd-cn/so-whats-so-good-about-acai-whole-lot, and "Rainforest Remedies." Dr. Oz Show Website, www.doctoroz.com/blog/lindsey-duncan-md/rainforest-remedies.

[19] Nancy Stepan, *Picturing Tropical Nature* (Ithaca, NY: Cornell University Press, 2001), ch. 2.

[20] Andrew Downie, "Beautifying the World with Amazon Ingredients," *New York Times*, August 24, 2007, www.nytimes.com/2007/08/24/business/worldbusiness/24beauty.html?pagewanted=all.

Natura is the best-known of the Brazilian companies that invoke this "Tropical Chic" marketing strategy pioneered by Aveda and The Body Shop. Whereas previous generations of Brazilians preferred imported cosmetics and body-care products over domestically produced goods, especially from Europe, companies like Natura have raised the profile of Brazilian beauty products and elevated the prestige of Amazonian ingredients both at home and abroad.[21] According to Natura's Website, Ekos, the name for the company's line of products derived primarily from Amazonian species, plays on three words: Greek "ôikos," or home; Tupi-Guaraní "ekó," the meaning of which is akin to "synonymous with life"; and the Latin "echo," or the reverberation of knowledge about the natural world that extends across generations. Ekos is also clearly meant to evoke the sense of "eco" as in ecological. The products are almost exclusively derived from plant species native to Brazil: *andiroba, breu branco, capitiú, priprioca, maracujá* (passion fruit), *cupuassu*, Brazil nuts, *guaraná, buriti,* and cacao, several of which were also listed in nineteenth-century exhibition catalogs.[22] On the company's Website, lush images of Amazonian *capitiú* leaves, *breu branco* sap, and *priprioca* root emphasize the purity of both the tropical forest and the imagined timelessness of the local knowledge upon which the products are based. Like the factories embedded in the fertile forest in Chapter 2, the jewel-colored elixirs contained within the sleek bottles of Natura's packaging represent a modernity that emerges out of the generative powers of the "uber-natural" Amazon forest.[23] Nineteenth-century modernizers also wrote treatises and catalog descriptions touting similar applications for an astonishingly diverse range of tropical species – including uses adopted from indigenous people. But it was, in part, their failure to develop a marketing scheme that prevented the raw materials of Brazil's forests from successfully penetrating North Atlantic markets. Natura has overcome the rough-hewn image of the Brazilian tropical frontier in selling products to North Atlantic consumers, illustrating that the nation's industrial forests have indeed endured into the twenty-first century.

[21] Mirelle de Franca, "Beleza Brasileira," *Revista do Globo* (O Globo Sunday Supplement), April 29, 2007, p. 50.

[22] Natura Website, www.natura.net/port/cosmoprof/ing/portfolio/corpo.asp.

[23] "Preciosidades da floresta," ("Treasures of the forest)," Natura Website, www.natura ekos.com.br/aguasdebanho.

Bibliography

Archives

Brazil

Arquivo Histórico do Exército, Rio de Janeiro
Archivo Nacional, Rio de Janeiro
Fundação Biblioteca Nacional, Rio de Janeiro
Instituto Histórico e Geográfico Brasileiro, Rio de Janeiro
Arquivo Edgard Leuenroth, Universidade Estadual de Campinas, São Paulo
Biblioteca Barbosa Rodrigues, Jardim Botânico do Rio de Janeiro

United States

Hispanic Reading Room, Library of Congress
Oliveira Lima Library, Catholic University of America, Washington, DC
Dibner Library of Science and Technology, Smithsonian Institution Libraries

Manuscripts

"Mémoire sur la comparaison d'une route ordinaire et d'un chem de fer entre Parahyba et Barbacena, et sur les limites qu'il convient d'adopter dans la trace d'une route pour les déclivités et les rayons des courbes," *Diversos Códices* 1612 a 1984, Códice 807 Volume 16, 1794–1883, *Arquivo Nacional.*
"Documentos sobre o recurso interposto por Dona Francisca Amalia de Oliveira Camargo, contra o ato de presidente do Estado de S. Paulo resolvendo as questões sussetadas sobre a abertura de uma estrada de Rodagem entre Capivary e a estação de Kilombo, de estrada de ferro Itaúna," manuscript, IT4 Maço[4], GIFI 43177, Código de Fundo: OI, Seção de guarda: SDE, *Arquivo Nacional.*

Newspapers and Journals

American Railroad Journal and Iron Manufacturer and Mining Gazette
O Agricultor Brazileiro
O Agricultor Progressista
O Auxiliador da Industria Nacional
O Corsário
Correio Mercantil
Gazeta Academico
Harper's Weekly
Jornal do Commercio
O Mosquito
Nature
New York Evangelist
New York Times
Revista Agricola do Imperial Instituto Fluminense de Agricultura
Revista do Globo
Revista Illustrada
Scribner's Monthly: an Illustrated Magazine for the People
Semana Illustrada

Primary Sources – Dictionaries

Diccionario da Lingua Portugueza, 4th ed., (Lisbon: Impressão Regia, 1831).
The Oxford English Dictionary, 2nd ed. (Oxford: Clarendon Press, 1989).
Aulete, F. J. Caldas, ed., *Diccionario Contemporario da Lingua Portugueza* (Lisboa: Imprensa Nacional, 1881).

Primary Sources – Publications

Almanak Administrativo, Mercantil, e Industrial (Rio de Janeiro: Tip. Laemmert, 1876).
Archivos da Exposição da Industria Nacional: actas, pareceres e decisões do jury geral da Exposição da Industria Nacional realizada no Rio de Janeiro in 1881 (Rio de Janeiro: Tip. Nacional, 1881).
O Brazil na Exposição Internacional dos Caminhos de Ferro em Pariz em 1887 (Rio de Janeiro: Imprensa Nacional, 1887).
Catalogo da Exposição Nacional em 1875 (Rio de Janeiro: Tip. e Lithographia Carioca, 1875).
Catalogo da Segunda Exposição Nacional de 1866 (Rio de Janeiro: Tip. Perserverança, 1866).
Catalogo dos Objectos Enviados para a Exposição Universal de Paris em 1867 (Rio de Janeiro: 1867?), bound with *Brazil na Exposição de 1867* (Rio de Janeiro: 1867?), Division of Rare and Manuscript Collections, Cornell University Library.
Catalogo dos Productos Naturaes e Industriaes que Figurárão na Exposição Nacional (Rio de Janeiro: Tip. o Diaro do Rio de Janeiro, 1862).

Catalogos dos productos naturaes e industriaes remettidos das provincias do Imperio do Brasil que figurárão na Exposição Nacional inaugurada na Côrte no Rio de Janeiro no dia 2 de Dezembro de 1861 (Rio de Janeiro: Tip. Nacional, 1862).

Commissão pela Expansão Ecônomica, *Il Mate del Brasile* (Roma: Tip. Enrico Voghera, 1910).

Le thé maté du Brésil: analyse chimique (?: Mission Brésillienne du Propagande, 1908).

The Empire of Brazil at the Universal Exhibition of 1876 (Rio de Janeiro: Tip. e Lith. do Imperial Instituto Artístico, 1876).

Official Catalogue of the British Section (London: Eyre and Spottiswoode, 1876).

Official Catalogue of the International Exhibition of 1876, rev. ed., (Philadelphia, PA: John R. Nagle & Co., 1876).

Official Descriptive and Illustrated Catalogue of the Great Exhibition, 1851 (London: Spicer Bros., 1851).

Recordações da Exposição Nacional de 1861 (Rio de Janeiro: Tip. Universal de Laemmert, 1862).

Swedish Catalogue (Philadelphia, PA: Hallowell and Co., 1876).

Viagem Imperial de Petrópolis a Juiz de Fóra por occasião de colleção de artigos publicados no "Jornal do Commercio" do Rio de Janeiro em 1861 e no "Diario Mercantil" de Juiz de Fóra em 1918 (Juiz de Fóra: Tip. Sul, 1919).

Agassiz, Elizabeth Cabot Cary and Louis Agassiz, *A Journey in Brazil* (Boston: Ticknor and Fields, 1868).

Almeida, Milguel Calmon du Pin e, *Ensaio sobre o fabrico do assucar offerecido a Sociedade D'Agricultura, Commercio, e Industria da Provincia da Bahia* (Bahia: Tip. do Diario, 1834).

Bennett, Thomas, *A voyage from the United States to South America, performed during the years 1821, 1822, & 1823. Embracing a description of the city of Rio Janeiro, in Brazil, of every port of importance in Chili; of several in Lower Peru; and of an eighteen months cruise in a Nantucket whaleship. The whole interspersed with a variety of original anecdotes*, 2nd ed. (Newburyport, MA: Herald Press, 1823).

Bentley, Thomas, *The Illustrated History of the Centennial Exhibition, Philadelphia, 1876* (New York: John Filmer, 1876).

Brandão, Ambrósio Fernandes (attributed), *Dialogues of the Great Things of Brazil (Diálogos das Grandezas do Brasil)*, Frederick Holden Hall, William F. Harrison, and Dorothy Winters Welker, trans., (Albuquerque: University of New Mexico Press, 1987).

Burlamaque, Frederico Leopoldo César, *Catechismo de Agricultura* (Rio de Janeiro: Tip. Deseseis de Julho, 1870).

Ensaio sobre a regneração das raças cavallares do Imperio do Brasil (Rio de Janeiro: Tip. Dous de Dezembro, 1856).

Manual de Maquinas, Instrumentos e Motores Agricolas (Rio de Janeiro: Tip. N. L. Vianna & Filhos, 1859).

Memoria analytica a'cerca do commercio dos escravos e a'cerca dos malles da escravidão domestica (Rio de Janeiro: Tip. Commercial Fluminense, 1837).

Burton, Richard, *Explorations of the Highlands of the Brazil; with a Full Account of the Gold and Diamond Mines, Also, Canoeing Down 1500 Miles of the Great River São Francisco, From Sabará to the Sea*, Vol. I (New York: Greenwood Press, 1869, 1969).

Câmara, Manuel Arruda da, *Dissertação sobre as plantas do Brazil, que podem dar linhos próprios e suprir falta do cânhamo, indagas de ordem do príncipe regente, nosso senhor* (Rio de Janeiro: Impressão Regia, 1810).

Condorcet, Marquis of, "The Future of Man," in *French Utopias: An Anthology of Ideal Societies*, ed., and trans., Frank E. Manuel and Fritzie P. Manuel (New York: The Free Press, 1966).

Couty, Louis, *A erva-mate e o charque* (Pelotas: Seiva, 1880, 2000).

Cunha, Antônio Luiz Fernandes da, *Relatorio Geral da Exposição Nacional de 1861 e Relatorios dos Jurys Especiaes Colligidos e Publicados por Deliberação da Commissão Directora* (Rio de Janeiro: Tip. Diario do Rio de Janeiro, 1862).

Dickens, Charles, *Hard Times* (Oxford: Oxford University Press, 2006).

Diderot, Denis, and Jean le Rond d'Alembert, eds., *Encyclopédie, ou dictionnaire raisonné des sciences, des arts et des métiers, etc.* University of Chicago: ARTFL Encyclopédie Project (Spring 2013 Edition), Robert Morrissey (ed.), http://encyclopedie.uchicago.edu/.

Durocher, M. J. M., *Idéias por coordenar a respeito da emancipação* (Rio de Janeiro: Tip. Diario do Rio de Janeiro, 1871).

Fletcher, James C., and D. P. Kidder, *Brazil and the Brazilians: Portrayed in Historical and Descriptive Sketches* (Philadelphia, PA: Childs and Peterson, 1857).

Brazil and the Brazilians, 9th ed. (Boston: Little, Brown, and Company, 1879).

Gama, José de Saldanha da, *Estudos sobre a Quarta Exposição Nacional de 1875* (Rio de Janeiro: Tip. Central de Brown & Evaristo, 1876).

Gaston, J. McFadden, *Hunting a Home in Brazil. The Agricultural Resources and Other Characteristics of the Country. Also, The Manners and Customs of the Inhabitants* (Philadelphia: King & Baird, Printers, 1867).

Jousselandiére, S. V. Vigneron, *Novo manual pratico da agricultura intertropical: seguido do calendario do agricultor de todos os mezes do anno e de conselhos de medicina, tudo fruito de 37 annos de experiencia de um lavrador pratico do Brasil* (Rio de Janeiro: E. & H. Laemmert, 1860).

Kenin, Richard, ed., *A Facsimile of Frank Leslie's Illustrated Historical Register of the Centennial Exposition, 1876* (New York: Paddington Press Ltd., 1976).

Kidder, Daniel P., *Sketches of Residence and Travels in Brazil Embracing Historical and Geographical Notices of the Empire and its Several Provinces* (London: Wiley and Putnam, 1845).

Leavitt, T. H., *Facts about Peat as an Article of Fuel* (Boston, MA: Lee and Shepard, 1867).

Lisboa, Baltasar da Silva, *Riqueza do Brasil em madeiras de construção e carpintaria* (Rio de Janeiro: n/p, 1823).

Macedo, Joaquim Manoel de, *A Carteira do Meu Tio* (Rio de Janeiro: Tip. Paulo Brito, 1855).

Machado de Assis, Joaquim Maria, "Bonde de Santa Teresa," *Obra Completa: Vol. III, Afrânio Coutinho*, Rio de Janeiro: Aguilar, 1962, in Antonio Luciano de A. Tosta, "Exchanging Glances: The Streetcar, Modernity, and the Metropolis in Brazilian Literature," *Chasqui*, 32:2 (Nov., 2003), pp. 35–52.

Philosopher or Dog? Clotide Wilson, trans., (New York: The Noonday Press, 1954, 1992).

Mansfield, Charles, *Paraguay, Brazil, and the Plate: Letters Written in 1852–1853* (Cambridge, UK: Macmillan, 1856).

Miers, John, *Illustrations of South American Plants* (London: Baillière, 1849).

Travels in Chile and La Plata: including accounts respecting the geography, geology, statistics, government, finances, agriculture, manners and customs, and the mining operations in Chile: collected during a residence of several years in these countries (London: Baldwin, Cradock, and Joy, 1826).

Moreira, Francisco Ignacio de Carvalho, *Relatorio sobre a Exposição Internacional de 1862* (London: Thomas Brettell, 1863).

Moreira, Nicolau Joaquim, *Diccionario de plantas medicinaes brasileiras contendo o nome da planta, seu genero, especie, familia e o botanico que o classificou; o logar onde é mais commun, as virtudes que se lhe atribue, e as doses e formas da sua aplicação* (Rio de Janeiro: Tip. de Correio Mercantil, 1862).

Historical Notes Concerning the Vegetable Fibers exhibited by Severino Lourenço da Costa Leite (New York: O Novo Mundo, 1876).

Nabuco, Joaquim, *Abolitionism: The Brazilian Antislavery Struggle, Robert Conrad, ed. and trans.*, (Urbana, IL: University of Illinois Press, 1977).

Netto, Ladislau, *Apontamentos sobre a colleção das Plantas Economicas do Brasil para a exposição internacional de 1867* (Paris: Ballière, 1866).

Pacova, Caetano da Rocha, *Apontamentos sobre a necessicade de uma escola de agricultura, theoria e pratica* (Rio de Janeiro: Tip. de N.L. Vianna e Filhos, 1859).

Pascual, Antonio Diodoro de, *Ensaio Crítico sobre a Viagem ao Brazil em 1852 de Carlos B. Mansfield* (Rio de Janeiro: Tip. Universal de Laemmert, 1861).

Pereira, Hipólito José da Costa, manuscript offered to the I.H.G.B. by Sr. Dr. Manoel Ferreira Lagos, *Revista do Instituto Histórico Geographico Brasileiro*, Tomo XXI. 2a edição, 1858.

Pinto, Joaquim de Almeido, *Diccionario de Botanica Brasileira ou compendio dos vegetaes do Brasil. tanto indigenas como acclimados* (Rio de Janeiro: Tip. Perserverança, 1873).

Documentos Officiaes da 3a Exposição Nacional inaugurada na cidade do Rio de Janeiro em 01 de Janeiro de 1873 (Rio de Janeiro: Tip. Nacional, 1875).

Rebouças, Andre, *Acondicionamento da Herva-Mate* (Rio de Janeiro: Tip. e Lith. Carioca, 1875).

Agricultura nacional: estudos econômicos: propaganda abolicionista e democrática, setembro de 1874 a setembro de 1883, 2nd ed. facsimile (Recife: Fundação Joaquim Nabuco, Editora Massangana, 1988, 1883).

Ensaio de indice geral das madeiras do Brazil, 3 vols. (Rio de Janeiro: Tip. Nacional, 1877).

Silva, José Bonifácio de Andrada e, "Representação á Assemblea Geral Constituinte e Legislativa do Imperio do Brasil Sobre a Escravatura," (Paris: Tip. de Firmin Didot, 1825) in *Obras Científicas e Sociais de José Bonifácio de Andrada e Silva, coligadas e reproduzidas por Edgard de Cerqueira Falcão,* Vol. II, (São Paulo: Revista dos Tribunais, 1963), pp. 115–58.

"Memoir addressed to the General Constituent and Legislative Assembly of the Empire of Brazil on Slavery!," William Walton, trans., (London: A. Redford and W. Robins, 1825) in *Obras Científicas e Sociais de José Bonifácio de Andrada e Silva, coligadas e reproduzidas por Edgard de Cerqueira Fálcão,* Vol. II (São Paulo: Revista dos Tribunais, 1963), pp. 159–218.

Silva, Rodrigo Augusto da, *Discurso Proferido por Occasião da Abertura da Primeira Exposição dos Caminhos de Ferro do Brazil,* in *O Brazil na Exposição Internacional dos Caminhos de Ferro em Pariz em 1887* (Rio de Janeiro: Imprensa Nacional, 1887).

Silveira, Urias A. da, *Fontes de Riqueza dos Estados Unidos do Brasil,* (S.L.P.: S.C.P., 1890), in Erdna Perugine, "A Palavra Indústria na Revista *O Auxiliador da Indústria Nacional* 1833–1843" (Master's thesis, Universidade de São Paulo, 1978).

Smith, Herbert H., *Brazil, the Amazons and the Coast* (New York: Charles Scribner's Sons, 1879).

Soares, Sebastião Ferreira, *Historico da Fabrica de Papel de Orianda ou a defesa do Dr. Guilherme Schüch de Capanema* (Rio de Janeiro: Tip. Universal de Laemmart 1860).

Sousa, Gabriel Soares de, *Tratado Descritivo do Brasil em 1587,* Francisco Adolfo de Varnhagen. ed., (Recife: Fundação Joaquim Nabuco, Editora Massangana, 2000).

Steuart, Sir James, *An Inquiry into the Principles of Political Oeconomy, Vol. I,* Andrew S. Skinner, ed., (Chicago: The University of Chicago Press, 1966).

Stewart, C. S., *Brazil and La Plata: the Personal Record of a Cruise* (New York: G. P. Putnam & Co., 1856).

Werneck, Francisco Peixoto de Lacerda, *Memória sobre a fundação de uma fazenda na província do Rio de Janeiro (Edição original de 1847 e edição modificada e acrescida de 1878)* (Rio de Janeiro: Fundação Casa de Rui Barbosa, 1985).

Wilberforce, Edward, *Brazil viewed through a naval glass: with notes on slavery and the slave trade* (London: Longman, Brown, Green, and Longmans, 1856).

Primary Sources – Provincial Reports

Provincial and Ministerial reports for nineteenth-century Brazil can be found online at the Center for Research Libraries' Brazilian Government Documents website, http://www-apps.crl.edu/brazil.

Primary Sources – Internet

Aché Website: www.ache.com.br/ingles/phytomedicines.shtml.

Agfax Online: http://agfax.com/2015/07/10/brazil-seeks-become-worlds-largest-ag-exporter/.

American Periodicals Series Online.

Dr. Oz Show Website: www.doctoroz.com/blog/lindsey-duncan-nd-cn/so-whats-so-good-about-acai-whole-lot

The Economist Online: www.economist.com/node/16886442

Embrapa Website: www.embrapa.br/english/embrapa/about-us

Forbes Magazine Online: www.forbes.com/free_forbes/2005/0725/080.html

National Public Radio Online: www.npr.org

Natura Website: www.natura.net/port/cosmoprof/ing/portfolio/corpo.asp; www.naturaekos.com.br/aguasdebanho/

New York Times Online: www.nytimes.com/2010/02/24/dining/24acai.html?page wanted=all&_r=0; www.nytimes.com/2007/08/24/business/worldbusiness/24beauty.html?pagewanted=all

Pinhalense Corporate Website: http://www.pinhalense.com.br/site/eng/index.htm

Senado Federal, official Website of the Brazilian Government: www.senado.gov.br/sf/

University of Chicago, The Project for the American and French Research on the Treasury of the French Language (ARTFL): http://artfl.uchicgao.edu/

Encyclopédie ou Dictionnaire Raisonné des Sciences, Des Arts et Des Métiers, artfl.uchicgao.edu/cgi-bing/philologic31/getobject.pl?c.90:282.encyclopedie 1207

Secondary Sources – Film

Mauá – O Imperador e o Rei. Directed by Sérgio Rezende. Rio de Janeiro: Riofilms, 1999.

Secondary Sources – Publications

Adas, Michael, *Machines as the Measure of Men: science, technology, and ideologies of western dominance* (Ithaca, NY: Cornell University Press, 1989).

Alden, Dauril, *Royal government in colonial Brazil; with special reference to the administration of the Marquis of Lavradio, viceroy, 1769–1779* (Berkeley, CA: University of California Press, 1968).

Alonso, Angela, *Idéias em Movimento: a geração 1870 na crise do Brasil-Império* (São Paulo: Editora Paz e Terra, 2002).

Amado, Janaina, Warren Dean, and Walter Nugent, "Frontier in Comparative Perspectives: The United States and Brazil," Working Papers No. 188, Latin American Program, The Wilson Center, Washington, DC, 1990.

Anderson, Rodney D., *Outcasts in their Own Land: Mexican Industrial Workers, 1906–1911* (DeKalb, IL: Northern Illinois University Press, 1976).

Andrade, André Luiz Alípio de, "Variações sobre um tema: a Sociedade Auxiliadora da Indústria Nacional e o debate sobre o fim do tráfico de escravos

(1845–1850)" (Master's thesis, Universidade Estadual de Campinas, Instituto de Economia, 2002).

Andrade, Joaquim Marçal Ferrera de, *História da fotorreportagem no Brasil: a fotografia na imprensa do Rio de Janeiro de 1839 a 1900* (Rio de Janeiro: Elsevier Editora Ltda., 2004).

Andrews, George Reid, *Blacks and Whites in São Paulo, Brazil: 1888–1988* (Madison: University of Wisconsin Press, 1991).

Araújo, Rosa Maria Barboza de, *A Vocação do Prazer: A cidade e família no Rio de Janeiro republicano* (Rio de Janeiro: Rocco, 1993).

Azevedo, Celia Maria Marinho de, *Onda Negra, Medo Branco: o negro no imaginário das elites século XIX* (Rio de Janeiro: Paz e Terra, 1987).

Azzi, Riolando, *A concepção da ordem social segundo o positivismo ortodoxo brasileiro* (São Paulo: Edições Loyola, 1980).

Baer, Werner, "Import Substitution and Industrialization in Latin America: Experiences and Interpretations," *Latin American Research Review*, 7: 1 (1972), pp. 95–122.

Balaban, Marcelo, *Poeta do Lápis: sátira e política na trajetória de Angelo Agostini no Brasil Imperial (1864–1888)* (Campinas, BR: Editora Unicamp, 2009).

Baptist, Ed, *The Half has never Been Told: Slavery and the Making of American Capitalism* (New York: Basic Books, 2014).

Barman, Roderick, *Brazil, the Forging of a Nation* (Stanford: Stanford University Press, 1988).

  Citizen Emperor: Pedro II and the Making of Brazil, 1825–91 (Stanford: Stanford University Press, 1999).

Barreto, Patrícia Regina Corrêa, "Sociedade Auxiliadora da Indústria Nacional: o templo carioca de palas atena," (Ph.D. dissertation, Universidade Federal do Rio de Janeiro, 2009).

Barros, Alvaro Paes de, *O Liceu de Artes e Ofícios e seu fundador* (Rio de Janeiro: n/p, 1956).

Bastos, Humberto, *O pensamento industrial no Brasil* (São Paulo: Martins Ed., 1952).

Bastos, Wilson de L., *Mariano Procópio Ferreira Lage: sua vida, sua obra, descendência, genealogia* (Juiz de Fora: Paraibuna, 1994).

Bauer, Arnold J., "Industry and the Missing Bourgeoisie: Consumption and Development in Chile, 1850–1950," *Hispanic American Historical Review* 70:2, (May 1990), pp. 227–53.

Beatty, Edward, *Technology and the Search for Progress in Modern Mexico* (Berkeley: University of California Press, 2015).

Beauclair, Geraldo de, *A Construção Inacabada: a economia brasileira, 1822–1860* (Rio de Janeiro: Vício de Leitura, 2001).

  Raízes da Indústria no Brasil: a pre-indústria fluminense, 1808–1860 (Rio de Janeiro: Studio F&S Editora, 1992).

Beintema, Nienke M., Antonio Flavio Dias Avila, and Philip G. Pardey, "Agricultural R&D in Brazil: Policy, Investments, and Institutional Profile," International Food Policy Research Institute, Empresa Brasileira de Pesquisa Agropecuaria, and Regional Fund for Agricultural Technology, *ASTI*

Country Report, Washington, DC; Brasilia, Brazil: International Food Policy Research Institute; Empresa Brasileira de Pesquisa Agropecuaria; Regional Fund for Agricultural Technology (August 2001).

Bell, Stephen, "Aimé Bonpland e a avaliação de recursos em Santa Cruz, 1848–50," *Estudos Ibero-Americanos*, PUCRS, XXI: 2 (1995), pp. 63–79.

A life in shadow: Aimé Bonpland in Southern South America, 1817–1858 (Stanford: Stanford University Press, 2010).

Benévolo, Ademar, *Introdução á História Ferroviária do Brasil: estudo social, politico e histórico* (Recife: Edições Fohda da Manhã, 1953).

Berg, Maxine, and Pat Hudson, "Rehabilitating the Industrial Revolution." *The Economic History Review*, New Series, 45:1 (Feb. 1992), pp. 24–50.

Berman, Marshall, *All That is Solid Melts into Air: the Experience of Modernity* (New York: Simon & Schuster, 1982).

Blasenheim, Peter L., "Railroad in Nineteenth-century Minas Gerais," *Journal of Latin American Studies*, 26:2 (May 1994), pp. 347–74.

Bleichmar, Daniela, *Visible Empire: Botanical Expeditions and Visual Culture in the Hispanic Enlightenment* (Chicago: University of Chicago Press, 2011).

Boxer, Charles, *The Golden Age of Brazil, 1695–1750: Growing Pains of a Colonial Society* (Berkeley: University of California Press, 1962).

Brunner, Herausgegeben von Otto, Werner Conze, Reinhart Koselleck, eds., *Geschichtliche Grundbegriffe: Historisches Lexikon zur politisch-sozialen Sprache in Deutschland* (Stuttgart: Klett-Cotta, 1982).

Burns, E. Bradford, *The Poverty of Progress: Latin America in the Nineteenth Century* (Berkeley: University of California Press, 1983).

Cabral, Diogo de Carvalho, "Floresta, política e trabalho: a exploração das madeiras-de-lei no Recôncovo da Guanabara (1760–1820)," *Revista Brasileira de História*, 28:55 (2008), pp. 217–41.

Caldeira, Jorge, *Mauá: empresário do Império* (São Paulo: Companhia das Letras, 1995).

Calhoun, Craig, ed., *Dictionary of the Social Sciences* (Oxford: Oxford University Press, 2002, 2012).

Camillo, Ema E. R., *Guia Histórica da indústria nascente em Campinas (1850–1887)* (Campinas, BR: Mercado de Letras, CMU, 1998).

Cannadine, David, "The Present and the Past in the English Industrial Revolution 1800–1900." *Past and Present*, 103 (1984), pp. 131–72.

Cardoso, Fernando Henrique and Enzo Faletto *Dependency and Development in Latin America*, Marjory Mattingly Urquidi, trans., (Berkeley: University of California Press, 1979).

Carone, Edgard, *O Centro Industrial do Rio de Janeiro e sua importante participão na economia nacional: 1827–1977* (Rio de Janeiro: Ed. Cátedra/Centro Industrial, 1978).

Carvalho, José Murilo de, *A Construção da Ordem: a elite política imperial*, e*Teatro de Sombras: a política imperial* (Rio de Janeiro: Editora Civilização Brasileira, 2006).

A Escola de Minas de Ouro Preto: o peso da glória (Río de Janeiro: FINEP, and São Paulo: Editor a Nacional, 1978).

"História intellectual no Brasil: a retórica como chave de leitura," *Topoí* 1 (2000), pp. 123–52.

Castilho, Celso, "Performing Abolitionism: The Social Construction of Political Rights in 1880s Recife, Brazil," *Hispanic American Historical Review*, 93:3 (2013), pp. 377–409.

Castilho, Celso and Camillia Cowling, "Funding Freedom, Popularizing Politics: Abolitionism and Local Emancipation Funds in 1880s Brazil," *Luso-Brazilian Review* 47:1 (2010), pp. 89–120.

Conrad, Robert, *The Destruction of Brazilian Slavery, 1850–1888* (Berkeley: University of California Press, 1972).

Costa, Emilía Viotti da, "Brazil: The Age of Reform, 1870–1889," in *The Cambridge History of Latin America*, Vol. V c. 1870–1930 (Cambridge: Cambridge University Press, 1986), pp. 725–78.

The Brazilian Empire: Myths and Histories (Chicago: The University of Chicago Press, 1985).

Cribelli, Teresa, "A Modern Monarch: Dom Pedro II's Visit to the United States in 1876," *The Journal of the Historical Society*, IX: 2 (June 2009), pp. 223–54.

O mais útil de todos os instrumentos o arado e a valorização da terra no Brasil no século XIX, in Márcia Motta and María Verónica Secreto, eds., *O Direito ás Avessas: por uma história social da propriedade* (Guarapuava, PR: Unicentro, and Niterói: Editora da Universidade Federal Fluminense, 2001), pp. 291–315.

Cronan, William, *Nature's Metropolis: Chicago and the Great West* (New York: W. W. Norton & Co., 1991).

Cunha, Luiz Antônio, *O ensino de ofícios artesanais e manufatureiros no Brasil escravocrata* (São Paulo: UNESP, and Brasília: FLACSO, 2005).

Dahlstrom, Neil and Jeremy Dalhstrom, *The John Deere Story: A Biography of Plowmakers John and Charles Deere* (Dekalb, IL: Northern Illinois University Press, 2005).

Dean, Warren, *Brazil and the Struggle for Rubber: A study in Environmental History* (Cambridge: Cambridge University Press, 1987).

"Deforestation in Southeastern Brazil," in Richard P. Tucker and J. F. Richards, eds., *Global Deforestation and the Nineteenth-Century World Economy* (Durham, NC: Duke University Press, 1983), pp. 50–67.

The Industrialization of São Paulo, 1880–1945 (Austin: Published for the Institute of Latin American Studies by the University of Texas Press, 1969).

With Broadax and Firebrand: The Destruction of the Brazilian Atlantic Forest (Berkeley: University of California Press, 1995).

Dias, Maria Odila da Silva, "Aspectos da ilustração no Brasil," *Revista do Instituto Histórico e Geográfico Brasileiro*, 278 (1968), pp. 105–70.

Domingues, Heloisa Maria Bertol, "A Nocão de Civilização na visão dos construtores do Império. (A Revista do Instituto Histórico e Geográfico Brasileiro: 1838–1850/60)," (Master's thesis, Instituto de Ciências Humanas e Filosofia, Centro de Estudos Gerais, Universidade Federal Fluminense, 1989).

"A Sociedade Auxiliadora da Indústria Nacional e as Ciências Naturais no Brasil Império," in Maria Amélia M. Dantes, ed., *Espaços da Ciência no Brasil: 1800–1930* (Rio de Janeiro: 2001), pp. 83–110.

Eakin, Marshall, *British Enterprise in Brazil: the St. John d'el Rey Mining Company and the Morro Velho Gold Mine, 1830–1960* (Durham, NC: Duke University Press, 1989).

Eisenberg, Peter L., *The Sugar Industry in Pernambuco: Modernization without change, 1840–1910* (Berkeley: University of California Press, 1974).

Elkin, Noah, "Promoting a New Brazil: National Expositions and Images of Modernity, 1861–1922," (Ph.D. dissertation, Rutgers, the State University of New Jersey, 1997).

Ermakoff, George, *Rio de Janeiro, 1840–1900: Uma Crônica fotográfica* (Rio de Janeiro: Casa Editorial, 2006).

Ferreira, Manoel Rodrigues, *A Ferrovia do Diabo* (São Paulo: Melhoramentos, 1959, 2005).

Fifer, J. Valerie, *United States Perceptions of Latin America, 1850–1930: a "New West" south of Capricorn?* (Manchester, UK: Manchester University Press, 1991).

Figueirôa, Silvia Fernanda Mendonça, *As Ciências Geológicas no Brasil: Uma História Social e Institucional, 1875–1934* (São Paulo: Hucitec, 1997).

Foot, Francisco, *Trem Fantasma: A Modernidade Na Selva* (São Paulo: Companhia das Letras; São Paulo: Editora Schwarcz, 1988).

Fox-Genovese, Elizabeth, *The Origins of Physiocracy: Economic Revolution and Social Order in Eighteenth-Century France* (Ithaca: Cornell University Press, 1976).

Franco, Maria Sylvia de Carvalho, "As idéias estão no lugar," *Cadernos de debate*, 1, (São Paulo: Brasiliense, 1976), pp. 61–4.

Frank, Zephyr, *Dutra's World: Wealth and Family in Nineteenth-Century Rio de Janeiro* (Albuquerque: University of New Mexico Press, 2004).

Freita, Marcus Vinicius de, *A Educação dos Negros: uma nova face do processo de abolição da escravidão no Brasil* (Bragança Paulista, SP: Coleção Estudos CDAPH, 2002).

Charles Frederick Hartt, um naturalista no império de Pedro II (Belo Horizonte, MG: Editora da UFMG, 2002).

Hartt: Expedições pelo Brasil Imperial (São Paulo: Metalivros, 2001).

Furtado, Celso, *Economic Development of Latin America* (Cambridge: Cambridge University Press, 1970).

Galloway, J. H., "Agricultural Reform and the Enlightenment in Late Colonial Brazil," *Agricultural History*, 53:4 (1979), pp. 763–79.

Giffoni, José Marcello Salles, "Trilhos Arrancados: história da Estrada de Ferro Bahia e Minas (1878–1966)" (Ph.D. dissertation, Universidade Federal de Minas Gerais, 2006).

Gilman, Nils, *Mandarins of the Future: Modernization Theory in Cold War America* (Baltimore, MD: The Johns Hopkins University Press, 2003).

Gootenberg, Paul, "A Forgotten Case of 'Scientific Excellence on the Periphery': The Nationalist Cocaine Science of Alfredo Bignon, 1884–1887," *Comparative Studies in Society and History* 49:1 (2007), pp. 202–32.

Graham, Richard, *Britain and the Onset of Modernization in Brazil: 1850–1914* (Cambridge: Cambridge University Press, 1968).

Patronage and Politics in Nineteenth-Century Brazil (Stanford: Stanford University Press, 1990).

Graham, Sandra Lauderdale, *House and Street: the Domestic World of Servants and Masters in Nineteenth-century Rio de Janeiro* (Cambridge: Cambridge University Press, 1988).

"The Vintem Riot and Political Culture: Rio de Janeiro, 1880," *The Hispanic American Historical Review* 60:3 (1980), pp. 431–49.

Grandin, Greg, *Fordlandia: The Rise and Fall of Henry Ford's Forgotten Jungle City* (New York: Picador, 2009).

Greenberg, Amy S., *Manifest Manhood and the Antebellum American Empire* (Cambridge: Cambridge University Press, 2005).

Greene, Ann Norton, *Horses at Work: Harnessing Power in Industrial America* (Cambridge, MA: Harvard University Press, 2008).

Greenhalgh, Paul, *Ephemeral Vistas: The Expositions Universelles, Great Exhibitions, and World's Fairs, 1851–1939* (Manchester, UK: Manchester University Press, 1988).

Grusin, Richard, *Nature, Technology, and the Creation of America's National Parks* (Cambridge: Cambridge University Press, 2004).

Guimarães, Carlos Gabriel, *A Presença Inglesa nas Finanças e no Comércio no Brasil Imperial: os casos da Sociedade Bancária Mauá, MacGregor & Cia. (1854–1866) e da firma inglesa Samuel Phillips & Cia. (1808–1840)* (São Paulo: Alameda Casa Editorial, 2012).

Guzmán, Tracy Devine, *Native and National in Brazil: Indigeneity after Independence* (Chapel Hill: University of North Carolina Press, 2013).

Haber, Stephen, ed., *How Latin America Fell Behind: Essays on the Economic Histories of Brazil and Mexico, 1800–1914* (Stanford: Stanford University Press, 1997).

Hanley, Anne G., *Native Capital: Financial Institutions and Economic Development in São Paulo, Brazil, 1850–1920* (Stanford: Stanford University Press, 2005).

Hardman, Francis Foot, *Trem-fantasma: a ferrovia Madeira-Mamoré e a modernidade na selva* (São Paulo: Companhia das Letras, 1988, 2005).

Hirschman, Albert O., *The Passions and the Interests: Political Arguments for Capitalism before Its Triumph* (Princeton: Princeton University Press, 1977, 1997).

Hoffenberg, Peter H., *An Empire on Display: English, Indian, and Australian Exhibitions from the Crystal Palace to the Great War* (Berkeley: University of California Press, 2001).

Holloway, Thomas H., *Immigrants on the Land: Coffee and Society in São Paulo, 1886–1934* (Chapel Hill, NC: University of North Carolina Press, 1980).

"Immigration and Abolition: The Transition from Slave to Free Labor in the São Paulo Coffee Zone," Dauril Alden and Warren Dean, eds., *Essays Concerning the Socio-Economic History of Brazil and Portuguese India* (Gainesville: University Presses of Florida, 1977), pp. 150–78.

Horn, Jeff, *The Path not Taken: French Industrialization in the Age of Revolution, 1750–1830* (Cambridge, MA; The MIT Press, 2006).

Horn, Jeff, Leonard N. Rosenband, and Merritt Roe Smith, eds., *Reconceptualizing the Industrial Revolution* (Cambridge, MA: MIT Press, 2010).

Hudson, Pat, *The Industrial Revolution* (London; New York: E. Arnold: Distributed in the USA by Routledge, Chapman, and Hall, 1992).

Ioris, Rafael R., *Transforming Brazil: A History of National Development in the Postwar Era* (New York: Routledge, 2014).

Jamieson, Ross W., "The Essence of Commodification: Caffeine Dependencies in the Early Modern World," *Journal of Social History*, 35:2 (2001), pp. 269–94.

Kearns, Kevin C., "Development of the Irish Peat Fuel Industry," *The American Journal of Economics and Sociology*, 37:2 (1978), pp. 179–93.

Klafke, Álvaro Antonio, "O Império na provincia: construção do estado nacional nas páginas de O *Propagador da Indústria Rio-grandense 1833–1834* (Master's thesis, Universidade Federal do Rio Grande do Sul, Brazil, 2006).

Klein, Herbert S., "The Supply of Mules to Central Brazil: The Sorocaba market, 1825–1880," *Agricultural History*, 64:4 (Fall, 1990), pp. 1–25.

Klink, Carlos A. and Ricardo B. Machado, "Conservation of the Brazilian Cerrado," *Conservation Biology*, 19:3 (June 2005), pp. 707–13.

Koerner, Lisbet, *Linnaeus: Nature and Nation* (Cambridge, MA: Harvard University Press, 1999).

Kraay, Hendrik, *Days of National Festivity in Rio de Janeiro, Brazil, 1823–1889* (Stanford: Stanford University Press, 2013).

Lamounier, Maria Lúcia, *Ferrovias e mercado de trabalho no Brasil do Século XIX* (São Paulo: Editora da Universidade de São Paulo, 2012).

Langfur, Hal, *The Forbidden Lands: Colonial Identity, Frontier Violence, and the Persistence of Brazil's Eastern Indians, 1750–1830* (Stanford: Stanford University Press, 2006).

Leff, Nathaniel H., *Underdevelopment and Development in Brazil, Vol. I: Economic Structure and Change, 1822–1947* (New York: George Allen & Unwin, 1982).

Lessa, Luiz Carlos Barbosa, *História do chimarrão*, 3rd ed. (Porto Alegre: Sulina, 1986).

Lesser, Jeffrey, *Negotiating National Identity: Immigrants, Minorities, and the Struggle for Ethnicity in Brazil* (Durham, NC: Duke University Press, 1999).

Lewis, Colin M., "Public Policy and Private Initiative: Railway Building in São Paulo 1860–1889," (London: Institute of Latin American Studies University of London, 1991), research paper.

Libby, Douglas Cole. "Notas sobre a produção têxtil brasileira no final do século XVIII: novas evidências de Minas Gerais." *Estudos Econômicos*, 27:I (1997), pp. 97–125.

Lima, Heitor Ferreira, *História do Pensamento Econômico no Brasil* (São Paulo: Editora Nacional, 1976).

Linhares, Temístocles, *História econômica do mate* (Rio de Janeiro: José Olympio Editora, 1969).

Lobo, Eulalia Maria Lahmeyer, *História do Rio de Janeiro (do capital comercial ao capital industrial e financeiro)*, 2 vols. (Rio de Janeiro: Instituto Brasileiro de Mercado de Capitais, 1978).

História político-administrativo da agricultura brasileira, 1808–1889 (n/p: 1979).

Lourenço, Fernando Antonio, *Agricultura Illustrada: liberalismo e escravismo nas origins da questão agraria brasileira* (Campinas, São Paulo: Editora Unicamp, 2001).

Luz, Nícia Vilela, *A Luta Pela Industrialização do Brasil* (São Paulo: Difusão Européia do Livro, 1961, Editora Alfa Omega, 1975).

MacCord, Marcelo, *Artífices da Cidadania: mutualismo, educação e trabalho no Recife oitocentista* (Campinas, BR: Editora Unicamp, 2012).

Majewski, John, Christopher Baer, and Daniel B. Klein, "Responding to Relative Decline: The Plank Road Boom of Antebellum New York," *The Journal of Economic History*, 53:1, March 1993, pp. 106–22.

Malavota, Leandro, *A Construção do Sistema de Patentes no Brasil: um olhar histórico* (Rio de Janeiro: Editora Lumen Juris, 2011).

Manthorne, Katherine Emma, *Tropical Renaissance: North American Artists Exploring Latin America, 1839–1879* (Washington: Smithsonian Institution Press, 1989).

Marinho, Pedro Eduardo Mesquita de Monteiro, "Engenharia Imperial, o Instituto Politécnico Brasileiro," (Ph.D. dissertation, Universidade Federal Fluminense, Niterói, Rio de Janeiro, 2002).

Marquese, Rafael de Bivar, *Ideias sobre a gestão da agricultura escravista brasileira* (São Paulo: Hucitec, 1999).

Marris, Emma, "Conservation in Brazil: The forgotten ecosystem," News Feature, *Nature* (October 13, 2005), pp. 944–5.

Martini, Augusto Jeronimo, "O Plantador de Eucaliptos: a questão da preservação florestal no Brasil e o resgate documental do legado de Edmundo Navarro de Andrade," (Master's thesis, Universidade de São Paulo, 2004).

Martins, Maria Fernanda Vieira, "O Imperial Instituto Fluminense de Agricultura: Elites, Política e Reforma Agrícola (1860–1897)," (Master's thesis, Universidade Federal Fluminense, 1995).

Marx, Karl, *A Contribution to the Critique of Political Economy*, Vol. I (Moscow: Progress Publishers, 1970).

   Capital: A Critique of Political Economy, Vol. I (London: Penguin Books, 1976).

Marx, Leo, *The Machine in the Garden: Technology and the Pastoral Ideal in America* (New York: Oxford University Press, 1964, 2000).

Mattoon, Robert H., Jr., "Railroads, Coffee, and the Growth of Big Business in São Paulo, Brazil," *The Hispanic American Historical Review*, 57:2 (May 1977), pp. 274–85.

Mattos, Ilmar Rohloff de, *O Tempo Saquarema* (São Paulo: Editora Hucitec, 1987).

Maxwell, Kenneth, *Conflicts and Conspiracies: Brazil and Portugal 1750–1808* (Cambridge: Cambridge University Press, 1973).

   Paradox of the Enlightenment (Cambridge: Cambridge University Press, 1995).

   Pombal: Paradox of the Enlightenment (Cambridge: Cambridge University Press, 1995).

Mayer, Jorge Miguel, "Raízes e crise do mundo caipira: o caso de Nova Friburgo," (Ph.D. dissertation, Universidade Federal Fluminense, 2003).

McCook, Stuart, *States of Nature: Science, Agriculture, and Environment in the Spanish Caribbean, 1760–1940* (Austin: University of Texas Press, 2002).

McGaw, Judith A., *Most Wonderful Machine: mechanization and social change in Berkshire paper making, 1801–1885* (Princeton, NJ: Princeton University Press, 1987).

Meade, Teresa, "*Civilizing Rio" Reform and Resistance in a Brazilian City, 1889–1930* (University Park: Pennsylvania State University Press, 1997).

Melo, Hildete Pereira de, "Coffee and the Rio de Janeiro Economy," in Clarence-Smith and Topik, eds., *The Global Coffee Economy in Africa, Asia, and Latin America, 1500–1989* (Cambridge: Cambridge University Press, 2003), pp. 360–84.

Melville, Herman, "The Tartarus of Maids," *Great Short Works of Herman Melville* (New York: Harper Collins Press, 2004), pp. 202–22.

Mendonça, Maria Luisa, "Brazil: Sugar cane plantations devastate vital Cerrado region," *Pacific Ecologist*, (Summer 2009), pp. 25–7.

Miller, Shawn William, *Fruitless Trees: Portuguese Conservation and Brazil's Colonial Timber* (Stanford: Stanford University Press, 2000).

Monzote, Reinaldo Funes, *From Rainforest to Cane Field in Cuba: an Environmental History since 1492* (Chapel Hill: University of North Carolina Press, 2008).

Morais, Viviane Alves de, *Carros, viandantes, cargas e as comunicações durante o Império: estudo sobre as estradas interprovinciais entre 1832 e 1860,* unpublished conference paper, *Anais do XIX Encontro Regional de História: Poder, Violência e Exclusão,* ANPUH/SP – USP, São Paulo, September, 2008, n.p.

Motta, Márcia Maria Menendes, ed., *Dicionário da Terra* (Rio de Janeiro: Civilização Brasileira, 2005).

Nas Fronteiras do Poder: conflito e direito à terra no Brasil do século XIX (Rio de Janeiro: Vício de Leitura, 1998).

Müller-Wille, Staffan, "Nature as Marketplace: The Political Economy of Linnaean Botany," *History of Political Economy*, 35, Annual Supplement (2003), pp. 154–72.

Needell, Jeffrey, *A Tropical Belle Epoque: Elite Culture and Society in turn-of-the-century Rio de Janeiro* (Cambridge: Cambridge University Press, 1987).

The Party of Order: The Conservatives, the State, and Slavery in the Brazilian Monarchy, 1831–1871 (Stanford: Stanford University Press, 2006).

Neves, Marcos Fava and Viníncius Gustavo Trombin, *The Orange Juice Business: A Brazilian Perspective* (The Netherlands: Wageningen Academic Publishers, 2011).

Oldenziel, Ruth, *Making Technology Masculine: Men, Women, and Modern Machines in America, 1870–1945* (Amsterdam: Amsterdam University Press, 1999).

Oliveira, Sérgio de, *Entrepreneurship in Nineteenth-Century Brazil: The Formation of a Business Environment* (New York: St. Martin's Press, 1999).

Pádua, José Augusto, *Um Sopro de Destruição: Pensamento Político e Crítica Ambiental no Brasil Escravista (1786–1888)* (Rio de Janeiro: Jorge Zahar, 2002).

Palti, Elías José, "The Problem of 'Misplaced Ideas' Revisited: Beyond the 'History of Ideas' in Latin America," *Journal of the History of Ideas*, 67 (January 2006), pp. 149–79.

Pena, Luís Carlos Martins, "Os Dous ou o Inglez Machinista," in *Comédias* (Rio de Janeiro: H. Garnier, n.d.).

Pérez, Louis A., Jr., *On Becoming Cuban: Identity, Nationality, and Culture* (Chapel Hill: University of North Carolina Press, 1999, 2008).

Perugine, Erdna, "A Palavra Indústria na Revista O Auxiliador da Industria Nacional 1833–1843" (Master's thesis, Universidade de São Paulo, 1978).

Pineda, Yovanna, "Financing Manufacturing Innovation in Argentina, 1890–1930," *Business History Review*, 83 (Autumn 2009), pp. 539–62.

Industrial Development in a Frontier Economy: The Industrialization of Argentina, 1890–1930 (Stanford: Stanford University Press, 2009).

Pinheiro, Luciana de Araújo, "A civilização do Brasil através da infância: propostas e ações voltadas à criança pobre nos anos finais do Império (1879–1889)," (Master's thesis, Universidade Federal Fluminense, 2003).

Plum, Werner, *World Exhibitions in the Nineteenth-century: Pageants of Social and Cultural Change, Lux Furtmuller*, trans., (Bonn-Bad Godesberg: Freidrich-Ebert-Stiftung, 1977).

Polanyi, Karl, *The Great Transformation: The Political and Economic Origins of our Time* (Boston: Beacon Press, 1944, 1957, 2001).

Pollard, Sidney, "Factory Discipline in the Industrial Revolution," *The Economic History Review*, New Series, 16:2 (1963), pp. 254–71.

Portuondo, Maria, "Plantation Factories: Science and Technology in Late-Eighteenth-Century Cuba," *Technology and Culture*, 44:2 (2003), pp. 231–57.

Prado Júnior, Caio, *História Econômica do Brasil* (São Paulo: Editôra Brasiliense, 1976).

Prasad, Ritika, "'Time-Sense': Railways and Temporality in Colonial India," *Modern Asian Studies*, 47:4 (July 2013), pp. 1252–82.

Pratt, Mary Louise, *Imperial eyes: travel writing and transculturation* (New York: Routledge, 1992).

Raison, Déborah, "Ventos da Modernidade: os bondes e a cidade do Rio de Janeiro – 1850/1880," (Master's thesis, Universidade Federal do Rio de Janeiro, 2000).

Ramos, Donald, "Social Revolution Frustrated: The Conspiracy of the Tailors in Bahia, 1798," *Luso-Brazilian Review*, 13:1 (Summer, 1976), pp. 74–90.

Renk, Arlene, *A luta da erva: um ofício étnico da nação brasileira no oeste catarinense*, 2nd ed. (Chapecó: Argos, 2006).

Rezende, Livia Lazzaro, "The Raw and the Manufactured: Brazilian Modernity and National Identity as Projected in International Exhibitions (1862–1922)," (Ph.D. dissertation, Royal College of Art, 2010).

Ribeiro, Luíz Cláudio M., *Ofício Criador: Invento e Patente de Máquina de Beneficiar Café no Brasil (1870–1910)* (Master's thesis, Universidade de São Paulo, 1995).

Richter, Amy G., *Home on the Rails: Women, the Railroad, and the Rise of Public Domesticity* (Chapel Hill: The University of North Carolina Press, 2005).

Ridings, Eugene, *Business Interest Groups in 19th-Century Brazil* (Cambridge: Cambridge University Press, 1994).

Robinson, Harriet, *Loom and Spindle or Life Among the Early Mill Girls*, revised edition (Kailua, HI: Press Pacifica, 1976).

Rocchi, Fernando, *Chimneys in the Desert: Industrialization in Argentina During the Export Boom Years, 1870–1930* (Stanford: Stanford University Press, 2006).

Roche, Jean, "La Colonisation Allemande et le Rio Grande do Sul," (Ph.D. dissertation, Faculté des Lettres de L'Université de Paris, Institut des Hautes Études de L'Amérique Latine, 1959).

Rock, David, *Argentina 1516–1987: From Spanish Colonization to Alfonsín* (Berkeley: University of California Press, 1985, 1987).

Rodgers, Thomas D., *The Deepest Wounds: A Labor and Environmental History of Sugar in Northeast Brazil* (Chapel Hill: University of North Carolina Press, 2010).

Rohter, Larry, *Brazil on the Rise: The Story of a Country Transformed* (New York: Palgrave MacMillan, 2010).

Roller, Heather Flynn, "Colonial Collecting Expeditions and the Pursuit of Opportunities in the Amazonian Sertão,' c. 1750–1800," *The Americas*, 66:4 (2010), pp. 435–67.

Russell-Wood, A. J. R., *The Portuguese Empire, 1415–1808: A World on the Move* (Baltimore: Johns Hopkins University Press, 1998).

Rydell, Robert, *All the World's a Fair: Visions of Empire at American International Expositions, 1876–1916* (Chicago: University of Chicago Press, 1984).

Safier, Neil, "A Courier between Empires: Hipólito da Costa and the Atlantic World," in Bernard Bailyn, ed., *Soundings in Atlantic History* (Cambridge, MA: Harvard University Press, 2009), pp. 265–93.

"Spies, Dyes, and Leaves: Agro-Intermediaries, Luso-Brazilian Couriers, and the Printed Worlds They Sowed," in Simon Schaffer, Lissa Roberts, Kapil Raj, and James Delbourgo, eds., *The Brokered World: Go-Betweens and Global Intelligence, 1770–1830* (Uppsala: Watson Publishing International, 2009), pp. 239–69.

Salsbury, Stephen, "The Emergence of an Early Large-Scale Technical System: The American Railroad Network," in Renate Mayntz and Thomas P. Hughes, eds., *The Development of Large Technical Systems* (Boulder, CO: Westview Press, 1988), pp. 37–68.

Samper, Mario and Radin Fernando, "Historical Statistics of Coffee Production and Trade from 1700 to 1960," in William Gervase, Clarence-Smith and Steven Topik, eds., *The Global Coffee Economy in Africa, Asia, and Latin America, 1500–1989* (Cambridge: Cambridge University Press, 2003), pp. 411–62.

Sanderson, Michael, "Education and the Factory in Industrial Lancashire, 1780–1840," *The Economic History Review*, New Series, 20:2 (August 1967), pp. 266–79.

Santos, Nadja Paraense dos, Angelo C. Pinto, and Ricardo Bicca de Alencastro, "Passando da Doutrina à prática: Ezequiel Corrêa dos Santos e a Farmácia Nacional," *Química Nova*, 30:4 (2007), pp. 1038–45.

"Theodoro Peckolt: Naturalista e Farmacêutico do Brasil Imperial," *Química Nova*, 21:5 (1998), pp. 666–70.

Sarmiento, Domingo, *Facundo: Or, Civilization and Barbarism*, Mary Mann, trans., and Ilan Stavans, ed., (New York: Penguin, 1998).

Sawyer, Donald, "Climate change, biofuels and eco-social impacts in the Brazilian Amazon and Cerrado," *Philosophical Transactions of the Royal Society B*: 363 (2008), pp. 1747–52.

Schultz, Kirsten, *Tropical Versailles: Empire, Monarchy, and the Portuguese Royal Court in Rio de Janeiro, 1808–1821* (New York: Routledge, 2001).

Schumaher, Schuma and Érico Vital Brazil, eds., *Dicionário Mulheres do Brasil de 1500 até a atualidade*, 2nd ed., (Rio de Janeiro: Jorge Zahar, 2000).

Schwarcz, Lilia Mortiz, *As Barbas do Imperador: D. Pedro II, um monarca nos trópicos* (São Paulo: Companhia das Letras, 2003).

Schwarz, Roberto, *Misplaced Ideas: Essays on Brazilian Culture*, John Gledson, ed., (London: Verso, 1974, 1992).

Schwartz, Stuart, "A Commonwealth within Itself: The Early Brazilian Sugar Industry, 1550–1670," Stuart Schwartz, ed., *Tropical Babylons: Sugar and the Making of the Atlantic World, 1450–1680* (Chapel Hill: University of North Carolina Press, 2004), pp. 156–200.

Scott, James C., *Seeing Like a State: how certain schemes to improve the human condition have failed* (New Haven, CT: Yale University Press, 1998).

Seemann, Jörn, "From Candle Wax to E 903: Commodity Geographies of the Carnaúba Palm (*Coperinicia cerifera*) from Northeastern Brazil," unpublished paper, *Brazilian Studies Association Conference*, 2008, New Orleans.

Segala, Lygia and Paulo Garchet, "Prescriptive Observation and Illustration of Brazil: Victor Frond's Photographic Project (1857–61)," *Portuguese Studies*, 23:1 (2007), pp. 55–70.

Sewell, William Hamilton, *Work and Revolution in France: the language of labor from the Old Regime to 1848* (New York: Cambridge University Press, 1980).

Sheriff, Carol, *The Artificial River: The Erie Canal and the Paradox of Progress, 1817–1862* (New York: Hill and Wang, 1996).

Silva, José Luiz Werneck da, "As Arenas Pacíficas do Progresso," 2 Vols., (Ph.D. dissertation, Universidade Federal Fluminense, Rio de Janeiro, 1992).

"Isto É O Que Me Parece: A Sociedade Auxiliadora da Indústria Nacional (1827–1904), na formação social brasileira: aconjuntura de 1871 até 1877" 2 vols., (Master's thesis, Universidade Federal Fluminense, Niteroi, 1979).

Silva, Maria Beatriz Nizza da, *A Gazeta do Rio de Janeiro (1808–1822): Cultura e Sociedade* (Rio de Janeiro: Editora UERJ, 2007).

Silveira, Mauro César, "Âs marcas do preconceito no jornalismo brasileiro e a história do Paraguay Illustrado," *Revista Brasileira de Ciências da Comunicação*, 30:2 (2007), pp. 41–66.

Skaggs, Jimmy M., *The Great Guano Rush: Entrepreneurs and American Overseas Expansion* (New York: St. Martin's Press, 1994).

Skidmore, Thomas, *Black into White; Race and Nationality in Brazilian Thought* (Oxford: Oxford University Press, 1974).

Smith, Adam, *An Inquiry into the Nature and Causes of the Wealth of Nations* (Chicago: The University of Chicago Press, 1976).

Sodré, Nelson Werneck, *História da Imprensa no Brasil* 4ª ed., (Rio de Janeiro: Mauad, 1998, 2004).

Soluri, John, *Banana Cultures: Agriculture, Consumption, and Environmental Change in Honduras and the United States* (Austin: University of Texas Press, 2005).

Sousa, Gabriel Soares de, *Tratado Descritivo do Brasil em 1587*, Francisco Adolfo de Varnhagen, ed., (Recife, PN: Fundação Joaquim Nabuco, Editora Massangana, 2000).

Spary, Emma, "Political, Natural, and Bodily Economies," in N. Jardine, J. A. Secord, and E. C. Spary, eds., *Cultures of Natural History* (Cambridge: Cambridge University Press, 1996), pp. 178–96.

Spence, Clark C., *God Speed the Plow: the coming of steam cultivation to Great Britain* (Urbana, IL: University of Illinois Press, 1960).

Stanley, Amy Dru, *From Bondage to Contract: Wage Labor, Marriage, and the Market in the Age of Slave Emancipation* (Cambridge: Cambridge University Press, 1998).

Stein, Stanley, *The Brazilian Cotton Manufacture: Textile Enterprise in an Underdeveloped Area, 1850–1950* (Cambridge, MA: Harvard University Press, 1958, 1985).

Vassouras, a Brazilian Coffee County, 1850–1900: The Roles of Planter and Slave in a Plantation Society (Princeton, NJ: Princeton University Press, 1958, 1985).

Stein, Stanley J., and Barbara H. Stein, *The Colonial Heritage of Latin America: Essays on Economic Dependence in Perspective* (New York: Oxford University Press, 1970).

Stepan, Nancy, *Beginnings of Brazilian Science: Oswaldo Cruz, Medical Research and Policy, 1890–1920* (New York: Science History Publications, 1976).

Picturing Tropical Nature (Ithaca, NY: Cornell University Press, 2001).

Summerhill, William, *Order Against Progress: Government, Foreign Investment, and Railroads in Brazil, 1854–1913* (Stanford: Stanford University Press, 2003).

"Railroads and the Brazilian Economy Before 1914," Summaries of Dissertations, *Journal of Economic History*, 56:2 (June 1996), pp. 464–7.

Telles, Pedro Carlos da Silva, *História da Construçao Naval do Brasil* (Rio de Janeiro: LAMN, FEMAR, 2001) as cited in Pedro Eduardo Mesquita de Monteiro Marinho, "Engenahira Imperial, O Instituto Politécnico Brasileiro," (Ph.D. dissertation, Universidade Federal Fluminense, Niterói, Rio de Janeiro, 2002).

Tenorio-Trillo, Mauricio, *Mexico at the World's Fairs: Crafting a Modern Nation* (Berkeley: University of California Press, 1996).

Terra, Paulo Cruz, *Cidadania e trabalhadores: cocheiros e carroceiros no Rio de Janeiro (1870–1906)*, (Ph.D. dissertation, Universidade Federal Fluminense, 2012).

"Conflitos cotidianos e motins: os usários de bondes no Rio de Janeiro no final do século XIX e início do XX," *História Social*, 22:23 (primeiro e segundo semestres de 2012), pp. 235–53.

"História social do transporte do Rio de Janeiro – final do século XIX e início do XX," *Núcleo Interdisciplinar de Estudos e Pesquisas sobre Marx e o Marxismo*, Universidade Federal Fluminense, 2011.

Thompson, E. P., *The Making of the English Working Class* (New York: Vintage Books, 1963).

Turazzi, Maria Inez, *Poses e Trejeitos: A fotografia e as exposições na era do espectáculo (1839–1889)* (Rio de Janeiro: Funarte, Editora Rocco Ltda., 1995).

Vardi, Liana, *The Physiocrats and the World of the Enlightenment* (Cambridge: Cambridge University Press, 2012).

Vinge, Joan, "Phoenix in the Ashes," in *Phoenix in the Ashes* (New York: Bluejay Books, 1985), pp. 1–34.

Vos, Paula de, "Natural History and the Pursuit of Empire in Eighteenth-Century Spain," *Eighteenth-Century Studies*, 40:2 (2007), pp. 209–39.

Walker, Timothy, "Acquisition and Circulation of Medical Knowledge within the Early Modern Portuguese Colonial Empire," in Daniela Bleichmar, Paula de Vos, Kristin Huffine, and Kevin Sheehan, eds., *Science in the Spanish and Portuguese Empires* (Stanford: Stanford University Press, 2009), pp. 247–70.

"The Medicines Trade in the Portuguese Atlantic World: Dissemination of Plant Remedies and Healing Knowledge from Brazil, c. 1580–1830," in Mobilising Medicine: Trade & Healing in the Early Modern Atlantic World, special issue, *The Social History of Medicine*, 26:3 (2013), pp. 403–31.

Watson, M. I., "Mutual Improvement Societies in Nineteenth-Century Lancashire," *Journal of Educational Administration and History*, 21:2 (1989), pp. 8–17.

Weinberg, Albert K., *Manifest Destiny: A Study of Nationalist Expansionism in American History* (Chicago: Quadrangle Press, 1963).

Weinstein, Barbara, *The Amazon Rubber Boom: 1850–1920* (Stanford: Stanford University Press, 1983).

The Color of Modernity: São Paulo and the Making of Race and Nation in Brazil (Durham, NC: Duke University Press, 2015).

Williams, Michael, "Industrial Impacts of the Forests on the United States: 1860–1920," *Journal of Forest History*, 31:3 (1987), pp. 108–21.

Zarth, Paulo Alfonso, *Do Arcaico ao Moderno: o Rio Grande do Sul agrário do século XIX* (Ijuí, RS: Editora UNJUI, 2002).

Zeller, Suzanne, "Darwin meets the Engineers: Scientizing the Forest at McGill University, 1890–1910," *Environmental History*, 6:3 (2001), pp. 428–50.

Index